RHYTHMS OF COLLEGE SUCCESS

A JOURNEY OF DISCOVERY, CHANGE, AND MASTERY

STEVE PISCITELLI

PEARSON

Prentice
Hall

Upper Saddle River, New Jersey
Columbus, Ohio

Library of Congress Cataloging-in-Publication Data

Piscitelli, Steve.
  Rhythms of college success : a journey of discovery, change, and mastery / Steve Piscitelli.
    p. cm.
  Includes bibliographical references and index.
  ISBN 0-13-238640-2 (pbk.)
1. College student orientation—Handbooks, manuals, etc. 2. College freshman—Handbooks, manuals, etc. I. Title.
LB2343.3.P53 2008
378.1'98—dc22

                                                                                    2006027231

Vice President and Executive Publisher: Jeffery W. Johnston
Executive Editor: Sande Johnson
Development Editor: Jennifer Gessner
Editorial Assistant: Lynda Cramer
Production Editor: Alexandrina Benedicto Wolf
Production Coordination: Thistle Hill Publishing Services, LLC
Design Coordinator: Diane C. Lorenzo
Text and Cover Designer: Candace Rowley
Cover Image: Alan Neider
Production Manager: Pamela D. Bennett
Director of Marketing: David Gesell
Marketing Manager: Amy Judd
Marketing Coordinator: Brian Mounts

This book was set in Weidemann Book by Carlisle Publishing Services. It was printed and bound by R.R. Donnelley & Sons Company. The cover was printed by Phoenix Color Corp.

Pearson Education Ltd.
Pearson Education Singapore, Pte. Ltd.
Pearson Education Canada, Ltd.
Pearson Education—Japan

Pearson Education Australia Pty. Limited
Pearson Education North Asia Ltd.
Pearson Educación de Mexico, S.A. de C.V.
Pearson Education Malaysia, Pte. Ltd.

10 9 8 7 6 5 4 3 2 1
ISBN-13: 978-0-13-238640-1
ISBN-10: 0-13-238640-2

This book is dedicated to all of the
student services support staff, advisors, counselors, and deans
in our colleges and universities.
Thank you for your daily commitment to student success.

BRIEF CONTENTS

CONTENTS

PART III: WELLNESS   210

Chapter 10   Building nutritious relationships: Harmonious connections   212

Chapter 11   Personal integrity: Hitting the right notes   236

INTRODUCTION

THE THREE LEVELS OF COLLEGE SUCCESS

Like most books, this book presents its topics in a linear fashion. The transitional adjustments of college life described in Chapter 1 will be followed by a discussion of motivation and goals in Chapter 2. This will then lead to strategies for classroom success—and so you will progress, reading one chapter after another.

But the realities of college life do not follow a linear path; they will move in many directions at once.

While you are trying to adapt to a new campus environment and the many different people around you, necessity requires that you attend classes, take notes, manage your time, establish new relationships, *and* successfully complete exams *at the same time.* During the first few weeks of school you will address each of the major topics described in this book's table of contents. Each concept is intertwined with the others. However, whereas book chapters represent artificial separations of these concepts, your college life will not be divided into neat little chapters.

You will need to be successful in the classroom and maintain a healthy lifestyle while you change, grow, and thrive in your new environment. For that reason, the chapters of this book will address the major issues of your college or university experience on three levels:

Level I: The 4 Rs

Level II: The Change Cycle

Level III: Tuning Your Life-Strings

LEVEL I: THE 4 RS

As you study the topics of each chapter you will be asked to do the following:

- *Reflect* on the skills and challenges you bring to college.

- *Respect* the skills, knowledge, and strategies that you already have as a student.

- Assume the *responsibility* to make necessary changes to address your challenges.

- Develop and maintain *renewal* strategies that foster balance, wellness, and growth in your life.

LEVEL II: THE CHANGE CYCLE

An old saying reminds us that the only *constant* in life is *change.* Whether we are old or young, a student or a college president, we look change in the face each day of our lives. To be sure, sometimes the change is minor and of little serious impact. An instructor modifying the reading assignment for today does not rank high on the scale of life changes. Other changes require significant thought and study—such as making the decision to invest your time, money, and emotions in a college education.

Martha Beck, an author and career development coach, maintains that "life transformation follows a cyclical course, one you've already negotiated several times."[1] College enrollment rep-

---

[1] Martha Beck, *Finding Your Own North Star: Claiming the Life You Were Meant to Have* (New York: Three Rivers Press, 2001), 244. An in-depth description of the cycle is found on pages 240–365.

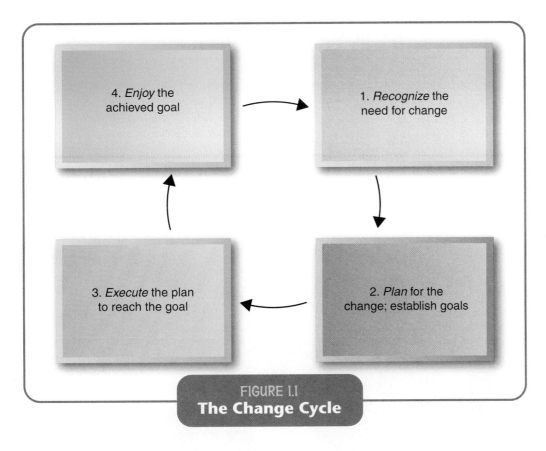

FIGURE I.1
The Change Cycle

resents one of those cyclical transformations. Figure I.1 graphically illustrates the four-stage process of Beck's cycle, which can be described as follows:

Stage 1: Recognize the need for change. The first stage represents a major event that stimulates a needed change. The event can be the physical death of a friend or loved one. More often, though, it represents the ending of one phase of life's experiences. At this point you recognize that life, as you knew it, is about to change. This may be a wrenching traumatic experience or it may be a wonderful opportunity. Graduation from high school, being laid off, getting divorced, or moving to the United States all provide an opportunity to move in a new and rewarding direction. Whatever the reason, a new road must be followed. Because that road may be unknown, this can be a time of elated anticipation or one of deep grief and anxiety.

Stage 2: Plan for the change. Once the need for change has become the new reality, you then move to the second stage where planning for the future starts to take place. The question "What do I want to do now?" is followed by brainstorming on how to find the correct road to your new goal. A plan of action needs to be established.

Stage 3: Execute the plan. Words and plans are put into action in the third stage—the execution of the plan. Beck cautions that this is a critical stage because possibilities for missteps and setbacks abound. At this point a student might get discouraged and decide to withdraw from a class or drop out of college. Or it can be time for a reality check to examine if the chosen direction is actually the correct road for the individual. The key lies in perseverance—keeping an eye on the final destination. Adjustments in your course might be necessary; maybe even a totally new road will be traveled. Keep the intent in mind and do not give up on yourself.

Stage 4: Enjoy the achieved goal. In the final stage with the desired goal accomplished, which Beck calls "the promised land," it is a time to sit back and enjoy your success. The hard work of planning and execution has resulted in reaching your goal. Notice, however, that in Figure I.1 an arrow moves from the "enjoy" phase to the "recognize" phase to emphasize the fact that change is always around the corner. For instance, once you earn your college degree, it will be time to enjoy your hard work and accomplishments—but, guess what? Your life as an undergraduate college student has ended. Recognition of this will lead you to start planning for your post-college life.

LEVEL III: TUNING YOUR LIFE-STRINGS

Personal growth will be continually stressed throughout each chapter. The *tuned strings of a six-string guitar* (see Figure I.2) graphically illustrates how balance and wellness through continuous personal renewal will strengthen the six dimensions of your life. Although this model is discussed in detail in Chapter 1, please note that each part of the book will focus on one or more of its six strings.

FIGURE I.2
Tuning Your Life-Strings

Part I (Chapters 1 through 4) discusses the transitions you face as you adapt from high school to college. Once you understand the challenges and strengths you bring to your college campus, it will become easier to focus on your academic goals. The diversity of students, professors, and belief systems will provide a rich network in which to foster meaningful growth. The chapters in part I connect directly to the *emotional* and *social* strings of your life.

Part II (Chapters 5 through 9) explores academic strategies. Your chances of academic success will be increased with effective study skills. Higher-order thinking skills will help you locate, evaluate, and use information effectively. The chapters in this part focus on the *intellectual* strings of your life.

Part III (Chapters 10 and 11) discusses the importance of wellness and balance. The number one "job" of the college student is to perform in the classroom. Intellectual development, however, is only one aspect of your entire self. In order to perform effectively and efficiently, you need to pay attention to your health and well-being. Whether you are building nutritious, healthy, and energizing relationships or concentrating on your own physical well-being, when you act in an honest, respectful, and responsible fashion you show respect not only for yourself but also for those around you. These chapters have a particular connection to your *physical* and *spiritual* strings.

Part IV (Chapters 12 and 13) explains the application of these concepts to lifelong learning. These last two chapters of the text explore how to apply and extend the strategies of the previous chapters beyond the classroom and the first-year college experience. You will have the opportunity to make clear connections between college majors and career fields. This concluding section addresses the *occupational* string of your life as it helps you build a bridge from the campus to the larger world beyond your school.

DEVELOPING THE SELF

Each of the three levels of student success is intimately related to your growth as an individual, as shown in Figure I.3.

Your first term of school will challenge you in a variety of ways. Some challenges will be exciting and you will embrace them. Others will be threatening and may cause you to entertain ideas of leaving school. In those difficult times of personal doubt, consider the three levels of student success discussed here. These concepts will not only assist you in making a successful adjustment to college life, but they will also prepare you to effectively handle changes during the rest of your life. Simply put, if you can master this now, there is nothing you cannot confront in the future.

Finally, review Figure I.4 and consider the following before you dive into the first chapter:

- As you embark on your college career, you bring old skills and talents with you. *Reflect* and *respect* them.

- You will need to develop some new strategies or, at the very least, refine some current strategies in order to meet the academic rigor of your campus successfully. *Reflect* and take *responsibility* for making appropriate adjustments in your new environment.

- Change, as you will see in this book, fosters *renewal;* a new and different you—even if only slightly—emerges from the process. *Reflect* and enjoy the journey!

FIGURE I.3
Three Levels of Student Success

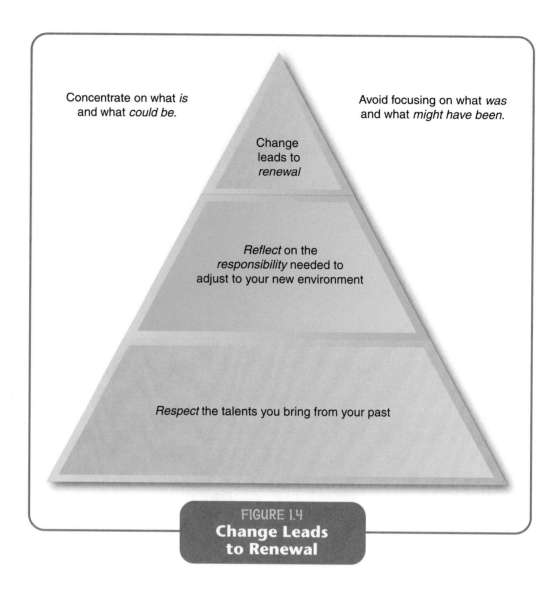

Concentrate on what *is* and what *could be*.

Avoid focusing on what *was* and what *might have been*.

Change leads to *renewal*

Reflect on the *responsibility* needed to adjust to your new environment

Respect the talents you bring from your past

FIGURE I.4
Change Leads to Renewal

A NOTE ABOUT LANGUAGE

This book uses the pronoun "you" freely. The intent is for the student to feel as though the author is speaking directly to him or her. From time to time the singular pronouns "him" and "her" are used for stylistic reasons. Rather than use just "him" or just "her," the pronouns have been alternated throughout the text.

A FLAMINGO, THE BEACH, AND A GUITAR: A PERSONAL NOTE FROM THE AUTHOR

As cliché as it might sound, my undergraduate college years hold some of the most cherished memories of my life. I had my difficult times like other students, but I fondly remember the good times, the challenging (and caring) professors, and my growth as an individual.

Your college experience should be fun and full of life; challenging but not overwhelming. The colorful cover of this book and the musical theme used throughout its pages reflect my belief that college *can be and should be an academically rewarding, fun, and energizing experience.*

In addition to my classroom teaching, I conduct motivational workshops all over the country to promote the importance of teaching student success strategies. In these workshops, I incorporate a beach theme complete with flamingoes, beach balls, sunglasses, and music. Why? Because they symbolize laughter, humor, and renewal. Yes, successful students will need effective study skills—but they will also benefit from maintaining a balanced and fulfilling life.

I loved college as a student—and still do as a professor. This book, with its flamingo, beach, and guitar images, reflects that enthusiasm and joy. I wish you every success in the coming term as you develop your own passion for this new phase of your life.

ACKNOWLEDGMENTS

At every step of the writing process I have been blessed with nurturing friendships, honest critiques, and professional guidance. Trying to thank everyone is impossible—but I would like to mention a few of the people who have added immeasurably to the book you now hold in your hands.

A number of my teaching colleagues unselfishly agreed to review initial chapters. They helped me shape rough and, at times, confused ideas into cogent and reader-friendly chapters. I would especially like to thank Amy Perkins, Sandy Willis, John Wall, Sheri Brown, Karen Reedy, Carl Brewer, Catherine Rifkin, and Dominique Dieffenbach. I would also like to thank the numerous colleagues and friends who continually inquired, "How is the book going?" Your encouragement meant a great deal to me.

Gratitude also goes to Robb Sherfield, who has never hesitated to share his thoughts and experiences when it comes to student success. He is a true leader of the profession. I would also like to thank each "guest speaker" for their chapter contributions. Their expertise and educational advice have improved the quality of this book. Their names and photos appear at the beginning of each chapter.

Thanks also to the following reviewers: Dr. Barbara Coan, Navarro College; Kelly Lowe, University of Wyoming; Grace Strong Kehrer, Middlesex County College; Lori Ruth Holtmann, USC Upstate; Judith B. Isonhood, Hinds Community College; Bea Gobeski, Hawkeye Community College; and Eric Grove, North Central State College.

If we are fortunate as we move through our professional careers, we get to work with one or two people who *really stand out* and exemplify professionalism, trust, and teamwork. I have been fortunate to have that relationship with Pearson Education. Amy Judd (senior marketing manager), Jenny Gessner (development editor), and my executive editor Sande Johnson kept me focused and balanced throughout the process. Sande, thanks for believing in me and supporting my efforts. You are a rare gem.

My wife, Laurie, has been there every step of the way. From reading all of the chapter drafts to giving up weekends and evenings as I wrote, she has been a model of patience. Without her nurturing and love this book would not have been completed.

I am a lucky man!

Steve Piscitelli
Florida Community College

ABOUT THE AUTHOR

Steve Piscitelli has more than two decades of teaching and professional development experience. He has taught students of varying abilities and grade levels, from middle school through the university level. He has been recognized for his effective teaching style with awards at the school, county, and international levels. Steve is also a seasoned workshop developer and presenter. He brings energy, humor, interaction, live original music, and practicality to his workshops.

Steve received degrees from Jacksonville University, the University of North Florida, and the University of Florida. He is currently a professor of history, education, and student success at Florida Community College at Jacksonville.

In addition to this textbook, he also published *Study Skills: Do I Really Need This Stuff?* (Prentice Hall, 2004). Steve has authored numerous articles and a history review book for students.

Steve lives with his wife, Laurie, and one canine companion, Buddy, in Atlantic Beach, Florida.

SUPPLEMENTAL RESOURCES FOR STUDENT SUCCESSES

INSTRUCTOR SUPPORT

Resources to simplify your life and engage your students.

BOOK-SPECIFIC

Print   Instructor's Manual, Test Bank   ISBN 0-13-229946-1
           PowerPoint Acetates   ISBN 0-13-229948-8

TECHNOLOGY

*"Easy access to online, book-specific **teaching support** is now just a click away!"*

Instructor Resource Center   Register. Redeem. Login. Three easy steps that open the door to a variety of print and media resources in downloadable, digital format, available to instructors exclusively through the Prentice Hall IRC.

www.prenhall.com

*"Teaching an online course, offering a hybrid class, or simply introducing your students to **Technology**, just got a whole lot easier!"*

OneKey Course Management   All you and your students need to succeed. OneKey is Prentice Hall's exclusive new resource for instructors and students providing access to the

best online teaching and learning tools—24 hours a day, 7 days a week. OneKey means all your resources are in one place for maximum convenience, simplicity and success. Visit *www.prenhall.com/onekey* and scroll to Student Success through the gallery option for additional information.

*"Reinforce strong **research skills, library usage,** and **combat plagiarism** with this tool!"*

Prentice Hall's Research Navigator   Designed to help students with the research process, from identifying a topic to editing the final draft, it also offers guidance on how to make time at the campus library more productive. RN includes four databases of credible and reliable source material to get your research process started: The EBSCO/Content Select, New York Times, Link Library, and The Financial Times. Visit *www.researchnavigator.com* for additional information.

"Choose from a wide range of video resources *for the classroom!"*

Prentice Hall Reference Library: Life Skills Pack   ISBN 0-13-127079-6 contains all 4 videos, or they may be requested individually as follows:

- Learning Styles and Self-Awareness, ISBN 0-13-028502-1
- Critical and Creative Thinking, ISBN 0-13-028504-8
- Relating to Others, ISBN 0-13-028511-0
- Personal Wellness, ISBN 0-13-028514-5

Prentice Hall Reference Library: Study Skills   Pack, ISBN 0-13-127080-X contains all 6 videos, or they may be requested individually as follows:

- Reading Effectively, ISBN 0-13-028505-6
- Listening and Memory, ISBN 0-13-028506-4
- Note Taking and Research, ISBN 0-13-028508-0
- Writing Effectively, ISBN 0-13-028509-9
- Effective Test Taking, ISBN 0-13-028500-5
- Goal Setting and Time Management, ISBN 0-13-028503-X

Prentice Hall Reference Library: Career Skills   Pack, ISBN 0-13-118529-2 contains all 3 videos, or they may be requested individually as follows:

- Skills for the 21st Century—Technology, ISBN 0-13-028512-9
- Skills for the 21st Century—Math and Science, ISBN 0-13-028513-7
- Managing Career and Money, ISBN 0-13-028516-1

Faculty Video Resources

- Teacher Training Video 1: Critical Thinking, ISBN 0-13-099432-4
- Teacher Training Video 2: Stress Management & Communication, ISBN 0-13-099578-9
- Teacher Training Video 3: Classroom Tips, ISBN 0-13-917205-X
- Student Advice Video, ISBN 0-13-233206-X
- Study Skills Video, ISBN 0-13-096095-0

Current Issues Videos

- ABC News Video Series: Student Success, ISBN 0-13-031901-5
- ABC News Video, ISBN 0-13-152865-3

Faculty Development Series Workshops

- Piscitelli: Classroom Motivators DVD, ISBN 0-13-178907-4

"Through partnership opportunities, we offer a variety of assessment options!"

LASSI   The LASSI is a 10-scale, 80-item assessment of students' awareness about and use of learning and study strategies. Addressing skill, will and self-regulation, the focus is on both covert and overt thoughts, behaviors, attitudes and beliefs that relate to successful learning and that can be altered through educational interventions. Available in paper, ISBN 0-13-172315-4, or online formats
ISBN 0-13-172316-2 (Access Card).

Noel Levitz/RMS   This retention tool measures Academic Motivation, General Coping Ability, Receptivity to Support Services, plus Social Motivation. It helps identify at-risk students, the areas with which they struggle and their receptiveness to support. Available in paper or online formats, as well as short and long versions.   Paper Long Form A: ISBN 0-13-0722588; Paper Short Form B: ISBN 0-13-079193-8; Online Forms A&B: ISBN 0-13-098158-3.

Robbins Self Assessment Library   This compilation teaches students to create a portfolio of skills. S.A.L. is a self-contained, interactive library of 49 behavioral questionnaires that help students discover new ideas about themselves, their attitudes, and their personal strengths and weaknesses. Available in paper,
ISBN 0-13-1738615; CD-Rom, ISBN 0-13-149804-5; and online,
ISBN 0-13-191445-6 (Access Card) formats.

Readiness for Education at a Distance Indicator (READI)   This is a Web-based tool that assesses the overall likelihood for online learning success. READI generates an immediate score and a diagnostic interpretation of results, including recommendations for successful participation in online courses and potential remediation sources. Please visit *www.readi.info* for additional information. ISBN 0-13-188967-2

"Teaching tolerance and discussing diversity with your students can be challenging!"

Responding to Hate at School   Published by the Southern Poverty Law Center, the Teaching Tolerance handbook is a step-by-step, easy-to-use guide designed to help administrators, counselors and teachers react promptly and efficiently whenever hate, bias, and prejudice strike. ISBN 0-13-028458-0

"For a terrific one-stop shop resource, utilize our Student Success Supersite!"

Supersite at (www.prenhall.com/success)   Students and professors alike may use the Supersite for activities, success stories, links, and more. For instructors to access PowerPoint slides, sample syllabi, articles and newsletters, supplemental information, and more, go to the Faculty Lounge. Contact your local representative for ID and password information.

"For a truly tailored solution that fosters campus connections and increases retention, talk with us about Custom Publishing."

Pearson Custom Publishing   We are the largest custom provider for print and media shaped to your course's needs. Please visit us at *www.pearsoncustom.com* to learn more.

STUDENT SUPPORT

Tools to help make the grade now, and excel in school later.

"We offer an online study aid to help students fully understand each chapter's content, and assess their knowledge through practice quizzes and exercises."

Companion Website   Please visit the site for this text at *www.prenhall.com/piscitelli*

Because students are pressed for time, we offer an alternative for studying on the go.

VangoNotes   Students are busy – we get it. With VangoNotes students can study "in between" all the other things they have to do to succeed in the classroom. These notes are flexible; just download and go. They're efficient; study in the car, at the gym or walking to class. Visit *www.prenhall.com/vangonotes* for additional information.

vango notes

Hear it. Get it.

"Time management is the #1 challenge students face—we can help."

Prentice Hall Planner   A basic planner that includes a monthly and daily calendar plus other materials to facilitate organization. 8.5" x 11".

Franklin Covey Planner   This specially designed, annual 4-color collegiate planner includes an academic planning/resources section, monthly planning (2 pages/month), weekly planning (48 weeks; July start date), which facilitate weekly as well as long-term planning. Spiral bound, 6" x 9".

"Journaling activities promote self-discovery and self-awareness."

Student Reflection Journal   Through this vehicle, students are encouraged to track their progress, share their insights, thoughts, and concerns. 8½" x 11". 90 pages.

"Our Student Success Supersite is a one-stop shop for students to learn about career paths, peer stories, and more!"

Supersite at (www.prenhall.com/success) Students will benefit from sections on Majors Exploration, Academic Skills, Career Path, Student Union, and more.

"Learning to adapt to the diverse college community is essential to student success."

10 Ways to Fight Hate   Produced by the Southern Poverty Law Center, the leading hate-crime and crime-watch organization in the United States, this guide walks students through 10 steps that they can take on their own campus or in their own neighborhood to fight hate everyday. ISBN 0-13-028146-8

"The Student Orientation Series includes short booklets on specialized topics for facilitating greater understanding by students."

S.O.S. Guides   Connolly, *Learning Communities,* ISBN 0-13-232243-9, and Watts, *Service Learning,* ISBN 0-13-232201-3. These booklets help students understand what these opportunities are, how to take advantage of them, and learn from their peers while doing so.

RHYTHMS OF COLLEGE SUCCESS

PART ONE

TRANSITIONS

WHAT'S ON YOUR MIND?

Thoughts from Fellow Students

Welcome to campus. When we first started college, it felt kind of overwhelming. We didn't know anyone on campus and had no idea what was expected of us. Truthfully, we just wanted to *survive* until the end of term. We had all sorts of questions racing through our minds, just as we imagine you have. Here are some of our original concerns and where they are addressed in this book:

- What's a safe way to meet people with interests similar to mine? (chapter 1)
- Will I be able to keep up with all the reading assigned in my courses? (chapter 4)
- My family expects so much from me. How can I deal with this stress? (chapter 4)
- What can I do if I fall behind in class? (chapter 6)
- What should I expect on my tests? Will they be harder than tests I've had before? (chapter 8)
- I don't know anyone at my school—will I make friends? What if I don't get along with my roommate and floor mates? (chapter 10)
- Am I going to have enough money to carry me through the term and have a little fun too? (chapter 11)
- I don't have a clue about what to major in. How do I try different things without wasting time and money? (chapter 12)

Just like you, we were anxious when we stepped on campus—but just like you will, we did survive. Probably the best advice we can offer is to give yourself time. Avoid the temptation to address all your concerns in the first week of school. Be yourself and don't be afraid to take chances—everyone is in the same stressful boat as you. Take it one step at a time and enjoy your college experience!

This book starts by asking you to reflect on key issues that face all students. It does not matter how long ago you were in high school, or if you had a previous try at college classes. Whether you feel panicky, apprehensive, or totally at home on campus, there is much to do and learn. In fact, before you can focus on long-term goals such as "earning a degree" or "career training," other more personal issues must be addressed—although this does not minimize your course work. After all, academic rigor will be expected of you by your professors.

College presents fresh challenges, but please understand that you do "bring something to the table." You have skills and strengths and resources that you have been drawing on all of your life. Make them work for you in college. Sure, there will be challenges—plenty of them. *But do not discount the talents you have.*

With that in mind, let's take a quick look at what you will find in this part of *Rhythms of College Success: A Journey of Discovery, Change, and Mastery.*

- **Chapter 1: Transitions and Adjustments.** College life presents many challenging opportunities. You have new freedoms, accompanied by new responsibilities. You have to negotiate a new campus environment. You have to establish connections with classmates and professors. Keep this question in mind as you read the chapter: *What knowledge, skills, and strategies do you bring to college that will help you be a successful student?*

- **Chapter 2: Motivation and Goal Setting.** Motivation provides the power to achieve goals. When you establish goals, you are actually putting together a strategy to obtain what you desire. Whether or not you achieve your goals depends in great part upon how effectively that strategy was planned and carried out. Properly motivated, you can accomplish remarkable feats. Keep this question in mind as you read the chapter: *How will you benefit from staying motivated and setting appropriate goals?*

- **Chapter 3: Open-Minded Observations of the World Around You.** Whether you participate in a classroom discussion, attend a forum on international events, or befriend a recent arrival from another nation, college presents many opportunities to challenge and/or reinforce your beliefs. Students can benefit from each other's knowledge and uniqueness—but such understanding requires a willingness to explore new ideas and diverse cultures. Keep this question in mind as you read the chapter: *How do open-minded observations of the world around you connect with college success?*

- **Chapter 4: Organizing Time and Space.** Although college does require considerable work, you also have more *unstructured* time than you have ever had. You will have to organize your schedule to include studies, family responsibilities, recreation, and the like, and also organize your study space so it will work efficiently. Keep this question in mind as you read the chapter: *How will you organize your time and space to help you effectively adjust to the college schedule and environment with minimal stress?*

When you walked on campus you were not a blank slate. You brought experiences, beliefs, and talents—but may also have brought some self-doubts. Research studies have found that the first few weeks of school are the most critical for students. The time has come to take some quality time and reflect on why you are here, what you want from college, and how you can grow from the experience.

Transitions and Adjustments

College Success Without the Blues

REFLECTIVE QUESTIONS

Keeping the following questions in mind will make this chapter more meaningful:

- What knowledge, skills, and strategies do you bring to college that will help you be a successful student?
- What is important to you about attending college now?
- What do you expect to gain from your college experience?
- What challenges (weaknesses) do you bring to college?
- How will you balance your academic demands and your personal responsibilities?
- How will you maintain a healthy lifestyle that will help you meet the challenges of college?

KEY TERMS

balanced life

C.A.P. principle

change cycle

dimensions of wellness

opportunity cost of a
college education

reflection

renewal

respect

responsibility

GUEST SPEAKER

MEET **SANDRA WILLIS**

Dean of Student Success

Florida Community College at Jacksonville

Jacksonville, Florida

Welcome to campus and all of the marvelous opportunities waiting for you. Like most students, you probably have a number of questions about college life. Find your school's Student Services office as soon as possible. In this area of the college you will find the resources to make your college experience a successful one. But you must seize the opportunity to utilize these resources. The assistance provided by the Student Services area is not just for students experiencing academic difficulty; even those who are excelling will benefit.

My top three suggestions to successfully adjust to college:

1. Learn what resources are available to you from the onset. Make a list and keep it handy for times of need.

2. Each term, make a calendar that lists all important dates—payment deadlines, class start dates, assignment due dates—and adhere to them.

3. Seek assistance early in selecting a degree choice. With federal and state requirements constantly changing, knowing your degree path will save you time and money.

INTRODUCTION

You have made it! You have purchased your books and hold the class schedule in your hand. With confidence and past experiences—and, yes, perhaps a bit of anxiety—you have arrived for the first week of classes. Your road to this point may have been short, leading directly from high school graduation to the college campus. Or perhaps the road first carried you through significant life events such as marriage, children, military service, or a stint in the workforce. Whatever the route, you are here and ready to begin a fascinating and challenging new stage of life.

Regardless of your personal history, you carry with you the most valuable resource of all—*you*. Remember this truth: *You have a lifetime of skills and strategies that can serve you well in college—if you know how to tap into them.*

Honestly reflect, and draw upon those skills as you tackle the new challenges in front of you and discover that you have a lot to offer to yourself. Rather than a time to sing the blues, college life provides the opportunity for students to find their own rhythm and harmony.

POINTS TO CONSIDER

- **What is your reason for attending college?** The college environment offers a large number of helpful resources. But before you can identify the correct resources, it will be helpful to understand why you decided to continue your schooling at this point in your life. Is your main motivation to earn lots of money—or did you enroll in college because you wish to pursue a particular passion? Or perhaps a combination of reasons fuels your motivation.

- **How does this benefit you?** Once you understand your reason for being here, ask yourself the following questions:

  "So what? How does knowing why I am here help me? Isn't it enough to be attending classes and exploring options? I'll figure out why I'm here as time goes by."

  In fact, it might be a wise idea to ask the "So what?" question throughout your entire college experience. When confronted with new information or options, understand why and how a particular path is beneficial. The college experience provides a range of choices and opportunities for growth; having a clear understanding of your direction will help you handle the various transitional issues that all first-year students must address.

- **How will you know if you have chosen the correct road to travel?** Even if you're driving with a road map beside you, it can be helpful every so often to pull into a rest area and reflect on your journey. Are you traveling a route that interests you? Do you still want to move toward the destination circled on your map? Although it is important to be focused, it is sensible to stop, reflect on your progress, and then make any adjustments necessary to bring the proper destination into focus.

WHY ARE YOU HERE?

Students enroll in college for various reasons. They come to campus with different abilities, desires, and unique challenges. You will meet these differences in the student center, the residential hall, and in the classrooms. In some situations you will casually converse with this diverse mix of people. In other instances you will need to work closely with these students. For that reason, it would be beneficial to take a generalized look at your prospective partners on a class assignment, a student government project, or a service learning activity.

Some students come to college with a very detailed and specific career goal in mind. They know exactly what they want and how to get it. These students will tell you exactly what they will be doing in two years, four years, and ten years down the road.

Others come to campus simply because they just got out of high school and college seems to be the next logical step in life. Other than that, they don't know why they are here. They just "know" that this is where they need to be. Not surprisingly, these students have only a vague idea, or none at all, about their life ambitions.

You will meet students who see the college experience as one continuous party. Socializing, sporting events, late-night clubbing, and road trips are their courses of study. Typically, students who follow this "curriculum" will receive personalized letters from the dean marked with either "Academic Probation" or "Academically Suspended."

Single parents who come to college must balance the needs of family and work. Unlike the partygoers who see college as an opportunity to escape responsibility, these students view campus as an important stop on their way to an improved life.

There may be a former member of the military sitting next to you in class. Having fulfilled a national commitment, this person now wishes to gain skills and knowledge that will help in a post-military life.

© *Stockdisc*

You will encounter students of all ages. Recent high school graduates—young and restless—will try to make meaning of their setting. Sitting next to them can very well be nontraditional students, such as the older student who has decided to return to school after many years away from the classroom, or the person with a full-time job who is taking just one course in order to secure a job promotion.

International students will be part of the classroom mix as well. These new arrivals experience the typical college transitional issues—but in a new culture while learning a new language. (Wow—talk about transitions!) You will also have a chance to meet and know students from different ethnic groups and socioeconomic backgrounds.

The diverse tapestry of your class fabric may include students with disabilities—hearing impaired students with signers, visually impaired students with guide dogs, physically impaired students in wheelchairs, and learning disabled students with note-takers.

Whatever your reasons for being here today, your fellow classmates have their own. Each of you will face both emotional and social challenges that will need to be addressed. Before you can successfully address these challenges, however, first reflect on why you are here by completing Activities 1.1 and 1.2.

The opportunity costs and the value of attending college

A college education represents a huge investment of time, money, and emotion.* For whatever reasons (see Activities 1.1 and 1.2) you made the choice to enroll in school rather than do something else with your precious resources. To be here, you have given up the opportunity to do something else.

Economists frequently refer to the concept of *opportunity costs.* When a choice is made, another option is eliminated, or at the very least, postponed. For instance, if a student decides to drop out of high school so that he can get a job, earn money, and buy a car, the opportunity cost of buying the car is the loss (or postponement) of his high school graduation.

Likewise, if a student decides to skip an evening with her friends so that she can study for a test, the opportunity cost of studying for the test is the lost time with her friends.

---

*Innumerable sources tout "the value of a college education." A recent Google search found *more than six thousand* sites. A few have been referenced in this section for your continued research.

WHY HAVE YOU DECIDED TO CONTINUE YOUR EDUCATION?

Why did you decide to come to college? Not the *actual* school you are currently attending, but why did you decide to continue your education at *any school?* Rate the following reasons for attending college on a scale from 0 (not at all) to 5 (a huge factor for attending college). Circle the numbers that most closely apply to you. Reflect on each item and honestly respond.

Reasons I am attending college now   **0 (not at all) to 5 (huge reason)**

_____ 1. I need career training.   0—1—2—3—4—5
_____ 2. I plan on earning a lot of money.   0—1—2—3—4—5
_____ 3. I want to explore different areas of interest.   0—1—2—3—4—5
_____ 4. I want to find a life partner.   0—1—2—3—4—5
_____ 5. I want to participate in college-level athletics.   0—1—2—3—4—5
_____ 6. My parents want me to attend.   0—1—2—3—4—5
_____ 7. My friends are going to college.   0—1—2—3—4—5
_____ 8. I want a better life for myself.   0—1—2—3—4—5
_____ 9. I want to make a better life for my family.   0—1—2—3—4—5
_____10. I want to be the first one in my family to attend.   0—1—2—3—4—5
_____11. I am divorced and need to support myself.   0—1—2—3—4—5
_____12. I want to party.   0—1—2—3—4—5
_____13. I need to experience life away from home.   0—1—2—3—4—5
_____14. All my children have left home—now it's my turn!   0—1—2—3—4—5
_____15. It has been my lifetime dream to earn a degree.   0—1—2—3—4—5
_____16. I need college courses for my current job.   0—1—2—3—4—5
_____17. It beats getting a "real" job.   0—1—2—3—4—5
_____18. Other: _____   0—1—2—3—4—5
_____19. Other: _____   0—1—2—3—4—5
_____20. Other: _____   0—1—2—3—4—5

21. Review the numbers you circled. Now put a check mark on the line in front of each reason that you rated either "4" or "5." These represent your major reasons for enrolling in college.

22. Reflect for a moment and then write your thoughts about your answers. In what ways do these rankings surprise you?

_____

_____

_____

23. Based on your rankings above, write one or two sentences as to why you are attending college classes.

_____

_____

_____

HOW DO YOU FEEL ABOUT BEING HERE?

At this point in a book such as this, it would not be unusual to ask you to consider your goals for the rest of the term. Although that can be a very worthwhile exercise—and one you will be asked to do in a later chapter—a different reality takes precedence at this time.

Before students can focus clearly on academic success or long-term goals such as "earning a degree" or finding "career training," other more personal issues must be addressed. There is much to do and learn about in your new environment.

For this activity please review your responses in Activity 1.1. Then respond to the following questions:

1. Whether you have been on campus one day or one month, how do you feel about being here? That is, do you feel emotionally or socially stressed, at ease, or somewhere in between by all the changes you are experiencing?

   _____

   _____

2. What do you think you can do now to help you successfully complete this term?

   _____

   _____

   _____

For everything we do, there is a cost of some sort. It is not, as the foregoing examples indicate, always directly related to dollars and cents—but something is gained and something is lost.

The same analogy holds true for a college education. Students sitting in class or completing a homework assignment have chosen *not* to do something else. Instead of attending college, they could be earning money in the workforce. The amount of money that they are *not* making because they are in school is an opportunity cost. If, instead of college, a student could be earning $20,000 a year, and he stays in college for four years, his opportunity cost equates to $80,000—the amount of money he could have earned in that same period of time.

When you add in the direct expenses of education—tuition, books, transportation, room and board, and fees—the cost to attend college increases considerably.[1]

With those kinds of numbers to consider, why do people decide to attend college? One explanation is because the value of a college education is greater in the *long term.* Whenever you feel emotionally drained, or maybe thinking of giving up on college, consider that the **opportunity cost of a college education** is an investment in your future.

And you may wish to consider the opportunity costs of *not* pursuing a college degree. According to the *U.S. Census Bureau News:*

> Workers 18 and over with a bachelor's degree earn an average of $51,206 a year, while those with a high school diploma earn $27,915. Workers with an advanced degree make an average of $74,602, and those without a high school diploma average $18,734.[2]

See Table 1.1 for a chart of this income comparison.

Another study reports that a community college education "more than doubles the full-time annual earnings potential of community college graduates" compared to those without a community college degree.[3]

Do the math (see Table 1.2). If the "accumulated earnings" (the amount that would be earned over the career span of a worker) are considered, the numbers are staggering. A person with a college

Table 1.1
Comparing income according to years of schooling

Amount of schooling	Less than a high school education	High school diploma	Bachelor's degree	Graduate degree
Income	$18,734	$27,915	$51,206	$74,602

Source: "College Degree Nearly Doubles Annual Earnings, Census Bureau Reports," *U.S. Census Bureau News,* March 28, 2005, U.S. Census Bureau, http://www.census.gov/Press-Release/www/releases/archives/education/004214.html (accessed July 7, 2005).

Table 1.2
Income differential according to level of education

Amount of schooling	No high school diploma	High school diploma	Bachelor's degree	Graduate degree
Income Earned per Year*	$18,734	$27,915	$51,206	$74,602
Total Income Earned in 30 Years	$562,020	$837,450	$1,536,180	$2,238,060

*Does not calculate inflation.

Source: Consumer Calcs, "What Is the Value of a College Education?" Financial Calculators Inc., http://www.fincalc.com/ (accessed July 7, 2005).

degree can expect to earn approximately *$1 million to $2 million more* than someone with no degree. Calculate the additional value of graduate degrees, and the money differential continues to widen.[†]

A college education has value beyond your savings account. A liberal arts education, for example, provides a broad base of knowledge to prepare you for many types of jobs. It exposes you to differing viewpoints, and it helps you to critically analyze material. Higher education provides advanced knowledge of history, politics, and culture. You discuss issues with like-minded individuals as well as debate issues with those who hold opposing beliefs. A college education allows you to broaden your knowledge base, reaffirm your beliefs and, at times, change your positions.

The value of a college education *is* dollars and cents—but it is so much *more.*

KEY TRANSITIONAL ISSUES FACING STUDENTS

This section presents quick overviews of some of the more common adjustment issues for college students. Think of these as "snapshots." The entire "photo" will come into focus over the course of this book.

[†] See, for instance, Consumer Calcs, "What Is the Value of a College Education?" Financial Calculators Inc., http://www.fincalc.com/

WHAT IS THE VALUE OF A COLLEGE EDUCATION?

This activity is different from most activities you will be asked to complete in this book, as it asks you to include feedback from a significant person in your life.* The idea is for you to reflect not only on your own views, but also on the views of a respected family member or friend—somebody in your home neighborhood. If that is not possible, then identify someone who has been a mentor or role model for you in the past—someone who has provided guidance over the course of your life. It does not matter whether the person attended college, or even if the person finished high school. The only requirement is that this person *has* been a part of your social and emotional network.

1. First, your thoughts. What is the value of a college education for you? That is, what will a college degree provide for you? How do you think it will be worth the opportunity costs?

   _____

   _____

   _____

   _____

   _____

   _____

2. Once you have reflected and written your thoughts, please forward the same questions to your identified significant person. What does this person think the value of a college education is in today's society? Call, write, e-mail, or sit down with the person. Write the person's responses on the lines provided.

   The name and relationship of your significant person: _____

   _____

   That person's response: _____

   _____

   _____

   _____

   _____

3. Once you have received that input from your significant person, reflect on the two responses. Are there similarities? What surprised you? Based on this new knowledge, what revisions, if any, would you make to your earlier thoughts about the value of a college education?

   _____

   _____

   _____

   _____

   _____

   _____

* I'd like to thank Eileen Crawford. After reading her book, *Mom's College Handbook* (2004), I was inspired to develop this particular idea.

Change: What do you bring to the table?

As described in the introduction to this book, the first stage in the **change cycle** is when people need or want to begin something new in their lives. You were at this stage when you decided to attend college.

In stage 2, you began planning for the day you would start college. You chose a college, filed an application, made financial arrangements, and enrolled in courses.

You are now at stage 3—execution of your plan. It is time to go to class and become a member of the student body at your college or university. You will experience many successes and also your share of setbacks. When you stumble, keep the following strategies—the 4 R's—in mind:

- **Reflect** on the reasons for the momentary disappointment. Do your best to understand what happened and why it happened.

- **Respect** the skills that you have to address the challenge. You have confronted obstacles before in your life. What did you do in past situations to solve problems?

- Take **responsibility** for any changes you will need to make—and move toward that change.

- Remember to develop and maintain **renewal** strategies that foster balance, wellness, and growth in your life.

College will present new challenges, but you have valuable past experiences to draw from. Consider the following facts:

Fact: College is different from high school, and it is different from the world of work.

Fact: College courses will require you to work with large volumes of material.

Fact: College-level work will require you to reevaluate the study skills and relational skills you bring with you to campus.

Fact: You already possess skills, knowledge, and strategies that will help you be successful in college.

Where you are now is different from where you were at this time last year. Whether you are a full-time student fresh from high school or a part-timer taking classes during your lunch hour from work, your new surroundings—the campus, the classrooms, the diverse mix of students and professors—look and feel different. Some students are energized by all the new sights, sounds, and smells of a college campus; others are overwhelmed. Activity 1.4 asks you to examine what you bring to the table—what you already know that can help you during this first term of change.

There are two points worth reflecting on from the preceding activity. First, there is no doubt that you will need to refine some of your old skills and even learn new strategies in your college classes. That is simply part of the educational process. As you ascend the educational ladder each term, you will be expected to grapple with ideas, issues, and skills that are foreign to you.

Second, as you face new challenges, it is understandable to be anxious about stepping outside of your comfort zone. At those times, think back to the activity. You have a larger and more developed skill base than you may give yourself credit for. Be willing to try your old skills in new situations—adjust and change as needed—but never forget that you have a great deal of experience on which to draw.

Emotional transition: Managing the freedom and responsibility of the first-year experience

College life demands a considerable amount of time. You must attend classes, read extensive assignments, complete research projects, involve yourself in lab work, and, possibly, engage in community service activities. Additionally, you may have to balance family, work, and/or cocurricular priorities. At times it may seem as though there are not enough hours in the day. Chapter 4 will suggest strategies for organizing time commitments, but for now let's take a look at the responsibility you signed on for when you walked on campus.

Even though rules and procedures vary from college to college and from instructor to instructor, the responsibility for getting to class and completing assignments rests squarely on the student's shoulders. If you miss an 8:00 a.m. psychology class every Monday, there is a better than

WHAT DO YOU BRING TO THE TABLE?

Your past experiences have already provided a knowledge base that will help you be successful. Read the items that follow and place a check mark in front of each skill you already possess (or have, at least, practiced in the past).

1. Right now, I can:

   _____ Read and understand instructions (such as a recipe for a meal or directions for downloading a computer program).

   _____ Read a newspaper article and summarize what it reported.

   _____ Watch a television program and explain what I saw to a friend.

   _____ Hear a song and later be able to remember the lyrics.

   _____ Prepare a reasoned argument as to why I deserve a pay raise.

   _____ Listen to a political speech and then develop an educated opinion about an issue.

   _____ Speak in front of more than 10 people (such as a group of friends, church group, or community organization).

   _____ Organize my day so that I can accomplish four or five tasks.

   _____ Meet a deadline (such as filing taxes, completing a college application, or registering for classes).

   _____ Persevere in the face of great odds to accomplish a desired goal (such as standing in line to get tickets for a sporting event or concert).

   _____ Prioritize a series of tasks so that I address important issues in my life.

   _____ Test successfully to achieve a goal (such as obtaining a driver's license).

   _____ Study to pass a test (such as a high school math exam).

   _____ Get along with diverse types of people.

   _____ Sit for long periods of time and listen to a person speak (such as at a business meeting or religious service).

   _____ Volunteer my opinion when a question is asked.

   _____ Assist group members to accomplish an assigned task.

   _____ Sleep an appropriate number of hours so that I am rested in the morning.

   _____ Focus my energies so that I can accomplish goals (such as participating on an athletic team, playing in a band, or getting accepted to college).

   _____ Others: What other skills do I have that will help me in college? List them here.

   _____

   _____

   _____

   _____

   _____

2. Now carefully examine the boxes that you checked. Maybe you checked more items than you thought you would. What does this inventory tell you about what you bring to the college table?

   _____

   _____

   _____

   _____

average chance that *no one* on the campus will come looking for you. You will have to make it to the class or scramble to get the notes and instructions you may have missed.

Perhaps you are taking only one course, slipping away during your lunch break at work to take an English class. If your boss requires you to take a different lunch shift and it interferes with your schooling, it will be your responsibility—not your instructor's—to handle the conflict. There will not be a counselor or parent to intervene on your behalf.* And when it comes to absences, many instructors will not make a distinction between "excused" and "unexcused" absences. Their view holds that a missed day of class participation *is* a *missed* day—there is no way to make that up. The class discussion occurred and cannot be repeated. Also, remember that the dynamics of the class will change without your presence. Your input in class discussions *is* important.

College life provides a great deal of personal independence but also requires a corresponding level of responsibility. Because no one will constantly be watching over you, you will need the self-discipline and emotional maturity to fulfill your obligations. Every so often it may be a good idea to reflect on why you are attending college (review Activity 1.2).

Many factors affect the manner in which students handle the freedom and responsibilities of campus life. For instance, family life will have an impact on how a student adjusts in college, as follows:

- Some students come from families where rigidly enforced rules were the order of the day. These students can go in a couple of directions. On the one hand, always having had the rules explicitly stated and enforced, they may not know what to do because no one is directing their every move; they are not used to making their own decisions. On the other hand, once away from the strict family rules, these students might "go wild" with their newfound independence.

- Other students have enjoyed more freedom, but perhaps with somebody always available to help in times of difficulty. For instance, parents may have been constantly on the phone to the guidance counselor, seeking assignment extensions for these students. It comes as quite a shock when they enter college and must live with the consequences of actions that cannot be "fixed" by someone calling the school.

- Still another group has had a great deal of responsibility placed upon them to raise siblings, care for an elderly relative, or work to help support the family. Such responsibilities may continue during college. These students will still be accountable for their home-based duties while trying to find time to tackle the expectations of college. Sometimes these overly responsible students may have a stressful time balancing everything they must do.

Emotional transition: Working through the change cycle

Life brings change—transitions from one place to another. Change can also bring *life*. Change is invigorating and passion producing. Each stage of the change cycle (see Figure I.2 in the book's introduction) can enhance renewal. And at times we may be undergoing a couple of different changes at the same time. For instance, there is the change of having to deal with the rigors of college academic expectations, while at the same time trying to adjust to a new roommate or determine where you will get day care for your child.

Social transition: The time crunch of balancing school, work, and cocurricular activities

Time-management skills—or the lack of them—will quickly become evident as you try to survive during the first term on campus. You might be one of those students who is actively involved in cocurricular activities like student government or intramural sports. Or you may only be on campus a short time each day, leaving campus immediately after class in order to go to

---

*In fact, due to confidentiality laws, schools are not allowed to release information to parents without student permission, if the student is older than 18 years of age. Although exceptions may apply, for further information see the Family Educational Rights and Privacy Act (FERPA), available on the Web site of the U.S. Department of Education, http://www.ed.gov/policy/gen/guid/fpco/ferpa/index.html.

WHERE ARE YOU IN THE CHANGE CYCLE?

Pause and reflect for a moment. For each stage listed here, identify *one* area of your life that finds you in that particular stage. Then answer the questions that follow.

1. *Stage 1: Recognize the need for a change.*   This is the point when you recognize that life as you know it is about to change, or already has changed. For example, graduating from high school represents the end of one phase of your schooling and the beginning of the next (college). Or the loss of a job might force you to recognize the need for new job training. The end of a relationship may also signal the end of one phase of life. What aspect of your life is in this particular stage of change? It could involve academic expectations, new relationships, or financial obligations. What has recently occurred that has caused you to recognize the need to establish a new goal or adjust a current direction in which you are traveling?

   _____

   _____

   _____

2. *Stage 2: Plan for the change.*   What are you doing in your life right now that indicates you are planning for a change in your life? Once again, it can involve any area of your life. For instance, perhaps you are changing where or with whom you live. Maybe the beginning of the school term means a new schedule for you and your family. Whatever the situation may be, you have established a goal and are making plans to reach it. What are you doing that will move you toward making this goal a reality?_____

   _____

   _____

   _____

3. *Stage 3: Execute the plan.*   On the way to your destination there will probably be unforeseen detours. What kind of obstacles have you encountered (or do you anticipate) on your way to your destination? Have you had to adjust your course? What do you do to keep a positive attitude and forward progress? _____

   _____

   _____

   _____

4. *Stage 4: Enjoy the achieved goal.*   How do you enjoy the accomplishment of a goal in your life? Maybe you have been accepted into a campus club or have received an A on your first college exam. What are you doing to savor the moment? That is, how are you enjoying the thrill of the achievement?_____

   _____

   _____

   _____

5. *Connections to college transitions.*   How can knowing about the change cycle help you deal with college transition issues? Why is it important to be able to recognize when there is a time for change, plan for the change, execute the change and, finally, enjoy the change that you have made? _____

   _____

   _____

   _____

work. Whatever the situation, time—finding enough of it to do everything you need and want to do—will present a new set of challenges. It is one area that can seem overwhelming. Specific strategies will be introduced in chapter 4, but you might find the following general strategies helpful now:

- On average, budget two hours of study time for each hour spent in a class.

- Commit to work and cocurricular activities once you know you have scheduled appropriate time for class, study, and sleep.

- Be sure to schedule time for physical, emotional, and social renewal.

- How you use time is your *choice.* Make the decision a wise one.

Social and emotional transitions: Key people to know— The C.A.P. principle

© Stockdisc

To name all of the key people on campus would require its own chapter. And a key person to one student might not be a key person to another student. For instance, a student needing financial assistance (grants, scholarships, or an on-campus job) may find the financial aid office initially to be the most important stop on campus. An athlete might find his coach to be the key contact.

Generally speaking, educators often mention the same "top three people to know" for a student to have an increased chance of college success. Make sure, as soon as possible, that you begin a working and trusted relationship with *at least:*

- One **c**lassmate

- One **a**dvisor or counselor

- One of your **p**rofessors

Note that the first letter of each name forms the acronym *C.A.P.* When you follow the **C.A.P. principle,** these three key people can help you connect with the physical campus, adjust to the college experience, and persist to graduation. In fact, don't settle for knowing just *one* of each; get to know as many as you possibly can. Make it a goal, for instance, to personally visit the office of each of your professors.

MAINTAINING A HEALTHY BALANCE

How do you develop and practice a healthy lifestyle in your new environment?

Yours is a busy world. You are pulled in a variety of directions. You have to choose appropriate classes, navigate the emotional roller coaster that sometimes accompanies relationships, eventually declare a major, and (down the road) graduate and find your place in the work-a-day world.

Do you take the time to "recharge your batteries" along the way? A battery-operated piece of equipment after extended use will steadily lose power and eventually stop working. Some batteries are renewable—that is, they can be recharged for extended life. Yet they, too, will eventually lose juice and, unless plugged into the charger, become useless as well.

If you consistently operate on too little sleep, eat less than nutritious food, or depend on the "help" of drugs and alcohol to cope with life's challenges, your "batteries" will eventually quit working, too. One result is fatigue, which can weaken your immune system, making you more susceptible to illness—and missed days from class.

The introduction to this book described how a **balanced life** will help renew the six dimensions of your life. Let's examine those dimensions on a deeper level.

Dr. Bill Hettler, cofounder of the National Wellness Institute (NWI), is credited with developing the *Six Dimensional Wellness Model.*[4] This very simple yet powerful model reminds us that a balanced life needs more than three good meals and a restful night's sleep. Each of the six dimensions has an impact on the other five. According to the NWI, no single category operates as a renegade; all six—social, occupational, spiritual, physical, intellectual, and emotional—work together for a balanced life. If ignored, any one of the dimensions can have a detrimental effect on the others. As you review each category below, think how your daily practices and overall lifestyle measure up to each description. The six **dimensions of wellness** are depicted in Table 1.3.

Table 1.3
Dimensions of wellness

Dimension	Description of a "well person"
Social	You maintain positive relationships with people around you and encourage a support network of family, friends, classmates, and coworkers. You have an awareness of your impact on society and the environment.
Occupational	You are involved in a profession (or course of study) that is personally satisfying. You learn new skills and develop career-oriented goals.
Spiritual	You stress the importance of finding your life's purpose by reflecting (meditating, praying) on the purpose of life, and then you act on your beliefs and values to reinforce your discovered purpose. You acknowledge and understand that "you are connected to the universe ... [and] woven into the fabric of this universe."[5]
Physical	You maintain a healthy lifestyle (diet, rest, exercise, strength, flexibility). You are able to recognize and appropriately respond to warning signs of ill health.
Intellectual	You actively seek to expand your knowledge base and skill base, and to develop your creativity and critical thinking skills.
Emotional	You have the ability to manage and express emotions appropriately and handle stress effectively.

Source: Adapted from "The Six Dimensional Wellness Model," National Wellness Institute, http://www.nationalwellness.org/index.php?id=391&id_tier=381 (accessed July 7, 2005).

Another way to think of this model is to visualize a six-string guitar. The guitar will be able to make sweet music with properly tuned strings. If one of the six strings falls out of tune or breaks, the guitar can still be played but the song will not be as pleasing. As more strings weaken or break from undue stress, the guitar loses its ability to play music.

Apply the guitar analogy to your life. The six dimensions ("strings") represent the six critical areas of your personality. You might be able to keep making music if one or two of the strings weaken or break. Eventually, though, the remaining strings will not be able to carry the tune, possibly leading to the total collapse of the song (mind, body, spirit).

We all need to tune our life-strings. After all, this instrument—our mind, body, and spirit—enables us to create the sounds and rhythms we choose.

Too often, people break down under the weight of life's daily stresses simply because they have not tended to one or another aspect of their lives. The same holds true for students. During the first year of the college experience, students can experience any number of stressors that will weaken one or more of the life-strings. You already possess healthy ways to strengthen each dimension in your life. You may have helped a friend weather a difficult time when his life was becoming dangerously imbalanced. Maybe someone has done the same for you.

Care for your life-strings, and the instrument will continue to play rich music.

SUMMARY

IT'S A NEW AND WONDERFULLY EXCITING LIFE ON CAMPUS

This chapter has introduced a number of issues. Your head could very well be swimming with ideas on how to embrace the rest of the term. On the other hand, you may be entertaining thoughts of leaving school and returning to more familiar and comfortable surroundings. Regardless of your direction, take a slow and deep breath, and review the following key points from this chapter:

- Understand your reasons for attending college at this time in your life. This will help you concentrate on beneficial activities.

- Take time to reflect on your decisions. Spontaneity can be a blessing, but deliberation has its advantages as well.

- Acknowledge the experiences and skills you bring to the classroom. Use and build on this reservoir of personal talent.

- Know the resources that will help you cope and thrive with change. Your school has a lot to offer.

- Take time to keep your life-strings in tune. Treat your body, mind, and spirit with respect.

The last three activities of this chapter will allow you to reflect on the three levels of student success as presented in the book's introduction:

Level I: The 4 Rs

Level II: The Change Cycle

Level III: Tuning Your Life-Strings

tuning your life-strings

the 4 Rs

self

change and personal growth

Your SELF:
Personal growth
and balance

Each activity will give you an opportunity to reflect and apply the chapter concepts in a way that is meaningful to you during this transitional phase of your life. For your convenience and reflection, similar activities will be placed at the end of each chapter so that you can apply newly acquired information and also keep an ongoing journal of growth in the various facets of your life.

The 4 Rs

Describe a personal example as to how you used each of the 4 Rs to effectively handle a transitional issue thus far in your college term.

1. *Reflection* (Example: Perhaps you gave careful consideration before deciding to join a club or study group.)

   _____

   _____

2. *Respect* (Example: To calm your anxiety about meeting new people, you reminded yourself that you have always had a talent for making friends easily.)

   _____

   _____

3. *Responsibility* (Example: You realized your writing skills need improvement so you took action and went to the campus writing lab to work with a peer tutor.)

   _____

   _____

4. *Renewal* (Example: To increase your energy level, you have started exercising three days per week.)

   _____

   _____

The Change Cycle

Thus far in the term, what has been the biggest change you have had to make as you adjusted to college life? Has it been an academic change, like revising your study habits? Or has it involved relationship issues (roommates, classmates, teammates)? Maybe the change was financial. Perhaps college life has inspired change in your family life.

1. What change have you identified as the biggest? _____

_____

_____

_____

_____

2. What led you to recognize that this change needed to be made? _____

_____

_____

_____

_____

3. What was (or will be) your plan to make the change a reality?_____

_____

_____

_____

_____

4. If you have put the plan into action (executed it), how are you progressing?_____

_____

_____

_____

_____

5. Once the change has become a reality, how do you plan to enjoy this achievement? _____

_____

_____

_____

_____

Tuning Your Life-Strings

Fill in the last two columns of the table that follows. With this activity you can regularly check the strength of each life-string, apply any needed repair work, and enjoy a more balanced and harmonious life. For instance, if you have been feeling unusually stressed during the first week of classes, you may decide that an appointment with a student services advisor will help you more effectively handle the emotional pressures you feel. It's worth a try, wouldn't you say?

Life-string	Questions to consider	What possible activities could help you tune this string?	Who can help you tune this string?*
Social	• Do you have a support network in place? • What is your place in the school community? • Who is the person with whom you can share most any concern?		
Occupational	• Earlier in this chapter you reflected on your reasons for coming to college. How does your reason (or reasons) for being in college bring you joy?		
Spiritual	• Have you recently explored or reexamined the deeper meanings of life—and your purpose in this life? • Do you have peace of mind?		
Physical	• How nutritious was your diet for this past week? • What kind of exercise schedule do you maintain? • What do you do for healthy relaxation? • Do you feel rested each morning when you awaken?		

(continued)

Life-string	Questions to consider	What possible activities could help you tune this string?	Who can help you tune this string?*
Intellectual	• What did you do this week that involved critical thinking? • How did this expand your knowledge and/or skill base?		
Emotional	• What strategies have you used to effectively deal with your college stressors? • On a scale of 1 to 5, how would you rate your self-esteem?		

*Many colleges and universities provide wellness strategies, programs, or models for students and employees. For an example, refer to the Web site of Clark State Community College, http://www.clark.cc.oh.us/clinic_well.html. What kind of a model does your school have?

Rhythms of Reflection

Because sound decisions require reflective consideration of all factors involved, this chapter will end with one last reflective activity.

Carefully read the following poem. Its words were penned more than *eight hundred years ago* but the thoughts are as pertinent as if the poet had just put them to paper this morning. Find a quiet place and read these few lines:

> *You were born with goodness and trust.*
> *You were born with ideals and dreams.*
> *You were born with greatness.*
> *You were born with wings.*
> *You are not meant for crawling, so don't.*
> *You have wings.*
> *Learn to use them and fly.*
> –*Rumi*[6]

Using Rumi's words for inspiration, explain how you will take the knowledge you have gained from this chapter's reflective activities and apply it to your life so that you will appreciate your "wings" and use them to fly.

_____

_____

_____

_____

_____

_____

To further respond online, please go to the *Rhythms of Reflection* module in chapter 1 of the Companion Website.

ENDNOTES

1. M. Cummings, *The Value of an Education,* Monmouth Housing Alliance, http://www.housingall.com/STEPUP/ValofEdu.htm (accessed May 30, 2006).
2. "College Degree Nearly Doubles Annual Earnings, Census Bureau Reports," *U.S. Census Bureau News,* March 28, 2005, http://www.census.gov/Press-Release/www/releases/archives/education/004214.html (accessed July 7, 2005).
3. Janice Motta, "Massachusetts Community Colleges Release Findings of Study on Economic Benefits of Community College Education on Graduates and the Commonwealth," April 6, 2004, 1, Massachusetts Community Colleges, http://www.masscc.org/pdfs/press_1759econreportrelease2.pdf (accessed October 1, 2005).
4. Bill Hettler, "The Six Dimensional Wellness Model," National Wellness Institute, http://www.nationalwellness.org/index.php?id=391&id_tier=381 (accessed July 7, 2005).
5. Robert M. Sherfield, *The Everything Self-Esteem Book* (Avon, MA: Adams Media., 2004), 94.
6. Rumi was a thirteenth century poet. This poem can be found on a number of Internet sites with inspirational messages. It can also be found in Wayne Dyer, *The Power of Intention: Learning to Co-Create Your World Your Way* (Carlsbad, CA: Hay House, 2004), 120.

Motivation and Goal Setting

Dancing to Your Own Beat

REFLECTIVE QUESTIONS

Keeping the following questions in mind will make this chapter more meaningful:

- What values (personal principles) guide you?
- What motivates you to achieve your goals?
- How do you know your goals are correct for you?
- What will you do to reach your goals?
- Do you have a realistic way to monitor your progress toward your goals?

KEY TERMS

action steps
belief system
goal
locus of control
motivation (extrinsic and
intrinsic)
motivational barriers
values

GUEST SPEAKER

MEET JANICE A. DALY

**Assistant Dean of Students and Director,
First-Year Experience Program**

Florida State University

Tallahassee, Florida

As a college student, you are frequently asked, "What do you want to do with your life?" Your answer to that question reflects your life's goals.

Goals may be set for personal, educational, social, physical, financial, or occupational areas of your life. Your dreams will become your goals. Motivation, like goal setting, is influenced by others, but it belongs to you. You can be motivated by challenge, hard work, risk, and the possibility of achievement. Goals give you direction; motivation gives you the drive to achieve your goals.

Every day of your life is shaped by the choices you make. Your goals reflect those choices.

My top three suggestions for reaching your goals:

1. Identify a realistic and specific goal. What is of value to you that you want to accomplish? How will it contribute to yourself and others?

2. Establish an action plan. Commit to small, specific, and manageable steps that you can measure and see a difference, so you can build on small successes. Others have had the same or similar goals. Seek advice and assistance from others.

3. Make your dream a reality. Remain focused on your goal. Remember that setbacks are not failures. Your action plan can be altered along the way.

INTRODUCTION

It is not unusual for first-year college students to look at the subject of goal setting with a raised eyebrow:

"Goal setting? Why do I need to think about that? After all, I'm here aren't I? My goal is to get a diploma. Why make it more difficult than it is?"

This chapter will look at what motivates students to achieve their goals. When you establish a goal, you are actually putting together a strategy to obtain what you desire. Whether or not you achieve the goal depends in great part upon how effectively your strategy was planned and carried out.

In the world of corporate leadership, the word *strategy* is used often. One company develops a strategy to market and sell computers directly to customers. A textbook publisher revises its strategy to sell more books to college students. A leading automobile manufacturer constantly refocuses its strategy to put drivers (buyers) in its vehicles.

Every successful corporation has to have a strategy—a plan of action—which simply and clearly places itself in a position to have an advantage in the marketplace. The corporate strategy is all about making winning choices and using available resources to bring about success.

Let's relate this example to you, the college student.

Your first term in college has been, and will continue to be, a series of learning experiences. You have had to find your classes, buy books, obtain a parking decal, locate the campus library, fight for a parking space, start tackling assignments, and maybe fit in with a new roommate or roommates. At times it might feel like you are moving in a cloud of dust. You might say, "Who has time for strategies? I'm just trying to survive!"

True enough. But a well-developed plan—a strategy to reach a goal—can provide an advantage in the classroom and on the larger campus.

POINTS TO CONSIDER

- **What motivates you to achieve a goal?** This question goes to the heart of what you value—what is important to you. These values determine what you want to accomplish by the end of this term—or even by the end of this week. What do you want to gain from college? Or asked another way, what is it that you value and how can college help you put your values into action?

- **How does this benefit you?** You may ask, "So what! Why do I need to know what motivates me? How does this benefit me now?" Once you know why you are here (college), it's time to focus on what you need to do. What steps do you need to take to achieve your goals, and when will you take those steps? College places great demands on your time. Once you establish academic goals, how will you stay motivated to make them become realities?

- **How will you know if you have chosen the correct road to travel?** As you move toward your goals it will be helpful to establish checkpoints along the way to help you assess the academic choices and priorities you have made. In addition to measuring progress toward achieving a goal, you will want to continually reflect on its appropriateness. Ask yourself, "Is the goal I established still right for me? Is this what I want to do?" Goals should be energizing rather than emotionally draining. As you work through this chapter, reflect on the manner in which your goals affect the dimensions of your wellness.

VALUES

A great deal has been written and said about values and their connection to education. Calls for character education and values-based courses have generated spirited political and social debate. Right or wrong, agree or disagree, this topic vibrates in our society.

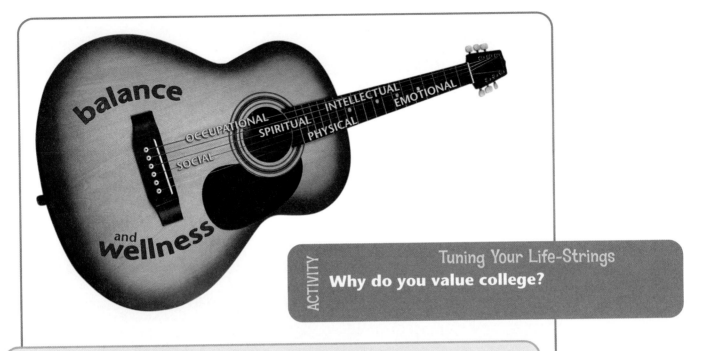

ACTIVITY

Tuning Your Life-Strings
Why do you value college?

Review your responses in Activity 1.1 ("Why Have You Decided to Continue Your Education?"). Now reflect on how your beliefs about the importance of a college education evolved over time.

1. **Belief system.** Think back to when you first remember hearing about "going to college." Over the years, as you heard more about college, what did you come to believe about college? That is, why did you come to value attending college? _____

_____

_____

_____

_____

In short, *character* refers to how you conduct yourself—how you behave. Your *behavior* indicates a great deal about what you value. Your *values* are reflected by your motivations and goals. (For instance, see the accompanying Tuning Your Life-Strings feature, "Why Do You Value College?")

Where do you "find" your values?

At its simplest level, your **values** represent what you see as important. For instance, you may value free time with your friends; you may value earning a spot on the Dean's List; you may value your professor's advice; and you may value the importance of an agreeable roommate.

But values do not "just happen." They are cultivated over time. In fact, your values evolve from your **belief system**—what you consider or believe to be true about the world (see Figure 2.1). This is how you see the world. And this view goes a long way in determining what you see to be important or significant.

For instance, maybe you grew up in a family of hardworking high-school-educated adults. Although they have been model employees their entire careers, they may have had difficulty making ends meet or "getting ahead." They may have worked two jobs to support their families. Perhaps you heard, "I want you to go to college because college-educated people earn more money and have a more comfortable life than I do." Over time, that became part of your belief system; *it is what you considered to be true about the world.* Because of this *belief* you then placed great *value* on getting a college degree. It became a *motivating force* in your life (see Figure 2.2).

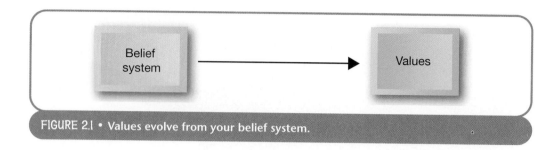

FIGURE 2.1 • **Values evolve from your belief system.**

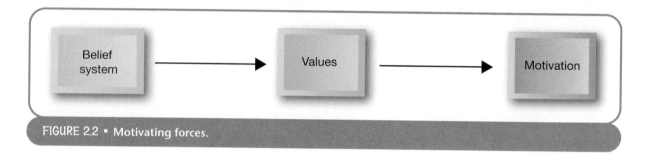

FIGURE 2.2 • **Motivating forces.**

MOTIVATION

Motivation moves you to act on or toward something. It can come from within you or can be the consequence of some outside force that drives you forward. Actually, you do not need this book or a teacher to tell you what motivation is. Before you ever set foot on this college campus you were driven by desires—and you acted on those desires. For instance, one of those desires was to attend college. You took action to make that happen and here you are, *just like you had the desire to do.* Motivation provided the fuel—the energy—to move toward your goal (go to college). That fuel came from your values. Understanding your value structure can help you understand these driving forces.

You *value* college because of the *belief system* that has shaped your worldview to this point in your life.

Consider, for example, what might motivate someone to become a teacher. Perhaps growing up in a family of educators has shaped a worldview; teaching has become part of the person's belief system. Dig deeper, and the person might find that what attracts him to teaching is the ability to help young people reach their potential and discover their dreams. With this deeper introspection, he discovers that he wants to be a teacher because he values helping young children. This becomes the fuel that propels this student ahead.

Where do you find motivation?

Human motivation varies from person to person depending on the opportunities, challenges, tasks, activities, and life experiences we face. An athlete's love for sport may motivate him to get to practice early and remain late. Or perhaps another student did not do as well on a reading quiz as she would

© Stockdisc

Table 2.1
Intrinsic and extrinsic motivation

	Why? Intrinsic motivation	Why? Extrinsic motivation
Attends school at night	She has always wanted to be the first in her family to get a college degree. She has always loved reading and learning—they give meaning to her day.	The only way she can advance in her job and get a pay raise is to have a college diploma.
Works a full-time job	She loves her job and would like to become a supervisor some day.	She has a child to raise and rent to pay each month.
Serves as treasurer for her child's school PTA	She is able to plan activities that will benefit the children of the school. It gratifies her to watch the children laugh and play with new playground equipment that the PTA was able to purchase.	She was told volunteer work would look good on her college application.
Awakens early each morning to study	She loves the classes she is taking and thirsts for as much knowledge as she can retain.	She has to maintain a C average if she wants to keep her financial aid.

have liked, so she pushes herself to improve by 10 points on the next quiz. Maybe you know a single parent who attends school at night, works a full-time job during the day, is the treasurer for her child's school PTA—and awakens early each day to study for her college classes. These are motivated individuals chasing after their goals. But what is it that creates the drive to accomplish these activities? Where does the drive come from?

Extrinsic and intrinsic motivation

Motivation either comes from within you (*intrinsic*) or from some source outside of you (*extrinsic*). The single mother who is a student may be moved intrinsically, extrinsically, or both. Table 2.1 provides a glimpse into her motivations. Obviously, this single mother is driven by a variety of factors. Whether they are intrinsic or extrinsic, she gets closer to her goal of college graduation.

Let's make this a little more personal. Think about the beginning of this school term. Your professors outlined course expectations in their syllabi. Whether or not you adhere to those requirements remains up to you. Will you attend class regularly because you enjoy the lectures, discussions, and classmates (intrinsic motivation), or because you know that attendance counts toward your grade (extrinsic motivation)?

Characteristics of a motivated learner: Can an individual *learn* to be motivated?

If you understand what makes up motivation, you can more effectively evaluate your behavior—and begin to make changes as needed. Let's review one model that further breaks motivated behavior into five distinct parts.[1]

1. Motivated behavior always involves making a *choice.* Chapter 1 examined the concept of opportunity costs—the cost incurred when you give one thing up to do something else. Because you are in college, you are sacrificing some other activity you could be doing with your time. Maybe your time in a college classroom means you cannot work as many hours at gainful employment, and, consequently, you will take a pay cut while pursuing your studies. But you still came to college for some reason. In short, you were motivated to make this choice.

2. A motivated person will put forth *effort* to achieve a goal. This person is not waiting for the goal to happen. The motivated individual chooses to make the goal happen.

3. The motivated individual chooses to be *persistent.* Simply put, this student has that trait known as stick-to-itiveness. He can stick with a task until it is completed.

4. Motivated students think—really think—about what they are doing. If they write an essay, they think about the topic, think about the outline, and think about the final product. They *engage* the topic. Like people who are engaged to be married, engaged students choose to be committed to their work.

5. Finally, if the preceding four characteristics—choice, effort, persistence, and engagement— are present, there will be a connection to a quality final product. There will be some form of *achievement*—a movement closer to a goal (see Figure 2.3).

If your final result is not what you had hoped for, that does not necessarily mean you lacked motivation. It simply indicates that it's time to reevaluate your choices and then recommit your efforts. *Flexibility* is important. You cannot control everything that will happen in college.

SELF-MONITORING CHECK: ARE YOU A MOTIVATED LEARNER?

Reflect on a time when you were committed to something. You may have been an athlete on a sports team, a club member, a student government officer, a recital performer, or involved in some other activity on which you worked diligently.

1. Can you specifically identify *why* you were committed to the task? What characteristics of motivation (choice, effort, persistence, engagement, and/or achievement) were present?

_____

_____

_____

2. Who was part of your social support system? That is, who helped to keep you moving toward your results? Was there someone or something else driving you (*extrinsic motivator*), or did some force within you (*intrinsic motivator*) drive you forward? _____

_____

_____

_____

3. How did you maintain your level of commitment over time? _____

_____

_____

_____

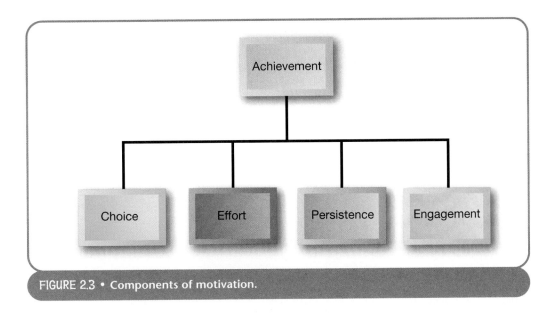

FIGURE 2.3 • Components of motivation.

WHO IS RESPONSIBLE FOR YOUR MOTIVATION?

Take a moment to reflect on the following questions:

1. **Personal success.** What motivates you to achieve personal success beyond the classroom?

   _____

   _____

2. How has this motivator (or motivators) changed since the same time last year?

   _____

   _____

3. **Academic success.** What motivates you at this time in the classroom?

   _____

   _____

4. How has this motivator (or motivators) changed since the same time last year?

   _____

   _____

5. What insights (inner flashes of understanding) do you get from your answers?

   _____

   _____

   _____

Overcoming motivational barriers

For the moment, consider that you are *not* able to control external forces that stand between you and what you would like to achieve. Whether it's an unfair instructor, an uncaring employer, or the state of the economy, we'll put those externalities aside for now. Instead, your target for this exercise will be *those things you can control*—that originate within you. How can you overcome these **motivational barriers?**

Attitude.[2] Think of something you have had difficulty staying motivated to achieve. Maybe you have not been able to get to the gym as often as you would like each week. Or perhaps you have not lost the weight you had hoped this year. Confront yourself—that is, *listen to your words.* Consider these statements:

> "I *hope* to lose weight."
>
> "I will *try* to lose weight."
>
> "I *think* I will be able to lose weight."

What do you notice about those words, especially the verbs? Compare them with the following statements:

> "I *will* lose weight."
>
> "I *shall* lose weight."
>
> "I *pledge* to lose weight."

This second set of statements present more forceful and more positive sentiments. There are no wishy-washy thoughts. Using this "language of action" states the point (the goal) in a very definite manner.

Suggestion: Listen to your words—they might very well reflect your commitment level. Are you using the language of commitment, or the language of doubt and uncertainty?

Mental Paralysis. Think of a Ping-Pong game. Two contestants paddle a small ball back and forth over the table net. One player makes an incredible shot, but the opponent makes a masterful return. Just when it looks like one person has made the defining shot that will end the match, it is countered with another unbelievable shot. Back and forth the game goes. Eventually, one player will win.

Sometimes your mind engages in a Ping-Pong game of sorts when you are trying to motivate yourself to accomplish something. Let's call the two opponents *Yes* and *But.* Every time *Yes* presents a reason to move forward with an action, *But* skillfully returns with a reason why you should stay put. Back and forth the exchange goes. While *Yes* makes good attempts, the back-and-forth exchange can become tiring and nothing is accomplished. *But* has been too persistent and eventually stops the progress. Here is what such a "match" might sound like:

> "*Yes,* I need to study more for my math exam."
>
> "*But,* I really don't have any more time to devote to that class."
>
> "*Yes,* I know that time is an issue. Still, I really must devote more time to math class."
>
> "*But,* I never have been any good at math. The extra time won't help anyway!"
>
> "*Yes,* I guess I'm just destined to be a poor math student."

In this exchange the person ended up talking himself right out of the commitment. As one professor of psychology has said, "The word *but* functions like an eraser, negating the motivation that went before—and nothing happens."[3]

Suggestion: Erase the word *but* from your motivational vocabulary before it erases your motivation.

Commitment. Sometimes the initial excitement to do something fades away quickly. Maybe it is difficult to maintain motivation because you lack passion for what you are trying to accomplish. For instance, perhaps you committed to play intramural sports with your friends. After two weeks of practice, however, you are not excited about continuing. When you examine the issue, you see that you participated only because you did not want to disappoint the friends who were going to play. You also have noticed that in order to devote time to the sport, you have had to stay up much later each night to complete your homework and have had to give up some hours from your part-time job. After careful analysis, you decide the intramural sport is not where you need—or want—to invest your energies.

Suggestion: Check your commitment as to why you want to do something. If you can honestly say that the "cost" is more than you are willing to pay, then maybe you should look for another road to follow.

Are You in the Way? Sometimes two motivators might conflict with one another. One might create an opportunity cost that hinders another. For instance, perhaps you have pledged that you will earn a 3.5 GPA this term. In addition, you have pledged to work at your part-time job as many hours as you can in order to save money for a car. You are motivated by the high GPA *and* you are motivated by the money to buy a car. But trying to get the one might have a negative effect on the other.

Suggestion: Examine your motivators. If one seems to have a harmful effect on another, you may wish to rethink what you are trying to do. Or look for alternatives. For instance, maybe you could work more hours on the weekends, leaving the nights during the school week for homework. Do not work at cross-purposes with yourself.

© Stockdisc

GOAL SETTING

What is a goal?

The first part of this chapter looked at what drives a person to a destination. Now let's turn our attention to that end point—to the goal your motivation moves you toward.

Generally, people think of a **goal** as a place they want to reach. The "place" can be academic ("I want an A in history"), or it can be personal and nonacademic ("I will run and finish a five-mile race"), or it can be community-oriented ("I will assist in painting the local community center").

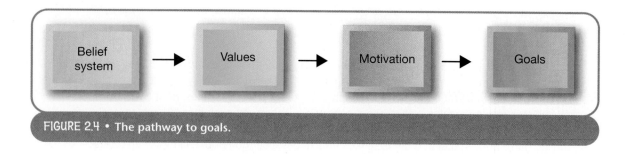

FIGURE 2.4 • The pathway to goals.

We all have goals of one kind or another. They can be simple short-term goals like cleaning a room, or more complex long-term destinations like becoming qualified for a particular career. Our goals come directly from our beliefs, values, and motivations (see Figure 2.4).

Why do you need a goal? Converting fantasies to dreams— and dreams to realities

You already know how to establish goals. Most everything you tried to do in your life—before ever stepping on a college campus—connected directly to goal setting. For instance, did you ever do any of the following?

Try out for an athletic team?

Decide to perform in a ballet?

Save your weekly allowance as a child to buy someone a gift?

Take certain high school courses so that you could apply to college?

Fill out an application for a summer job?

Muster up your courage to ask someone for a date?

If you have done any of these things, or anything similar, you have engaged in goal setting. And thus, because you have a history on which to build, what follows should not be intimidating. Consider the following example:

> **Perhaps when you were a child you picked up a basketball and started to throw it toward a basket. Eventually, a few years later, you found yourself on a community basketball team. By that time, you had been playing basketball in the local park for five or six years. You knew how to dribble a ball, pass a ball, and toss the ball through the hoop. You had the basic skills, *but* your new team coach still provided instruction. He built upon your skill base. Possibly, some of those previous skills were not adequately learned. Maybe your body was in the wrong position when shooting a jump shot. The coach gave some advice; sometimes it was just a little tweak here or there. In the end, you became a much better all-around ball player.**

That's the idea with the rest of this chapter. (And in reality, that analogy will hold true for the entire book.)

Don't forget what you have learned, but be open-minded enough to examine and use some new strategies. In other words, *respect* your past experiences while taking *responsibility* to build new experiences.

Goal setting allows you to focus your sights on something you want to achieve, make a plan, and finally move toward that result. Effective goals, whether long-term or short-term, address the *why, when,* and *how* of our lives. If your goals lack these components, then your goals turn out to be daydreams or mere fantasies.

Goals provide a challenge. Some may have an impact on more than one aspect of your life. Quitting your job, for instance, so that you can attend school on a full-time basis will have a far-reaching impact on your life. Whether the goal is large and long-term or small and short-term, it should set forth a challenge.

UNDERSTANDING YOUR GOALS

Reflect on one of your current goals. It can relate to one of your classes, a campus club of which you are a member, your current job, or some other part of your life.

1. State the goal: _____
   _____
   _____

2. Why do you have this goal? Why is it something you want to do? Are you being encouraged by someone else to achieve this goal? Which of your values is behind this goal?
   _____
   _____

3. When do you wish to accomplish this goal? (Have you set a date for completion?)
   _____
   _____

4. How will you accomplish this goal? That is, what resources will you need to achieve your goal? _____
   _____
   _____

5. How will you know when you accomplish your goal? What will have specifically happened?
   _____
   _____

6. Finally, here is a question that many times is ignored: How do you know that this is the correct goal for you to pursue at this time of your life? Does the goal move you toward an emotionally satisfying end result? _____
   _____
   _____
   _____

What does a clearly stated goal look like?

The questions in Activity 2.3 provide a glimpse into the parts of a goal.[4] A useful goal—as opposed to mere fantasy—must provide the means to help you reach your desired destination (see Figure 2.5).

The first step to reach your challenge involves developing a clear *goal statement*—a concrete step to make your dreams become reality. A clearly stated goal has the following six properties:

1. *A clear goal is written.* This is the step in which you state precisely *what* you want to achieve. Once in writing, it becomes an affirmation of intent. Put it where you will see it every day. Some people find the process of actually *writing* a goal to be awkward and a waste of time. Nevertheless, this is a valuable exercise as you develop the habit of establishing long-range plans. So, sharpen that pencil and get ready to write.

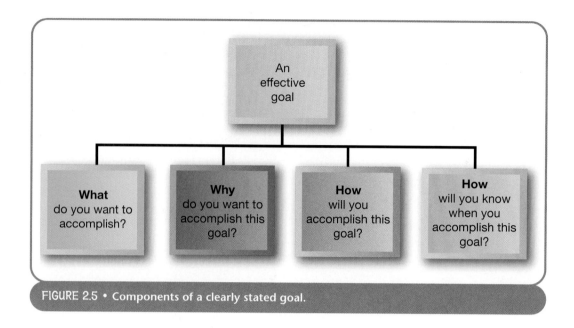

FIGURE 2.5 • Components of a clearly stated goal.

2. *A clear goal must be specific and measurable.* Exactly what will be accomplished? Saying "I want to have a better English grade" is admirable, but it is incomplete. How do you define "better"? If your current grade is a D, would you be satisfied with a D+ (which, after all, is "better" than a D)? By *how much* do you wish to raise your grade? By *when?* How will you know when you have achieved the goal? Write in concrete terms so that you clearly know when you have achieved the goal: "I want to get a B in my English class by the end of the semester" is a much clearer statement. There is no doubt as to what you want to accomplish. You have also identified the time frame in which the goal will be accomplished.

3. *A clear goal has to be realistic.* It should be challenging, yet attainable. Saying you will raise your English grade from an F to an A by the end of the week is not realistic. Challenge yourself, but do not frustrate yourself. Many students have tried to turn around an abysmal term, only to become discouraged because they set their sights unrealistically high—and waited too long to begin moving toward the goal.

4. *A clear goal must have a practical road map.* Know where you are going, how you are going to get there, and when you plan on arriving. Aimlessly wandering toward a goal will waste your valuable time. Simplify the goal into manageable, bite-size action steps. In other words, once you have a long-range goal, establish short-range steps to achieve that goal. *Do not skip this important step.* You want to motivate, not overwhelm yourself. Here is an example of a road map:

Long-term: To attain an A in math by the end of the semester.
Short-term: Complete all assigned homework.
          Correct and rework any problems marked as incorrect on homework or tests.
          See the instructor at least once a week for extra help—for a second
            explanation or a chance to work additional problems.
          Find a study group.
          Participate in class.
          Get A's on all the tests.*

5. *A clear goal anticipates potential problems or obstacles.* Stage 3 of the change cycle—executing the plan—is the time when obstacles present themselves. Your goals will not be immune to twists and turns of the road. Don't become paranoid or obsessive about potential problems, but do try to anticipate some of the problems you may encounter. If you do so, obstacles will not be a surprise—and they will not be as demoralizing.

---

*Remember to check your instructor's grading scale. An A in one class might be 90 percent whereas an A in another class might require 95 percent.

6. *A clear goal has built-in incentives.* Even though you want to reach a point where your goals are intrinsically motivating, it is a good idea to recognize (and enjoy) your achievements. Provide appropriate rewards for yourself as you make progress. In fact, establish a schedule of incentives (rewards) that coincide with your "bite-size" action steps. Perhaps, after doing all of your homework, you could reward yourself with a pizza or a video game or a game of basketball. When you get that hard-earned A, treat yourself to a movie with friends. It really does not make any difference what that reward is just so long as it provides you with a little fuel (motivation) to keep plugging away at your goal. Remember that in stage 4 of the change cycle you get to enjoy your accomplishment.

In any first-year college experience textbook or study skills book you will find suggested steps to follow in goal setting. And incorporated into these plans you will usually find all (or most) of the foregoing six properties of a clearly stated goal. One model, for instance, uses the acronym *S.M.A.R.T.*[5]—that is, goals need to be *specific, measurable, attainable, realistic,* and *tangible.* Whatever works for you, use it.

Long-term and short-term goals

Goals go beyond the classroom. In fact, goals address many issues in life. Figure 2.6 gives a broad overview of different categories of goals.

The four main categories of goals, in the middle tier of Figure 2.6, can be classified as *long-term goals*—larger goals that will be accomplished in the future. These goals will not be reached in a day or two. In the case of career goals, years will be required. These goals help define who you are as a person—and they reflect your *belief system* and *values.*

Some people may shy away from long-term goals because they appear intimidating and so far in the future as to be disconnected from the present. Specific, measurable, and responsible *short-term goals* have two useful functions.

For one, they focus on small, incremental steps toward a larger goal. Rather than tackling too much at once, short-term goals establish manageable and action-oriented steps. For many people, a tiny bite-size move forward is not as overwhelming as a more complex and long-range goal. These **action steps** get a person moving in the right direction.

Secondly, specific short-term goals will help you mark your progress, step by step, toward your ultimate goal. If one of your academic goals is to get an A in your English class by the end of the term, a short-term goal may be to find a study group, or to attend tutoring sessions, or to visit the professor once per week with specific questions.

Tips on How to Develop Your Action Steps

- Once you have identified a goal, identify the most important step you can take to reach it.

- Make a commitment to take that important step as soon as possible. Can you do it tonight? Tomorrow?

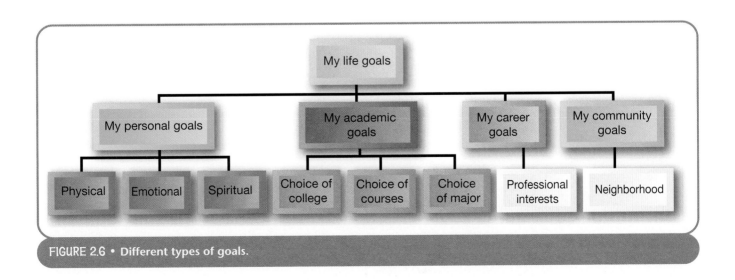

FIGURE 2.6 • Different types of goals.

ESTABLISHING SHORT-TERM GOALS TO REACH YOUR LONG-TERM GOALS

For this exercise, determine a long-term personal goal and an academic goal for one of your courses. Then, for each of these long-term goals, identify two short-term goals (specific action steps) that will take you closer to the bigger goal. As the term implies, these will be *action-oriented* movements toward your destination. Remember to keep the goals measurable—state them in terms that will enable you to know when you have achieved them.

1. Personal goal: _____

   Short-term goals (or action steps) to reach the personal goal:

   a. _____

   b. _____

2. Academic goal: _____

   Short-term goals (or action steps) to reach the academic goal:

   a. _____

   b. _____

- Be diligent, but be flexible. That is, treat your goals and their action steps with respect, but understand that you may need to make adjustments. As the Dalai Lama has said, "Remember that not getting what you want is sometimes a wonderful stroke of luck"—as you will be forced to look in a new direction.

- Be willing to ask for help. The 3 Fs—friends, family, and faculty—can be wonderful resources.

Obstacles, missteps, and detours

Think about your favorite movie or novel for a moment. Can you remember the hero or heroine? That person started at a certain point in his life and ended at another at the conclusion of the story. The final scene usually represented some type of success or progress for the main character. However, that achievement did not occur without twists and turns of the plot. Those adventures—or misadventures—kept you turning the pages of the book or sitting in your seat watching the screen. As the hero made his way toward a particular goal, an obstacle presented itself and the hero detoured from his goal. He had to gather his thoughts, refocus, and then move back up the road toward the goal. This continues until he reaches the final scene. Plotting the journey of the lead character would look more like the up-and-down path you see in Figure 2.7 rather than a straight line.

Just like the hero and heroine, you, too, will probably have missteps along the way. Goals are set in the *real world*. Problems, unforeseen circumstances, and "bad luck" are also part of the *real world*. Expect them, plan for them, and keep moving toward the desired result.

Here are some common obstacles to achieving goals.[6]

- **Not expecting mistakes.** If you expect to move along without any glitches, and then one occurs, you may become so dejected that you will give up. For instance, when planning the steps to finish a term paper (identify a topic, research your topic at the library, establish an outline, write a rough draft, proofread your paper, and revise as necessary), leave flexibility and "breathing room" for an unexpected detour like a computer malfunction. Being prepared for missteps and wrong turns, you will be able to handle them better. They won't be pleasant, but you will be able to remain focused.

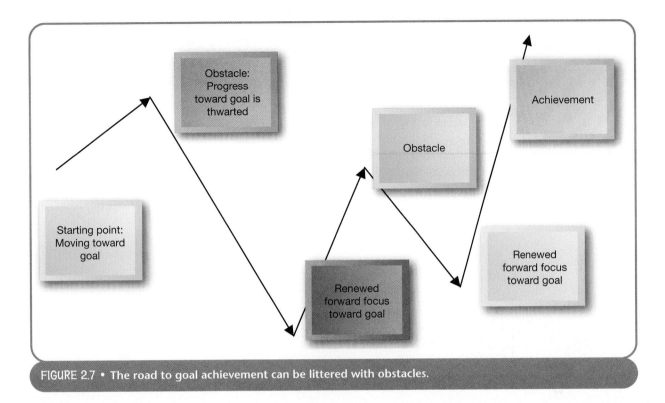

FIGURE 2.7 • The road to goal achievement can be littered with obstacles.

- **Blaming obstacles on your lack of abilities.** Sometimes an obstacle is beyond your control; sometimes it happens because you never tried to reach this type of goal before. You might become frustrated with a particular instructor's teaching style. Or the content may stretch you beyond your previous experiences. It can become too easy to say "I'm stupid" or "I don't *do* history!" Abilities can change. Each time you enter a classroom you bring your *old skills* to a *new situation.*

- **Not changing your environment.** If you want to increase your biology grade by one letter grade by the end of the term, you may need to change your study environment. Or maybe the study group you work with is not working for you. Take stock of where, when, and how you are doing things and then make a well-planned move. It may mean you have to make choices regarding when and where to meet with your friends. Learn to say no, if saying yes to a particular situation would compromise your goals. Refer to the topics titled "Commitment" and "Are You in the Way?" discussed earlier in the chapter.

Locus of control

There is one more obstacle, one that springs from how you see yourself in the world. Do you believe that your actions can influence the way things turn out? Do things just "happen" to you—or do you cause things to happen? How you answer questions like these reflects your **locus of control,** a concept attributed to psychologist Julian Rotter[7] that refers to how much you believe your actions can affect the future.

A simplified description of locus of control is the *focus of one's power.* Do you believe your power to control events resides within you—or do you believe events are controlled by outside forces?

Generally speaking, a person's locus of control can be either internal or external. A student with an *internal* locus of control, for example, explains a poor test grade by looking into the mirror, pointing at himself, and saying, "I should have studied more" or "Before the next exam I will be sure to visit my professor in his office." The responsibility is placed squarely on that student's shoulders *by that student.* On the other hand, a student who is more apt to blame the teacher exhibits an *external* locus of control. Statements such as "That teacher is not fair" or "How could I possibly do well when the teacher covers so much material each class period?" characterize a student looking to assign responsibility elsewhere.

IDENTIFYING LOCUS OF CONTROL

Read the following scenario and then identify and support whether the person exhibits an external or internal locus of control.

> **Natasha has missed a number of math classes lately due to child care difficulties. She recently missed two quizzes—and the instructor does not allow makeup quizzes. She fears that her grade may be severely reduced as a result. Yesterday morning, Natasha went to the instructor's office. "I know it is my responsibility to get to class and take the quizzes on time," she said. "But my babysitter is no longer available. I think I have a new person lined up. Is there any extra credit I can do to make up for the lost points on those two quizzes?"**

1. Did Natasha exhibit an internal or external locus of control? Briefly explain your answer.

   _____

   _____

   _____

2. How can this knowledge benefit you?

   _____

   _____

   _____

   _____

   _____

Refer to Figure 2.8. As with any continuum, few people are found on either extreme. Most of us fall somewhere in between. But if we are honest with ourselves, we will notice that we *tend* to *lean* to one end or the other. Are you a person who generally takes responsibility for your actions? Or are you someone who is more apt to blame someone else? Use this information to heighten your awareness.

Recognize that there are times we all face when *other people* (external) will have significant influence or control over what we will or will not do. For instance, the college or university sets the final exam schedule; the students must adjust their own schedules to meet those dates. The point is to understand what *you* (internal) can have an impact on—and what you may be avoiding because it is easier to do so.[8]

External locus ⟵⟶ Internal locus

FIGURE 2.8 • Locus of control continuum.

Summary

WHERE ARE YOU HEADING?

This college term will pass quickly. The weeks ahead will require completion of academic work, focused planning, a strong knowledge of yourself, and strategies to take responsibility for your time and behavior (*an internal locus of control*). You control your fate. In the end it will be up to you to stay motivated, set goals, and set your course for success. By following the strategies outlined in this chapter you will be on your way to a path of success. Keep the following points in mind as you move with determination through your semester:

- Values determine direction in life.

- Motivation is the driving force to move toward goals.

- Goals provide purpose and meaning to life. They can help energize you to reach the destination by keeping the end in focus.

- Short-term goals—the action steps to reaching one's dreams—need to be specific, measurable, and responsible.

- Goals are set in the real world. Problems, unforeseen circumstances, and bad luck are also part of the real world. Expect them and plan for them.

- Locus of control influences whether you believe life will *just happen,* or that you will be able to *influence what happens.*

tuning your life-strings

the 4 Rs

self

change and personal growth

Your SELF:
Personal growth
and balance

The last three activities of this chapter will allow you to reflect on the three levels of student success as they apply to the major concepts introduced in this chapter. Each activity will give you an opportunity to reflect and apply the chapter concepts in a way that is meaningful to you during this transitional phase of your life. Use this opportunity to apply newly acquired information and also keep an ongoing journal of growth in the various facets of your life.

The 4 Rs

Describe a personal example of how you used each of the 4 Rs with motivation and/or goal setting.

1. *Reflection* (Example: Perhaps you examined why a particular goal is important to you.)

_____

_____

2. *Respect* (Example: Perhaps you have set and achieved goals all of your life. What experiences can you now draw upon?)

_____

_____

3. *Responsibility* (Example: Describe responsible steps you have taken to achieve a goal.)

_____

_____

4. *Renewal* (Example: Do you have passion for your goals? Do they energize you?)

_____

_____

The Change Cycle

Goals are intimately connected with the change cycle. Very simply, when you reach a goal something in your life has changed. For this activity, reflect on a goal you have or one that you are thinking of pursuing. (Recall the four stages of the change cycle: *recognizing* the need for change, *planning* for the change, *executing* the plan, and *enjoying* the achieved goal.)

1. What is your goal? State it in measurable terms.

_____

_____

2. What led you to *recognize* that this was the right goal for you?

_____

_____

3. What is (or will be) your *plan* to make the goal a reality?

_____

_____

4. If you have put the plan into action (*executed* it), how are you progressing?

_____

_____

5. Once the goal has become a reality, how do you plan to *enjoy* this achievement? How will you reward yourself?

_____

_____

Tuning Your Life-Strings

As you complete the table that follows, pause and reflect on the balance—or lack of balance—in your life at this point in the semester. Use this activity to apply newly acquired information from this chapter to gauge the level of strength in the various facets of your life.

Life-string	Questions to ask yourself	What possible activities could help you tune this string?	Who can help you tune this string?
Social	• How have you adapted to your new college environment? • Do you have any short-term goals to make new social contacts on campus?		
Occupational	• Have you established any goals that will impact your major or career interests? • Have you taken a moment to visit the campus career center?		
Spiritual	• What types of explorations have you been involved in on campus that can help you examine the deeper meanings of life—and your purpose in this life?		
Physical	• What are your short-term goals for a healthy lifestyle? • Have you participated in any recreational activities this week? • What kind of exercise schedule do you maintain?		

(continued)

Life-string	Questions to ask yourself	What possible activities could help you tune this string?	Who can help you tune this string?
Intellectual	• What did you do this week that involved critical thinking? • How did this expand your knowledge and/or skill base?		
Emotional	• What strategies have you used to deal effectively with your college stressors? • What is one goal that you can set to sharpen your emotional strength?		

Rhythms of Reflection

To complete this chapter, please reflect on the following words:

Nothing happens until something moves.

–Einstein

Consider the goals you now have. Apply your reflections from this chapter and describe what needs to *move* so that what you desire will *happen*.

_____

_____

_____

_____

_____

_____

_____

 To further respond online, please go to the *Rhythms of Reflection* module in chapter 2 of the Companion Website.

ENDNOTES

1. Scott W. VanderStoep and Paul R. Pintrich, *Learning to Learn: The Skill and Will of College Success* (Upper Saddle River, NJ: Prentice Hall, 2003), 40–41.

2. Based on William Miller, "Resolutions That Work," *Spirituality and Health* (February 2005): 44–47.

3. Miller, "Resolutions That Work," 46.

4. For a more detailed discussion, refer to Susan B. Wilson, *Goal Setting* (New York: American Management Association, 1994), 4–9. Information for this section can also be found in Steve Piscitelli, *Study Skills: Do I Really Need This Stuff?* (Upper Saddle River, NJ: Prentice Hall, 2004), 50–51.

5. Paul Meyer, "Creating S.M.A.R.T. Goals," 2004, Top Achievement, http://www.topachievement.com/smart.html (accessed on January 3, 2005).

6. For a more in-depth discussion, see VanderStoep and Pintrich, *Learning to Learn*, 32–35.

7. See, for example, Jack Mearns, "The Social Learning Theory of Julian B. Rotter," Department of Psychology, California State University–Fullerton, http://psych.fullerton.edu/jmearns/rotter.htm. In 1966 Rotter developed a locus of control personality test. Variations of the Rotter test can be found at http://www.dushkin.com/connectext/psy/ch11/survey11.mhtml and http://www.prenhall.com/rolls_demo/sal_demo/wam/q3.html.

8. For a discussion and activity that addresses the issue of "Fix What?"—that is, what is in your control to fix and what is not—see Steve Piscitelli, *Study Skills: Do I Really Need This Stuff?* (Upper Saddle River, NJ: Prentice Hall, 2004), 49.

3 Open-Minded Observations of the World Around You

Getting to Know All the Members of the Band

REFLECTIVE QUESTIONS

Keeping the following questions in mind will make this chapter more meaningful:

- How do "open-minded observations" connect with college success?
- How will you benefit from understanding the various faces of diversity?
- How will other people benefit from knowing your uniqueness?
- Why does discussion of diversity bring fear to some people?
- Does diversity strengthen or weaken a community of people?

KEY TERMS

cultural frame of reference
discrimination
diversity
hyphenated-Americans
intersection of cultures
"isms"
multiculturalism
prejudice
stereotyping

GUEST SPEAKER

MEET GARDNER "SPUD" REYNOLDS

College Success Instructor and Program Chair

South Texas College

McAllen, Texas

There is no greater gift that a man or woman can give him or herself than an open mind. An open mind allows the user to think objectively and critically, to accept or reject new ideas on the basis of their merit rather than on preconceived notions, and generally to receive information in a mind-set of "Hmmm, let's see what this is all about." A closed mind is completely counterproductive.

Apply this open mind to the diversity of the human species and you will quickly come to see that we are all much more alike than we are different. We all have the same basic needs—air, water, food, clothing and shelter, companionship, and a means of sustaining our lives. The differences among us— skin color, ethnicity, religion, socioeconomic status, and so on—are much more superficial. Like one of my students once told me: "I don't care what color you are on the outside, we all bleed red. We're all the same on the inside."

My top three suggestions concerning open-mindedness and cultural diversity:

1. Develop and maintain an open mind. An open mind invites new ideas and clear thinking. It is a powerful tool for effectively comprehending the world around you.

2. Give value to difference. Different is not bad, it is merely different. Variety is the spice of life.

3. Empathize with others. In the words of the Native American proverb: *"O great spirit, grant that I not criticize my neighbor until I have walked a mile in his moccasins."* Empathy is one of the best ways to understand others.

INTRODUCTION

College campuses reflect the larger society. Whether your campus has 1,000 students commuting from around the city or 35,000 students converging from around the world, you can be sure there are more differences than meet the eyes and ears. As this chapter points out, diversity involves more than racial makeup, gender, and national origin.

Often the concepts of *multiculturalism* and *diversity* are used interchangeably. There is some overlap, but the two concepts do differ.

Multiculturalism most accurately describes a variety of *cultures.* That can include religious practices, fashion, history, cuisine, language, and customs. **Diversity** is a more inclusive term. Although it can refer to cultures, it has a longer reach including social class distinctions, racial classifications, sexual orientation, learning styles, communication styles, and physical, mental, or emotional disabilities.

Too often diversity is only associated with appearances: "He is black; she is white." "That group has different facial features than we do." "They dress oddly." "Her language is nothing like I have ever heard." Although the observations may be accurate perceptions, such reductionism minimalizes the broad scope and significance of the concept of diversity.

For instance, a campus whose students are of only one race can still be *diverse.* These students, even while sharing the same skin pigmentation, may practice a variety of religions or have varying political affiliations. A religiously affiliated school that is homogeneous in terms of race and religion can still have a diversity of social class, disabilities, and political preferences. Avoid jumping to conclusions—diversity is all around us. To fully understand it requires open-minded observations of the world around you.

POINTS TO CONSIDER

- **Why should you consider diversity?** Any American schoolchild is well aware of our nation's rich history of immigration. But how is that knowledge useful now, when you are in your college years? Does the dusty story of our nation's past really make a difference as you navigate the various challenges of college life? And if you are one of the increasing numbers of international students entering our nation's institutions of higher learning, do *you* need diversity education? After all, you have come to a foreign land. Well, the short answer remains that *all of us* can benefit from an open-minded approach to the diversity around us. We do not live in a vacuum. Group work, residential arrangements, class discussions, and social relationships will be enhanced with a broader knowledge of our fellow humans.

- **What can you do to learn about the diversity around you?** Colleges and universities provide ample opportunities for students to experience the world. Whether you participate in a classroom discussion, attend a forum on international events, or befriend a recent arrival from another nation, choices abound to increase your understanding of the variety of people around you. Ask questions, listen to others, read books, and attempt to understand the controversies of the day through the eyes of other people. Diversity is more than knowing the names of famous foreigners. It involves understanding the differences that surround us in everyday life.

- **How will knowing about diversity be of benefit to you?** *E pluribus unum*—"Out of many, one"—has been our national motto since 1776. What emerged from the fight for national independence has come to take on an expanded meaning over the years. An old saying holds that "All of us is better than any of us."[1] Very simply, by working together—and not against one another—we increase our chances of creating a more meaningful life. Not only can others benefit from your knowledge, expertise, and uniqueness, but you can likewise benefit from others. Misunderstandings, hurt feelings, and stalemates result when communication and respect for one another diminish. A stronger community develops when respect and openness are nurtured.

WHY CONSIDER DIVERSITY?

Gazing into the future

The top ten nations from which foreigners came to the United States in 1970 were as follows:

1. Italy
2. Germany
3. Canada
4. Mexico
5. United Kingdom
6. Poland
7. Soviet Union
8. Cuba
9. Ireland
10. Austria

Thirty years later (2000), the top ten list looked like this:

1. Mexico
2. China
3. Philippines
4. India
5. Cuba
6. Vietnam
7. El Salvador
8. Korea
9. Dominican Republic
10. Canada[2]

Now consider the following facts:

- Figures released by the U.S. Census Bureau project that by 2010 the foreign-born population of the United States will increase to 11.2 percent of the total U.S. population.[3]

- According to the U.S. Census Bureau report of 2000, nearly 18 percent of the U.S. population speaks a language other than English in their homes. Of this number, nearly 90 percent "speak English less than well."[4]

- One prediction holds that by the year 2020, students of color will make up close to 46 percent of the student population in the United States.[5]

- The 1990 U.S. census figures tell us that "African Americans, Hispanics, and Asians make up the fastest growing consumer group in the country. In fact, in certain cities—Washington, D.C., Los Angeles, and Miami, for example—the minority now represents the majority of the population."[6]

IS DIVERSITY A DIRTY WORD?

Diversity is a fact of life. Anywhere you look, diversity exists. In its simplest form the word refers to *variety, differences, heterogeneity, uniqueness,* and *a range of possibilities.* Something that is not diverse tends to be homogeneous, the same, alike, and uniform.

Diversity is . . . well, *diverse!*

Many times the true nature of diversity gets lost in political arguments.* One group argues that diversity celebrates and respects the glorious array of people in our country. Another perspective counters that diversity education actually harms our nation by encouraging difference at the expense of a unitary national pride. Sometimes, as the rhetoric turns to yelling, an observer may wonder if the opposing sides understand what the other side believes *diversity* to mean.

Before we examine that debate, let's briefly review vocabulary associated with diversity.

- *Age* refers to one's chronological years of life. Generational differences provide clear examples of diversity of age. For instance, an adolescent group will have (more than likely) different tastes in music and fashion from a group of retirees.

---

*Ironically, when liberals, conservatives, and those in between argue about diversity, they exemplify one type of diversity—political diversity.

IMPLICATIONS OF POPULATION STATISTICS

Based on the population information presented in this chapter, respond to the following questions:

1. What observations can you make about the statistics?

    _____

    _____

    _____

2. What significance does this information have for colleges and universities in particular, and the United States in general?

    _____

    _____

    _____

3. What insights do you get from the data provided?

    _____

    _____

    _____

- *Culture,* in its broadest interpretation, refers to the way in which a particular group of people live. They share language, history, cuisine, dress, religion, and traditions.

- *Educational levels* of our population range from illiterates to PhDs, from high school dropouts to college-educated professionals.

- *Ethnicity* refers to people who share the same culture. Italians, for example, are an ethnic group in the United States; so are Poles, Chinese, French, Mexicans—and many more.

- *Gender* refers to the biological makeup of an individual: female or male.

- *Geographic location* can have an impact on a person's manner of speech (dialect), types of foods eaten (regional cuisine), and leisure activities (snowboarding or surfing waves, for example).

- *People of color* is an inclusive term for nonwhite people that includes African-Americans, nonwhite Hispanics, Asians, and Pacific Islanders.

- *Physical and mental abilities* cover a broad range. Some individuals are gifted with high intellectual capabilities and/or physical abilities. Others may have a physical disability that limits mobility, sight, or hearing. Still others may have a mental disability that interferes with cognitive reasoning.

- *Race* is a sociological concept that categorizes people according to physical characteristics. Skin color, eye shape, hair texture, and facial features are a few of the traits used to classify people.

- *Religious beliefs* represent one component of culture. From worship practices to beliefs about afterlife, religion shapes the values and daily routines of millions of people around the world.

- *Sexual orientation* refers to the attraction of one person for another. *Homosexuality* is a same-gender attraction: male to male (gay) or female to female (gay or lesbian). Attraction to the opposite gender is *heterosexuality.* Some people who are attracted to both males and females are known as *bisexual.* People who have undergone gender change surgery are referred to as *transgender.*

WHAT DO YOU THINK OF WHEN YOU HEAR THE WORD DIVERSITY?

3.2
ACTIVITY

1. Write at least five words that come to mind when you hear the word *diversity*.

   a. _____

   b. _____

   c. _____

   d. _____

   e. _____

2. Compare your list with a classmate's. What similarities and what differences exist?

   _____

   _____

   _____

   _____

3. How do you think these similarities and differences have come about? Is it due to family background, birthplace, or some other factors?

   _____

   _____

   _____

   _____

4. How would you explain the negative—and in some cases, hostile—reactions some people have to the concept of diversity?

   _____

   _____

   _____

   _____

- *Socioeconomic class* categorizes people within the same nation according to lifestyle, occupations, and income levels. Typical descriptors include working class, middle class, and upper class.

Although the foregoing concepts represent a few of the major categories of diversity, others exist as well. While they can be viewed as smaller pieces of the broad terms above, these categories further delineate how people differ from one another. A short list looks like this:

- Communication styles

- Learning styles

- Marital status

- Parental status
- Personality styles
- Political philosophies
- Teaching styles
- Work experience

© *BananaStock Ltd.*

The many faces of diversity

Think of your best friend or, if you have one, your roommate. Perhaps you both enjoy the same type of music, or attend the same church, or come from the same part of the country. Whatever the shared commonalities, you feel comfortable around one another.

You also may very well enjoy each other's company because of your differences. Possibly your friend's outgoing personality counters your tendency to be shy and withdrawn. Or your beliefs about political issues have been moderated by her actual life experiences. Each person has a positive impact on the other.

Earlier in this book (chapter 1) you were asked to reflect upon what you bring to the college experience. You examined the skills and abilities that would help you in your college years. All of your past experiences make you who you are. These elements help to form your **cultural frame of reference**.

Imagine a picture frame for a moment. It places boundaries around a piece of art or a photograph to focus attention on the artist's work. A cultural frame of reference acts in much the same manner, as it helps "a cultural group interpret the world . . . in a particular manner. A cultural frame of reference is a filter for impressions from the outside world."[7]

In addition to your cultural frame of reference, your worldview is also affected by the dimensions of your life. The accompanying Tuning Your Life-Strings feature—"Identifying Your Cultural Frame of Reference: What Is Your Diversity Profile?" on page 54—examines your life-strings in the context of your life's experiences and beliefs.

Communication: Understanding differences

As stated earlier, diversity goes beyond physical appearances and religious beliefs. For instance, one of the adjustments of college life involves working and possibly living closely with a wide variety of people. Whether in the classroom, at the student center, or on the athletic field, students will need to communicate with one another.

When most (or all) of a person's experiences are within one culture, that individual will likely have difficulty understanding how someone from another group communicates. For instance, you may have learned from an early age that it is polite, when talking with someone, to look that person in the eye. Some cultures, however, find direct eye contact to be rude. In fact, in these cultures avoiding eye contact with someone who is respected or in authority is considered polite behavior.[8]

"OK, that's nice," you say. "But why do I need to know that? After all, I'm a student trying to finish my requirements and get a degree."

As will be discussed in chapter 10, you *will* find yourself in a number of collaborative activities throughout your college experience. During the initial meetings with a group, it can be easy—and even disastrous—to misinterpret the manner of communication and body language from a group member. Some people, for example, would never think of interrupting another person; they listen, reflect, and then respond. Others have a more assertive—and maybe even aggressive—communication style that is characterized by rapid-fire response—even when it means interrupting someone. One group member may briefly describe her position, while a second person tends to be long-winded and detailed. One style is not necessarily "good" or "bad." But because differences *do* exist, it would be helpful to recognize that in any given group situation these styles will be present.

Table 3.1 describes some common communication styles. As you read the explanations, do not get lost in the details. Rather, appreciate that there are a variety of styles that can have an impact

Table 3.1
Diversity of communication styles: Who is around you?

Type of communication style	Characteristics of the style
Relating to others: *High consideration*	• Is generally polite • Generally does not interrupt • Takes time framing a response • Generally will not embarrass someone • Uses respectful tone of voice
Relating to others: *High involvement*	• Tends to be very verbal • Tends to be argumentative • Increases volume of speech • Interrupts a lot • Responds rapidly
Explaining a viewpoint: *Indirect*	• Explains reasoning • Might appear to hesitate and avoid confrontation • Does not wish to anger or embarrass another person • Takes time to understand and agree with a particular position
Explaining a viewpoint: *Direct*	• Presents views concisely and succinctly • Starts with conclusions or main points first • Presents evidence last, and only if needed
Interacting with the environment: *Field dependent*	• Works well with others to achieve a common goal • Will readily assist others • Is responsive to feelings and opinions of others
Interacting with the environment: *Field independent*	• Prefers to work independently • Likes to compete and earn individual recognition • Is task oriented, unmindful of social environment when working

Source: See *TEACH Session 2 Trainer's Manual,* 159, 161. The information on field dependent and field independent styles can be found in Orlando Taylor, "Appendix II: Some Attributes of Field Independent and Field Dependent Cognitive Styles (adapted from Ramirez and Castaneda, 1974)," *Cross-Cultural Communication: An Essential Dimension of Effective Education,* rev. ed. (Chevy Chase, MD: Mid-Atlantic Center, 1990), Mid-Atlantic Equity Consortium, *http://www.maec.org/cross/11.html* (accessed February 12, 2006). See also Susan Githens, "An excerpt from 'Men and Women in Conversation: An Analysis of Gender Styles in Language,'" May, 1991, *http://www.georgetown.edu/faculty/bassr/githens/tannen.htm* (accessed August 9, 2006).

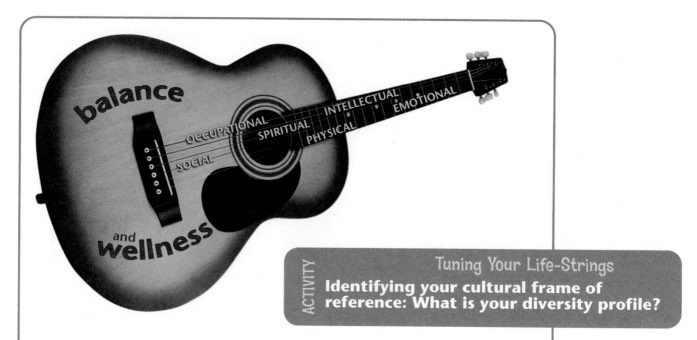

Tuning Your Life-Strings
Identifying your cultural frame of reference: What is your diversity profile?

For each dimension of your life, list the various characteristics and traits that help to describe you as a person. That is, how does each dimension identify who you are as a person?

1. **Social.** For this dimension you may wish to list the type of family from which you come—large, divorced, only child. Are you a person who has a large network of friendships or do you tend to be more of a loner? Has your culture, ethnicity, gender, or race had an impact on your social relationships? What else in your social dimension helps to define who you are as a person? _____

   _____
   _____
   _____
   _____

2. **Occupational.** What job skills, academic talents, and experiences do you have? You may be a recent high school graduate with minimal work experience, or you may be an older student returning to school after spending twenty-five years in the work world. What in your occupational dimension helps to define you as a person? _____

   _____
   _____
   _____
   _____

3. **Spiritual.** How do your spiritual beliefs identify you as a person? Are you affiliated with a specific religious denomination, or do you follow a more solitary spiritual practice? How do your spiritual views shape your view of the world around you? _____

   _____
   _____
   _____
   _____

4. **Physical.** Do you have physical disabilities? How have they shaped your life? If you are in top-notch physical shape, how has that had an impact on your life?

_____

_____

_____

5. **Intellectual.** Are you academically gifted? Do you have disabilities that hinder your intellectual functioning? How has this dimension of life had an impact upon your development as a person?

_____

_____

_____

6. **Emotional.** How have your emotional states affected you as a person? Are you emotionally strong, fragile, or somewhere in between? How has this dimension of your life-strings had an impact upon your development as a person?

_____

_____

_____

7. Based on your responses above, write a description of yourself. That is, if you were to describe yourself to a classmate, what would an accurate description sound like?

_____

_____

_____

8. In what ways, if any, do your answers provide insights about your cultural frame of reference?

_____

_____

_____

on how you effectively or ineffectively communicate with another person or group. This can have an impact on your relationship with a roommate, spouse, sibling, child, group member, or teacher.

Sexual orientation

Diversity also includes sexual orientation—a hot-button issue in our society. Lesbian, gay, bisexual, and transgender (LGBT) students—who hold a variety of personal, political, and religious

MOVING FROM THE THEORETICAL TO THE PRACTICAL

Understanding and applying the knowledge of diverse communication styles may help to minimize miscommunication and conflict within group settings. Refer to Table 3.1 as you answer the following questions.

1. First, reflect on your communication style. Identify which styles described in Table 3.1 best describe you. Provide a brief example of each to support your choices.

   _____

   _____

   _____

2. Explain how this knowledge can benefit you.

   _____

   _____

   _____

3. Carefully pay attention to your interactions over the next week. Whether speaking with a roommate, partner, classmate, teammate or coworker, pay attention to the manner in which that person communicates. For each of the communication styles listed in Table 3.1, identify one person who exhibits that trait *and* describe how you feel when interacting with this person.

   a. *High consideration*

   The person: _____

   How do you feel when interacting with this person?

   _____

   _____

   b. *High involvement*

   The person: _____

   How do you feel when interacting with this person?

   _____

   _____

   c. *Indirect*

   The person: _____

   How do you feel when interacting with this person?

   _____

   _____

d. *Direct*

The person: _____

How do you feel when interacting with this person?

_____

_____

e. *Field dependent*

The person: _____

How do you feel when interacting with this person?

_____

_____

f. *Field independent*

The person: _____

How do you feel when interacting with this person?

_____

_____

4. How can these reflections be of benefit to you?

_____

_____

_____

beliefs—enroll in colleges and universities. As members of the student body, they have the same rights to a quality education and safe environment as all other students. Unfortunately, harassment based on sexual orientation is not uncommon. Consider the following:[9]

- In one study, gay teens were five times more likely than heterosexual teens to miss school because they feared for their safety.

- The same study found that gay teens were four times more likely than their heterosexual classmates to be threatened at school with a weapon.

- A 2001 study found gay teens twice as likely to attempt suicide as heterosexual students.

- One nationwide study of gay and lesbian youth found that 69 percent experienced verbal harassment, 65 percent encountered sexual harassment, and 42 percent reported physical harassment.[10]

If a person experiences and suffers from feelings of isolation, acts of violence, episodes of harassment, and loss of self-worth, success in school becomes much more difficult.

GOD AND FEDERAL LAW[11]

Your sociology class has been talking about gay rights in the United States. There has been spirited discussion in class. One day the professor divides the students into groups to discuss gay rights and hate crimes. He asks for each group to determine whether anti-gay attacks should be considered hate crimes.

As your group begins the discussion, one student confidently and calmly says, "Homosexuals deserve what they get. They violate the teachings of God. Why in the world should we protect immoral behavior with a federal law?"

1. How do you respond to this statement and view?

_____

_____

_____

_____

_____

_____

Addressing Hate and Intolerance

The Southern Poverty Law Center has a long history of fighting for justice and tolerance. The following ideas from its "101 Tools for Tolerance" are designed to improve open-minded acceptance in families, schools, the workplace, and the community.[12]

- Volunteer for a social services organization.

- Speak up when you hear racial slurs being used.

- Share information about your family heritage.

- Read a book or watch a movie about another culture.

- Promote good sportsmanship. Do not "boo" the opponents.

- Create a diversity discussion group to examine issues pertinent to your campus.

- Explore the possibility of building a "peace garden" on your campus.

For all our differences, we share one world. To be tolerant is to welcome the differences and delight in the sharing.

—Southern Poverty Law Center

DIVERSITY: DIVIDING OR UNITING?

Hyphenated-Americans

> The paradox, which began in colonial America, is this: While on the one hand we have welcomed strangers to work and live among us, on the other hand we have scorned and abused immigrants of minority groups who have deviated from the dominant culture.[13]

Such has been our history. Over the centuries, the nation has opened—and continues to open—its doors to immigrants and refugees. The Statue of Liberty stands ready to welcome the "huddled masses yearning to breathe free" as she lifts her "lamp beside the golden door."[14]

But a simultaneous reaction seems to fear the differences of language, religion, and customs these strangers bring to our shores. Historically, citizens of our nation have expected the arriving immigrants to readily accept the culture of their newly adopted home—and to become Americanized by dropping allegiances to their native cultures.

In 1892, the Pledge of Allegiance was penned and soon thereafter became a morning ritual for U.S. schoolchildren. One reason for its writing and recitation was concern about the rising number of immigrants in the United States. The Pledge, it was reasoned, would help to Americanize the immigrant schoolchildren.

Today, the common practice of referring to U.S. citizens according to the ethnic or racial background has produced a wide variety of **hyphenated-Americans**, who emphasize their ethnic pride by identifying themselves as a distinct group or subculture within American society. (Hence we hear, for instance, reference made to Mexican-Americans, African-Americans, Italian-Americans, and German-Americans.) But while the practice may be common, it does not mean it is without controversy. Rather than being seen as pride in both family heritage and the current country of citizenship, some view this practice as a disuniting force in America—one that creates a division of loyalties that will ultimately harm the United States.

The Balkanization of America?

In his 1991 book, *Disuniting of America*, Arthur Schlesinger identified what he believed to be the dangers that multiculturalism held for the United States. Referring to the history of ethnic conflict

WHAT IS THE AMERICAN CULTURE?

1. The debate has raged about whether schools should teach a multicultural curriculum celebrating the many cultures of our nation or concentrate solely on educating children about *the* American culture. For the moment, let's assume that you and a committee of peers has the opportunity to draw up a definition of *the* American culture. This definition would be the basis for all school instruction. What definition clearly encompasses *the* American culture? Write that definition here.

_____

_____

_____

_____

_____

on the Balkan Peninsula,* which split families, communities, and nations, he argued that the increasing emphasis on multiculturalism would have a disuniting effect. Maybe a civil war would not develop in the United States, but he maintained that the increasing emphasis on hyphenated-Americans would hinder, if not destroy, the nationalistic need for pride in a common culture.

As our opening quote to this section demonstrated, such concerns are not new to the nation. Nearly a century ago, then-former President Theodore Roosevelt railed against the hyphenation of America:

> But a hyphenated American is not an American at all. . . . There is no such thing as a hyphenated American who is a good American. The only man who is a good American is the man who is an American and nothing else.[15]

During the same period, Congress had concerns about the increasing number of immigrants arriving on our shores. In the early part of the twentieth century it passed a law requiring the administration of a literacy test to foreigners wishing to gain entrance into the United States. President Woodrow Wilson believed such a law went counter to our national history. In his veto message he said:

> The right of political asylum has brought to this country many a man of noble character and elevated purpose who was marked as an outlaw in his own less fortunate land. . . . The [literacy test is] . . . not [a] test of quality or of character or of personal fitness, but tests of opportunity.

Congress enacted the law over the president's veto.

Fear and misunderstanding: The "isms"

Fear is a powerful force. It can paralyze even the strongest among us. Fear can have a very real identity and reference point. If you were to see a person wildly run toward you pointing a gun at your head, you would have reason to fear for your safety. You can see the gun, the wild look, the closing distance between you and the imminent danger. You might run, you might fight, or you might panic and do nothing. But the fear has a real and tangible source.

Talk of diversity creates a similar reaction in some people. For some the fear may have a real source. Perhaps someone of a different race or ethnicity had caused injury or insult in the past. Or perhaps a female had been continually abused by males with whom she had relationships. Each of these people may unjustly generalize about a particular group of people based on past experiences—but the source of the judgment lies with a real situation.

For others, their fears come from the unknown. They see a group of "foreign-looking and foreign-sounding" people and their imagination begins to run. "What are they talking about?" "They look like terrorists." "Why can't they speak our language?" The judgments tumble like a waterfall.

These reactions reflect **prejudice**—a prejudgment or attitude that may have little connection to actual facts. These attitudes can lead to **stereotyping**—viewing all people of a particular group as being the same regardless of individual distinctions. If such prejudices are acted on without careful examination, the result can range from a simple misunderstanding to a devastating act of **discrimination**—an act treating otherwise equal people in different ways. Discrimination usually arises from prejudicial or stereotypical thinking. It can be found in various "**isms**" such as ageism, classism, ethnocentrism, racism, regionalism, and sexism. Each of these "isms" tends to negatively stereotype a group: old people fearing young people; poor people sneering at rich people; one race insulting another racial group.

---

*Region in southeastern Europe that takes its name from the Balkan Mountains.

WHAT'S IN A NAME?
POINT AND COUNTERPOINT

In what ways does it matter (or not matter) which name Americans use to refer to themselves? Should the emphasis be on how people *behave* toward their nation? Or does the *label* carry significance as well?

1. Write an argument that clearly and logically explains why there is *no harm*—and maybe even a *benefit*—in allowing U.S. citizens to refer to themselves as hyphenated-Americans.

   _____

   _____

   _____

   _____

2. Write an argument that clearly and logically explains why there *is harm*—and *no benefit*—in allowing U.S. citizens to refer to themselves as hyphenated-Americans. _____

   _____

   _____

   _____

   _____

3. *Follow-up activity.* Talk with a classmate or friend who considers himself or herself to be a hyphenated-American. In a *reasoned discussion* find out why this is important to that classmate or friend. Write your findings here.  _____

   _____

   _____

   _____

   _____

Positive assumptions of multiculturalism and diversity

If fear, prejudice, discrimination, and the division of a nation are the by-products of the push for a more inclusive society, one could not be faulted for wondering if maybe this is the wrong agenda for our nation.

Positive change, however, often comes with struggle. For instance, although the Thirteenth, Fourteenth, and Fifteenth Amendments to the U.S. Constitution freed the slaves, provided citizenship for the freed slaves, and guaranteed suffrage for all males regardless of race, it took more than a century to continue combating racism just so black and white children could sit side by side in a classroom. The fight has been ongoing and agonizing for the participants in particular and for the nation as a whole. But it has been a necessary struggle to provide equal access and acceptance for fellow Americans.

There is no reason that cultural diversity cannot continue to be a positive and strengthening force for our society. One myth to debunk is that effective diversity education is about glorifying minority groups while denigrating other groups. Just because one group is celebrated does not mean that another group must be diminished.

CAMPUS PREJUDICE AND DISCRIMINATION

3.7 ACTIVITY

1. Since you have been attending classes at your school, what instances of prejudice and discrimination have you witnessed? Have you witnessed or experienced any of the "isms" listed above? Briefly describe one such incident.

_____

_____

_____

2. What do you think caused this incident of prejudice or discrimination?

_____

_____

_____

3. Using your critical thinking skills (discussed in chapter 5), describe a solution to this problem.

_____

_____

_____

_____

© BananaStock Ltd.

Multicultural education is for *all* members of the campus community (and the larger society). Recognizing, understanding, and respecting the cultural frame of reference each person brings to the table can help to increase the level of intelligent discussion while at the same time lowering the volume of intolerant voices.

Reasoned discussion encourages harmony, a sense of community, and a thriving economy. After all, nations that are torn asunder by ethnic rivalries have a difficult time progressing socially or economically.

Intersection of cultures

As you see in Activity 3.8, the United States has been likened to a *melting pot.* Each new immigrant group has added to the flavor of American culture. From the initial exchange in which the Native Americans and Europeans shared ideas, customs, and beliefs, the various cultures coming to these shores have created a unique culture, one that bears the contributions (warts, beauty marks, and all) of all comers.

The melting pot metaphor holds that once the new cultures arrive in the United States, their old cultural ways mix with the American culture so that they are no longer distinguishable as immigrants. Pour all the ingredients into the pot, stir it up—and out comes a new mixture. They, in effect, trade the old for the new. They are no longer Italians, Puerto Ricans, Mexicans, or Japanese—but rather, Americans. And all Americans change as a result of this additional "seasoning."

DOES MULTICULTURALISM DISCOUNT WESTERN VALUES?

React to the following quote by a newspaper columnist:

> If multiculturalism actually meant striving to understand other cultures, that would be a genuine contribution of seasoning to the melting pot, enabling young people, especially, to contrast and compare differences. But multiculturalism has become the prevailing euphemism for discounting Western values and celebrating every ideology and mindset with an anti-American core.[16]

1. What *evidence* can you provide that multiculturalism (or diversity) either does or does not "discount Western values"?

_____

_____

_____

_____

_____

A more recent metaphor holds that U.S. society has become a *salad bowl* society. This theory holds that when the ingredients (immigrant cultures + American culture) are placed in a bowl and mixed, they do not lose their individual identities. Think of a salad in which you find lettuce, tomatoes, carrots, cucumbers, onions, croutons, and cheese. Once the ingredients are thoroughly mixed together, the newly made dish (the salad) is different from its individual components—but the ingredients, though altered, still retain their individual flavors and looks.

Whatever metaphor you wish to use, one thing remains certain: For more than four centuries the **intersection of cultures** has been—and continues to be—a major part of our nation's historical development.

The concept of the intersection of cultures adds a different twist to multicultural education. It requires an open-minded understanding of *all* cultures. One professor describes it in this manner:

> One advantage the concept of the intersection of cultures adds . . . is that it puts European cultures into the picture. Often, multicultural education is taught from the standpoint of preparing "white" teachers for educating "minority" children. What about the situation of preparing African-American or Native-American teachers to educate the children of European descendants?[17]

Yes, an open-minded review and understanding of cultures is for *everybody.*

SUMMARY

DIVERSITY IS NOT A DIRTY WORD

Before leaving this chapter, keep the following points in mind:

- Diversity is a fact of life. Anywhere you look, diversity exists.

- Cultural frames of reference help people interpret the world around them.

- When most (or all) of your experiences are within one culture, it is understandable if you have difficulty understanding how someone from another group interacts with you.

- Understanding and applying the knowledge of diverse communication styles may help to minimize miscommunication and conflict within group settings.

- For more than four centuries the intersection of cultures has been—and continues to be—a major part of our nation's historical development.

Your SELF:
Personal growth
and balance

The following activities will allow you to reflect on the three levels of student success as they apply to the major concepts introduced in this chapter. Each activity will give you an opportunity to reflect and apply the chapter concepts in ways that are meaningful to you during this transitional phase of your life. Use this opportunity to apply newly acquired information and also keep an ongoing journal of growth in the various facets of your life.

The 4 Rs

Describe a personal example of how you used each of the 4 Rs as you have interacted with the diversity on your campus.

1. *Reflection* (Example: In what ways have you experienced diversity?) _____
   _____

2. *Respect* (Example: How do your past experiences add to your worth as a person?) _____
   _____

3. *Responsibility* (Example: Describe a responsible step you have taken to be open-minded about the world around you.)
   _____
   _____

4. *Renewal* (Example: In what ways does the diversity of your campus energize you?) _____
   _____
   _____

The Change Cycle

For this activity, reflect on a situation or issue concerning diversity that you have confronted this term—and that has required change on your part.

1. What is the situation that requires change? _____
   _____
   _____

2. What led you to recognize this? _____
   _____
   _____

3. What is (or will be) your plan to address this situation? _____
   _____
   _____

4. If you have put the plan into action (executed it), how are you progressing? _____
   _____
   _____

5. Once the plan has become a reality, how do you plan to enjoy this achievement? How will you reward yourself?
   _____
   _____

Tuning Your Life-Strings

Chapter 1 introduced the concept of tuning your life-strings. Before you move on to chapter 4, pause for a moment and reflect on the balance—or lack of balance—in your life at this point in the school term. As you fill in the table that follows, apply newly acquired information from this chapter.

Life-string	Questions to ask yourself	What possible activities could help you tune this string?	Who can help you tune this string?
Social	• How has your social network become more diverse during the course of this semester? • How has your association with diverse groups helped (or hindered) your well-being?		
Occupational	• What role will diversity play in your major and/or chosen career field?		
Spiritual	• What do you know about spiritual beliefs other than your own?		
Physical	• Are you gifted with above-average physical abilities—or do you have a disability that requires accommodations? • Have you had the opportunity to work with a disabled student? • If you have, what impact did this opportunity have on you—and the disabled person?		

Life-string	Questions to ask yourself	What possible activities could help you tune this string?	Who can help you tune this string?
Intellectual	• What books or articles have you recently read about diversity? • Do you feed your mind with responsible thought-provoking material about diversity? • Do you respectfully listen and discuss differing points of view?		
Emotional	• How does the diversity of your emotional states affect your interactions with people around you? • What kind of an impact has your background (heritage) had on your emotional development?		

Rhythms of Reflection

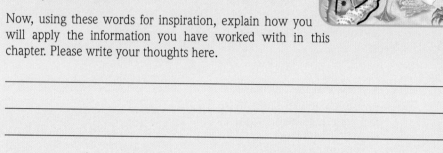

To complete this chapter, please reflect on the following words:

> *We have become not a melting pot but a beautiful mosaic. Different people, different beliefs, different yearnings, different hopes, different dreams.*
>
> *—Jimmy Carter, thirty-ninth President of the United States*

Now, using these words for inspiration, explain how you will apply the information you have worked with in this chapter. Please write your thoughts here.

_____

_____

_____

_____

_____

 To further respond online, please go to the *Rhythms of Reflection* module in chapter 3 of the Companion Website.

ENDNOTES

1. This saying is attributed to Ray Kroc, the founder of McDonald's.
2. From "Countries of Birth of the Foreign-Born Population, 1850–2000," *Profile of the Foreign-Born Population in the United States: 2000,* U.S. Census Bureau, 2001, Pearson Education's Infoplease Web site, http://www.infoplease.com/ipa/A0900547.html (accessed February 8, 2006).
3. "Projections of the Resident Population by Race, Hispanic Origin, and Nativity: Middle Series, 2006 to 2010," Population Projections Program, Population Division, U.S. Census Bureau, http://www.census.gov/population/projections/nation/summary/np-t5-c.txt (accessed February 8, 2006).
4. "Ability to Speak English: 2000," U.S. Census Bureau Quick Tables, http://factfinder.census.gov/servlet/QTTable?_bm=y&-geo_id=01000US&-qr_name=DEC_2000_SF3_U_QTP17&-ds_name=DEC_2000_SF3_U&-redoLog=false (accessed July 12, 2006).
5. Aaron M. Pallas, Gary Natriello, and Edward L. McDill, 1989, cited in James A. Banks, *Teaching Strategies for Ethnic Studies,* 6th ed. (Needham Heights, MA: Allyn & Bacon, 1997), 5.
6. Lafayette Jones, "Marketing Realities for the 'Browning of America,' " *Black Collegian,* October 1998, http://www.findarticles.com/p/articles/mi_qa3628/is_199810/ai_n8823185#continue (accessed February 12, 2006).
7. Joel Spring, *The Intersection of Cultures: Multicultural Education in the United States* (New York: McGraw-Hill, 1995), 5.
8. Ann Caddell Crawford, "Customs and Rites," chapter 6 in *Customs and Culture of Vietnam,* 2000, Go Asia, About.com, http://goasia.about.com/gi/dynamic/offsite.htm?site=http://www.militaryliving.com/vietnam2/index.html (accessed February 15, 2006).
9. Jennifer Middleton and Joshua Freker, *Making Schools Safe: Anti-Harassment Training Program* (New York: American Civil Liberties Union, 2002), 2, http://www.aclu.org/images/asset_upload_file681_24003.pdf (accessed February 12, 2006).
10. Kelli Evans, "The Rights of Gay and Lesbian Students," cited in Middleton and Freker, *Making Schools Safe,* 51.
11. Adapted from Middleton and Freker, *Making Schools Safe,* 67–68.

12. Southern Poverty Law Center, "101 Tools for Tolerance: Simple Ideas for Promoting Equity and Diversity," 2005, Fight Hate and Promote Tolerance, http://www.tolerance.org/101_tools/index.html (accessed February 12, 2006).

13. Leonard Dinnerstein and David M. Reimers, *Ethnic Americans: A History of Immigration and Assimilation* (New York: Harper & Row, 1975), 3.

14. From Emma Lazarus's poem "The New Colossus," which can be found on the base of the Statue of Liberty.

15. Theodore Roosevelt, in a 1915 speech in New York before the Knights of Columbus, cited in "History of the Term 'Hyphenated American,' " Answers.com, http://www.answers.com/topic/hyphenated-american (accessed February 11, 2006).

16. Suzanne Fields, "A Way out of the Balkans," *Washington Times,* June 13, 2004, http://www.washingtontimes.com/op-ed/20040613-102532-4353r.htm (accessed February 3, 2006).

17. Spring, *The Intersection of Cultures,* 5.

Organizing Time and Space
Finding Your Rhythm and Beat

4

REFLECTIVE QUESTIONS

Keeping the following questions in mind will make this chapter more meaningful:

- How can you effectively and efficiently organize your time and space?

- How can four classes per term end up taking so much of your time?

- What is the benefit of establishing priorities?

- Why do people procrastinate?

- What connection exists between organization and stress?

KEY TERMS

calendar

effective

efficient

personal storage areas

personal study area

priorities

procrastination

stress

study time

GUEST SPEAKER

MEET **MARIA D. SALINAS**

Freshman Seminar Coordinator/Instructor

Del Mar College

Corpus Christi, Texas

Organizing time and a study place are critical to a student's academic performance. Students who learn how to organize and manage their time help make their college experience more efficient and less challenging. Equally important, students who use a routine study area, free of distractions, will enhance concentration and improve effective study habits.

Time management is a lifelong skill. Students who use time effectively know how to set priorities, what their goals are, and how to carry out their plans. With proper development, time management is a valuable asset students can apply as they enter the workforce.

My top three suggestions for organizing time and space:

1. Monitor your time for a week. This is one way to determine exactly where your time is spent and how to find your time wasters. Adjustments to your schedule can be made once you have determined how you spend your time.

2. Begin *now* to organize the things that you need to do in order to prioritize. To-do lists can be fun when you challenge yourself to accomplish them, one task at a time.

3. Identify a specific place where you live as your personal space. Organize this space with good lighting, supplies, and a comfortable chair. Your space should provide a comfortable but effective learning environment.

INTRODUCTION

Time management challenges even the best students during their first term in college. For those recently out of high school, the flexible time schedule of college classes represents new territory. Whereas a typical high school day is planned and structured from early morning to midafternoon, a typical college student may only have two or three hours of class on a particular day. The increased amount of *unstructured* time can be troublesome for some college students. Even if it has been years since you were last in a classroom, returning to school can create a new set of challenges as you try to juggle family, work, and school.

But time is only one resource you have to organize. You also need to consider space: Where will you study, how will you file your papers, and where will you keep your supplies? Whether you live on campus, in an off-campus apartment, or at home with your family, you will benefit by designating a place for your out-of-class study time.

Finally, besides the impact that poor organization will have on your academic progress, if you are surrounded by chaos—overextended with commitments or overwhelmed by clutter—stress can result. Organization will not only improve your study habits and grades, but it will also allow you to feel in control of your life and thus keep your life-strings in tune.

POINTS TO CONSIDER

- **How do you organize your time now?** By this point in your school term you have experienced the rhythms of college life. Classes have regular meeting times; the assignment pages specify due dates; cocurricular activities and work hours take time from your schedule; and, possibly, family obligations compete for your waking hours. How do you keep track of your commitments and priorities? Is your organization of time both effective and efficient?

- **How do you organize your space now?** Have you established a personal study space to complete your out-of-class activities? Such a place can help you organize your school materials as well as provide you with a quiet area for reflection about your academic assignments. If you do have a space, is it organized in an effective and efficient manner?

- **How have you handled the stress of college life?** College life is filled with magnificent opportunities. From classroom experiences to campus and community events, there will be more activities available than you can possibly attend. Do you try to fit more into your schedule than you can handle? Do you seem to run out of time each day—and still have a long list of things that need to be accomplished? If so, stress can result from the seeming chaos. Can you recognize the signals your mind and body give you when you are stressed? How do you cope with stress?

ORGANIZATION AND TIME[1]

Did you ever wonder why students feel overwhelmed and swamped? Between course work, homework, after-school activities, family responsibilities, and personal activities, there are many demands on your time. To effectively manage time, it will help to understand the following:

- What you need to accomplish

- When you need to accomplish it

- What resources you will need for the tasks

The clock keeps ticking—no matter what you do. You cannot control time. You cannot create time. However, you *can* effectively use time for your benefit. The strategies discussed here will help you juggle all the obligations that look you in the face each day.

Study time: How much?

This is nearly an impossible question to answer. If you are taking a full load of classes, then your homework and class time could very well add up to a forty-hour workweek—based on the long-referenced formula of spending two or three hours a week *out* of class for every hour you spend *in* class. In this way, if you were spending twelve hours in class each week, you would need to devote another twenty-four to thirty-six hours to **study time**—reading, writing, researching, meeting with study groups, completing assignments, and preparing for tests outside of class.

That is a lot of time.

Some educators, however, refer to this as "insane arithmetic."[2] They maintain that

© *Stockdisc*

what counts is the *quality* of time students spend on-task. And the type of work that is being done will also dictate how much time is necessary. For instance, if you are reviewing elementary concepts in an introductory math course, your amount of homework time may be less than for someone tackling higher-level calculus for the first time.

One truism does exist: It will be difficult to go through your college career without a clear-cut idea of the time commitments needed to successfully make it to graduation.

Let's ask the study time question in a different way: How much time *do you have available* for homework and study purposes? In Activity 4.1, notice that your last entry in the table reflects the amount of time you have *available* to study. There is no magic number to strive for, but consider the formula introduced earlier: two or three hours a week *out* of class for every hour you spend *in* class. If you are taking a full load of courses (four or five for a term) and your available time for homework only amounts to five hours, you will more than likely have a problem completing your college requirements.

Table 4.1 (p. 75) clearly shows that the more classes you take, the greater is the demand on your time. That sounds simplistic—but many students fail to look at the big picture when planning a semester. There is a reason that twelve credit hours is considered full-time by most colleges. Looking at the table, you can see that those twelve credit hours require a time commitment of thirty-six hours. If you're also planning on working a forty-hour-per-week job, then you must schedule seventy-six hours a week for school and work. *That is the equivalent of two full-time jobs.* That will leave you with ninety-two hours a week for *everything else* in your life. If you hope to get eight hours of sleep per night (fifty-six for the week), you now have only thirty-six hours remaining to fashion a life outside of work and school. If you can do it, great! If not, stop and reevaluate before you put yourself—and your friends and family—through a nightmarish schedule.

If you are exhausted by the end of your week, remember that you—not your instructor—established the schedule. You have control of how your day goes.

WHERE DOES YOUR WEEK GO?

4.1 ACTIVITY

There are 168 hours in every week. Whether you are a first-year student or a graduating senior, the number of hours remains constant. We cannot create or eliminate any of them.

In the first column of the table that follows, list all of the things you do in a week. You will find some common categories already entered for you. Add as many as apply to your week's schedule. Once you have completed that, go back and estimate the number of hours *per week* that you devote to each category, and enter these numbers in the right-hand column. (Recognizing that it is difficult to be exact with this type of exercise, estimate as best you can.) Then complete the last two rows of the table.

What I do each week	Number of hours I spend doing it
Sleep	
Eat meals	
Hygiene (showers, haircuts, general grooming)	
Time in class	
Time at employment	
Practice (sports, music, theater)	
Travel (time spent on the road)	
Child care	
Religious or spiritual activities	
Recreation	
Chores and errands	
Other family obligations	
Club activities	
Other	
Total time spent on all of the above activities	
Time remaining from my 168-hour week (the amount of time I could use for homework and study purposes)	

1. How does knowing this information help you become a better student?

_____

_____

_____

		Table 4.1 Determining study time			
Number of courses you are taking this semester	Course name	Number of credits/ hours in the classroom for this course	Study time (based on 2 hours for each hour in class)	Total hours per week for the course (in class and out of class)	Cumulative hours for all courses you are taking this term
1	English	3	6	9	9 (if you take just this one course)
2	Math	3	6	9	18 (for 2 courses)
3	History	3	6	9	27 (for 3 courses)
4	Humanities	3	6	9	36 (for 4 courses)
5	Biology (and lab)	4	8	12	48 (for 5 courses)

Source: Steve Piscitelli, *Study Skills: Do I Really Need This Stuff?* (Upper Saddle River, NJ: Prentice Hall, 2004), 65–66.

An additional strategy that evolves from Activity 4.1 and Table 4.1 is to complete similar tables *before* you register for next term's classes. Recognize what your time constraints are before you commit to more classes than you will be able to successfully handle. True, you can always withdraw from a class, but that can become costly in the long run—and it can tarnish your transcript as it reflects an individual who has difficulty completing tasks.

Keeping track of your time and commitments

Once you have an understanding of how much time you must devote to school and studies, you'll need a way to manage that time. Whatever strategy you choose, make sure it is something you will *use*. Some students have complex and expensive technological gadgets to track their obligations—but never use them. A **calendar**—or even a simple piece of paper—can work wonders *if* it helps you manage your time. Like your note-taking style (discussed in chapter 6), whatever you decide to go with, make sure it works for you—and use it consistently. Three common tools for keeping track of priorities and managing time are the monthly calendar, the weekly calendar, and the daily to-do list.

Monthly Calendar. This format allows you to "see" up to four weeks at a time. You can easily spot conflicts, upcoming tests, personal commitments, and the like (see Figure 4.1).

Weekly Calendar. Although, with a weekly calendar, you won't be able to see the entire month at a glance, it will allow you to enter more details for each day (see Figure 4.2). Some weekly calendars will even provide space to schedule specific appointment times (say, a study group meeting).

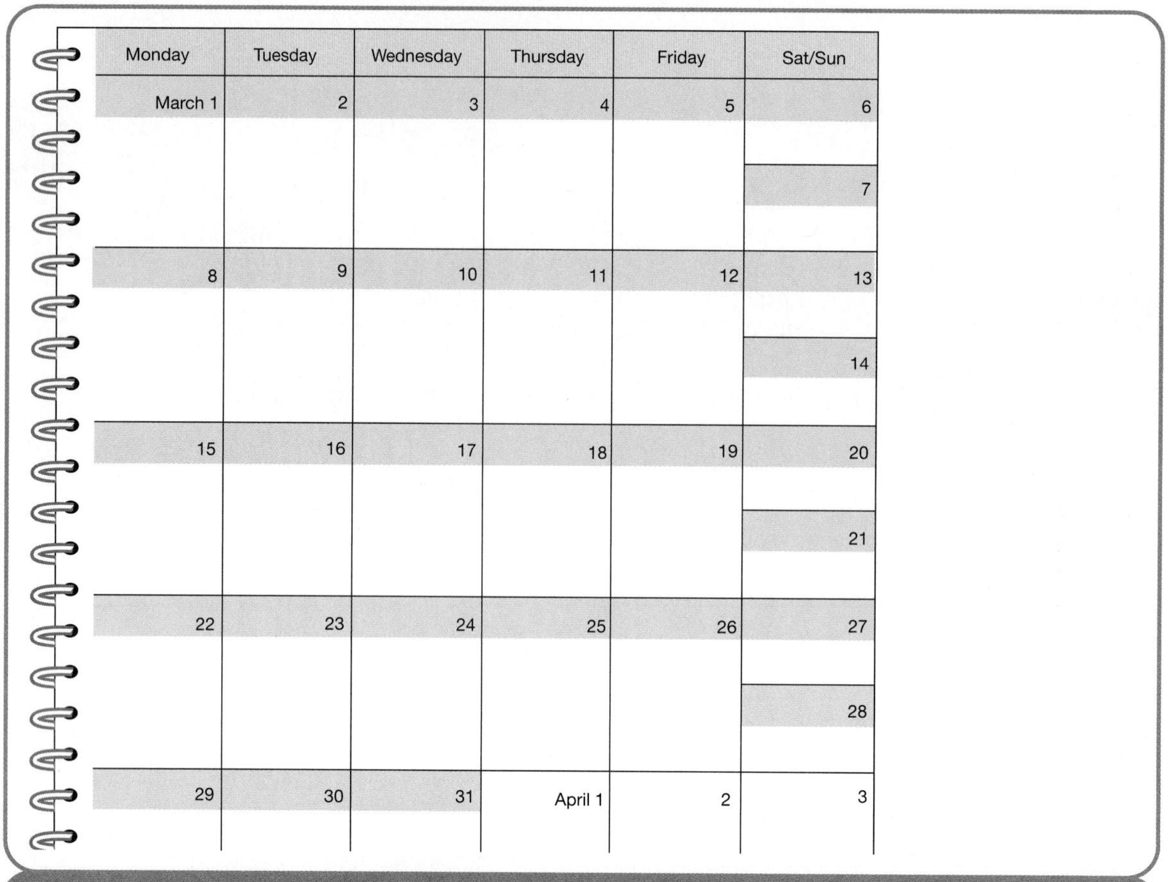

Monday	Tuesday	Wednesday	Thursday	Friday	Sat/Sun
March 1	2	3	4	5	6
					7
8	9	10	11	12	13
					14
15	16	17	18	19	20
					21
22	23	24	25	26	27
					28
29	30	31	April 1	2	3

FIGURE 4.1 • Monthly calendar.

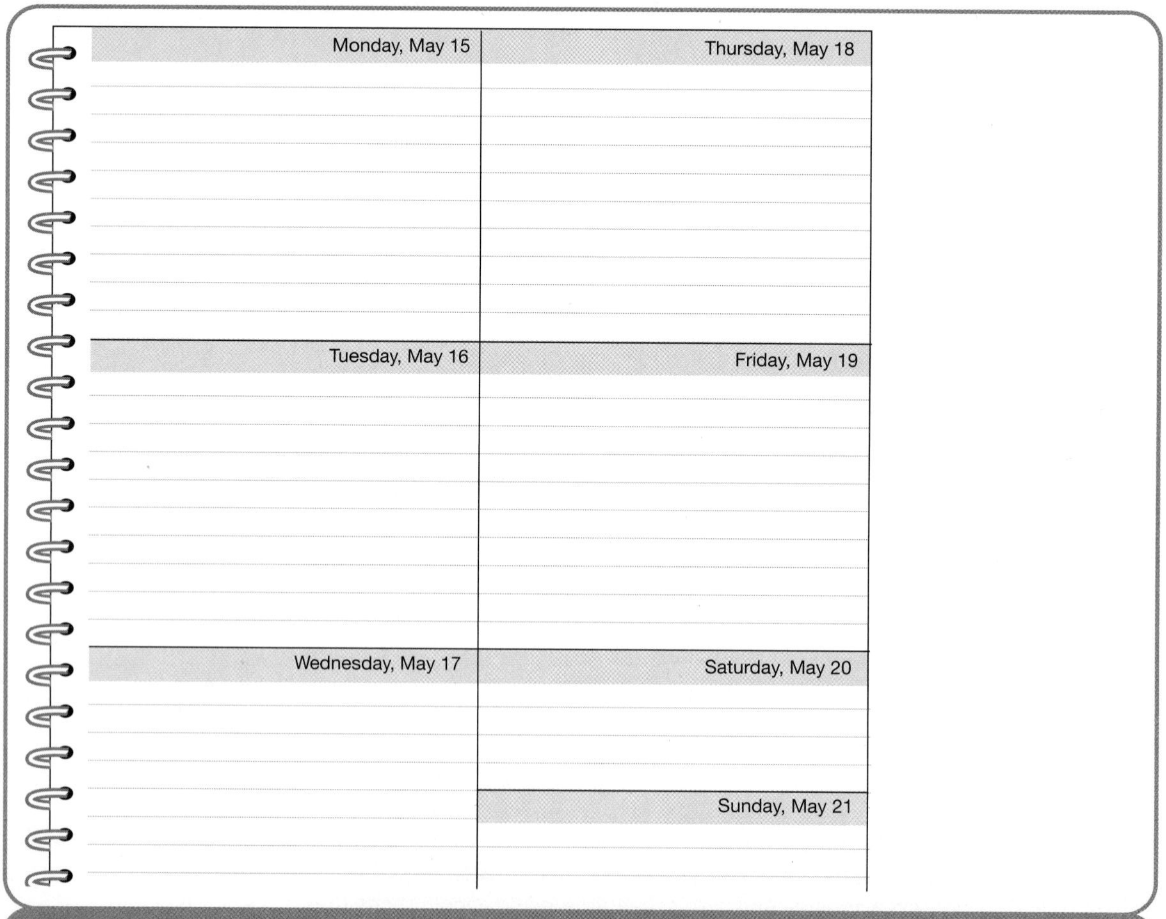

Monday, May 15	Thursday, May 18
Tuesday, May 16	Friday, May 19
Wednesday, May 17	Saturday, May 20
	Sunday, May 21

FIGURE 4.2 • Weekly calendar.

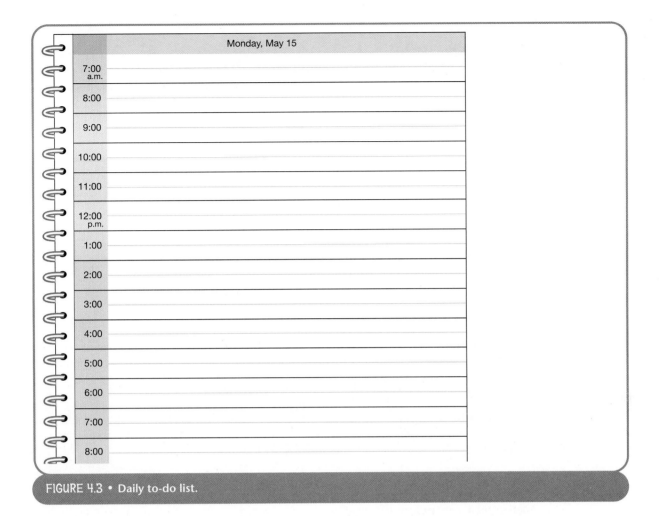

Monday, May 15

7:00 a.m.
8:00
9:00
10:00
11:00
12:00 p.m.
1:00
2:00
3:00
4:00
5:00
6:00
7:00
8:00

FIGURE 4.3 • Daily to-do list.

Daily To-Do List. You can be very detailed with a daily calendar. A variation of this format is the tried and true "to-do" list (see Figure 4.3). This can be a simple piece of notebook paper. Write the date across the top. Down the side of the paper, list and number the items you need to do today. As you finish an item, cross it off. A daily to-do list has two advantages:

1. You have a concrete record of what you actually accomplished.

2. You have immediate proof (gratification) of task completion.

If you don't finish an item today, transfer it to tomorrow's list. You probably will not check off every item every day. There is nothing wrong with that. Simply progress toward your goals one task at a time.

What should you do first? Establishing priorities

OK, let's recap. You have an idea of where your time goes each week. You know how many hours are available for homework and studying. You even adopted a method for keeping track of your commitments. Now, you must determine what to do first, second, and so on. Then, once you have established your list of things to do, you are ready to address the most important aspect of time management—prioritization.

Without establishing **priorities** (an order of importance) you can easily end up spending time on minor tasks while ignoring the major projects that require immediate attention. Many books have been written that address this important point in minute detail.[3]

Let's consider a few basic tips. After you have your list of things to do, make the following determinations:

• **Which items must be addressed immediately?** Studying for a quiz that will be given at 8:00 a.m. tomorrow has more immediacy than typing a research paper that is due two months from today.

THE BENEFITS OF TIME MANAGEMENT

Before moving on, take a moment to reflect on the time management concepts you just read about.

1. How does managing your time benefit you in your personal life and in the classroom?

_____

_____

_____

_____

_____

- **Which items represent a crisis?** You are scheduled to meet with your chemistry study group at noon today. But you just got word that the financial aid counselor wants to discuss your scholarship, also at noon today. Both are immediate. But the scholarship is critical to your continuing in college.

- **Can you plan ahead?** Using your syllabi and assignment pages, map out your entire semester. On your calendar, record when each exam, quiz, and assignment is due. Then you will be able to see the big picture—and there will be fewer surprises.

Backward planning

Another time management strategy is to plan *backwards*.[4] Suppose you have a test scheduled in one week. So you start with the end product—walking into class prepared for the exam. Now work backward: How will you get to this point? Table 4.2 provides a quick guide.

"I'll do all of this tomorrow!" Dealing with procrastination

All the tips, strategies, calendars, and campus resources to help you with classroom success will do absolutely nothing if you don't take the first step toward putting them into action. **Procrastination**—avoiding and postponing what should be taken care of now—can rob your time and derail your best intentions.

Procrastinators may have various reasons for their behavior, but regardless of the motivation, the habit is usually self-defeating. Psychologist Linda Sapadin says that procrastination is "a complex pattern of avoidance caused by an internal conflict: You want or need to do something, but you also feel a resistance toward doing it."[5] What is a student to do?

To begin, remember that procrastination is not synonymous with laziness. In fact, suggests Sapadin, procrastinators have energy to spare—it just is not focused in the appropriate direction. And there is usually an excuse attached to why an assignment or task is not completed. Thus, the first step in dealing with your procrastination is to "listen" to your excuses and then develop a plan to refocus your efforts. (This is similar to what you did in chapter 2 when you were asked to listen to your "language of action.") Table 4.3 provides a brief overview of Sapadin's six styles of procrastination, along with suggestions on how to fight these time-wasting behaviors.

ORGANIZATION AND SPACE

Once you have organized your time, examine your space. For the purposes of this section, *space* refers to those areas around you that may relate to your studies outside of the classroom: your

Table 4.2
A quick guide to backward planning goal: To receive an A on the next biology exam

Day	Task
Thursday	Successfully take the biology exam (the end result).
Wednesday	Briefly review major topics—no cramming necessary (☺).
Tuesday	Review vocabulary and potential exam questions.
Monday	Review your class notes again (reread).
Sunday	Review chapter questions in textbook; try to identify potential exam questions.
Saturday	Review class notes; review vocabulary and study guide sheets.
Friday	Review class notes; reorganize; write a brief summary of your notes; provide a descriptive title for your notes.
Thursday (the day you started)	Make sure all textbook readings are complete.

home study area, your book bag or purse, and, if you have one, your car. The time that you spend searching your space for a book, notes, or a syllabus is time taken from the priorities you had established on your calendar or to-do list.

Home study area

Whether you have a completely separate room dedicated to studying or just a small corner of a larger room, there are ways to organize your space so it works for you.

Workspace. The first thing to do is to mark an area that will be yours for schoolwork—a **personal study area.** For students living in on-campus residential halls, there will be a built-in desk and bookshelf area (or something similar). For those living off campus, a small desk or table can work as well. Do whatever you can to clearly "mark your territory." Make sure others in your residence know this area is for your studies—not for stacks of laundry, not for someone else's personal items, and not for trash or miscellaneous items. Do whatever you can to establish your workspace in a quiet area that will be conducive to uninterrupted study time.

Storage Areas. For an organized and clutter-free workspace, you will need practical storage for your papers, books, supplies, and other items. Such **personal storage areas** could include desk drawers,

© *Corbis*

Table 4.3
Strategies to deal with procrastination

Type of procrastinator	Description	What can you do?
Perfectionist	You don't want to let yourself or others down. Everything you do has to be "just right." You end up postponing completion by doing more work on the task than is needed.	Change your thinking from everything *must* be perfect to everything will be as good as possible. Know the difference between *practical* and *ideal.* (This does not mean you have to settle for inferior work. It simply means you should allow yourself some leeway. Don't unduly pressure yourself.)
Dreamer	Big plans and big ideas—but you never put them into action. You hope someone else will take care of the details for you.	Replace your dreams with *plans.* Develop *action steps* (see chapter 2)—and then follow them one at a time.
Worrier	You fear taking a risk. So rather than do something different or challenging that may be risky, you avoid commitment and/or following through as long as possible.	Speak confidently about your abilities. Associate with people who are positive and will help you see your talents. Each week take a little calculated risk (nothing foolish) in order to get used to stretching your abilities.
Crisis-maker	You live for adrenaline rushes! You wait until the last minute to study or complete a paper. The more pressure involved with a project, the better. You may even secretly like the attention that this type of behavior brings. Unfortunately, as more projects stack up, you are not able to complete the tasks satisfactorily.	Write assignment goals (see chapter 2) that include specific due dates that come *before* a course deadline— maybe two or three days before the due date. Use sports or some other activity to satisfy your adrenaline needs.
Defier	Ever the maverick or rebel, you don't see why your time should be affected by other people's demands (like class attendance or completing a written assignment).	Re-focus. "What can *I* do?" and "What do *I* need to do?" should be asked, rather than "Why do I have to do what *they* want me to do?" *You* made the choice to come to school and *you* (probably) made the choice to take the particular class.

Type of procrastinator	Description	What can you do?
	Table 4.3 (continued)	
Overdoer	You do not know how to say no. You do not want to disappoint people so you take on too much, run out of time, and turn in a half-done or unsatisfactory project. You can do certain tasks very well but you eventually run out of energy and crash. Ironically, you then *do* disappoint the very people you were trying to please, as well as yourself.	Learn that the healthiest word in the English language can very well be *no.* Reevaluate your goals (see chapter 2). Before taking on too much to do, make sure your goals are being advanced. Obviously, there is a fine line between being self-centered and willing to help others. But if you are an overdoer, you probably have long ago crossed this line and have failed to take proper care of your needs.

Source: From Linda Sapadin with Jack Maguire, *Beat Procrastination and Make the Grade: The Six Styles of Procrastination and How Students Can Overcome Them* (New York: Penguin Books, 1999), 15–20.

bookshelves, file boxes, or a file cabinet. Whatever you use, the following tips will help you stay organized:

- **Develop a filing method.** Desk drawers can be notorious agents of chaos. Avoid the urge to "toss and close" (toss an item in and then close the drawer). Designate specific drawers for specific functions. One may hold supplies like pencils, pens, tape, and staples. Another drawer—or perhaps a file box or shelf—may be home to paper, envelopes, computer disks, and ink cartridges.

- **Use file folders to organize papers.** Create a file folder for each class. Clearly label the folder. You can keep a copy of the syllabus or assignment sheet here (as well as another copy in the notebook that you carry to class each day). The folder can be a logical place to file returned papers or drafts of assignments. Don't forget to "file the file folders." You can use a small file cabinet, a desk drawer, or a file-folder holder that can sit on a corner of your desk.

- **Use technology when available.** Computer folders provide an efficient manner to manage documents. Perhaps your computer already has a file folder labeled "My Documents." Within this folder create subfolders for each class you have. You may even desire to create separate folders for each major assignment or unit of material. You can do the same with most e-mail servers. Create folders for each class and then file correspondence with your instructor and classmates, as well as any papers you submit. Also, file any comments you receive from your instructor. Whatever works for you, use it. Be sure to back up all your document files on a disk or flash drive.

- **Create a message center to hold important notices.** This can be as simple as a small wall-mounted cork board on which you tack important reminders. Or you can use a chalkboard or laminated wall poster to write important dates and tasks.

Personal portable storage

Whether you use a book bag, a purse, or some other item to carry your books and supplies to class, the item should be both **effective** and **efficient** for your needs. For instance, a book bag can be an effective way to carry a number of books, notebooks, supplies, and assignments. But if *finding*

EVALUATE YOUR HOME STUDY AREA

Is your home study area well planned? How efficiently does it fulfill its intended purpose? Use the following scale to rate it.

1. On a scale from 0 to 5, rate your home study area. A rating of 0 indicates the item does not exist in your study area. A totally efficient and effective feature of your study area will rate a 5. Circle the numbers that most closely apply to you.

My workspace	0—1—2—3—4—5
My filing system	0—1—2—3—4—5
My drawers for supplies	0—1—2—3—4—5
My computer files	0—1—2—3—4—5
My e-mail files	0—1—2—3—4—5
My message center	0—1—2—3—4—5
Other: _____	0—1—2—3—4—5
Other: _____	0—1—2—3—4—5

2. Based on your ratings, what can you do to improve the efficiency and effectiveness of your home study area?

    _____

    _____

    _____

    _____

any one of those things from the deep recesses of the bag proves to be time-consuming and frustrating, then perhaps the manner in which you are using the bag is not efficient.

Keep the following points in mind:

*   **Type of bag.** Give consideration to using a bag that has a couple of compartments. Many book bags have two main compartments, plus a smaller zippered area in front of the bag and possibly one or two side areas. The main compartments can be used to hold books, notebooks, assignments, and a laptop computer. The smaller compartments work well for pens, pencils, and other supplies, as well as keys, cell phones, computer disks, or digital handheld devices.

*   **Identification.** Have some form of identification attached to your bag in the event you ever leave it in a classroom or the cafeteria.

*   **Nightly review.** Each night empty the book bag to make sure you have not overlooked an important piece of paper that you shoved into the bag earlier in the day. Once you complete this, pack the bag for the next day. Place it where you will not forget it in the morning when you leave for class.

Car

Has your car become a mobile storage area? Has the trunk become a large black hole that has swallowed up books and important papers? Do you need a shovel to clear out the backseat?

If you do use your car for a storage area, consider placing a plastic or vinyl tub, with a lid, in the trunk. This will accomplish three things:

1. The tub will keep your materials in one neat location.

2. The lid and the plastic or vinyl construction will protect your material in case the trunk leaks.

3. When you place valuables in the backseat of your car, they are more visible to would-be thieves. The trunk, while not totally invulnerable, does offer a bit more security.

EVALUATE YOUR PERSONAL PORTABLE STORAGE

Do you have a book bag or other portable storage for the things you carry to class each day? Is your personal portable storage both effective *and* efficient? Use the following scale to rate it.

1. On a scale from 0 (does not exist) to 5 (totally effective and efficient), rate your personal portable storage. Circle the numbers that most closely apply to you.

My bag has a number of separate compartments.	0—1—2—3—4—5
I tend to "lose" things in my bag.	0—1—2—3—4—5
My bag is appropriately identified.	0—1—2—3—4—5
I review the contents of my bag daily.	0—1—2—3—4—5
Other: _____	0—1—2—3—4—5

2. Based on your ratings, what can you do to improve the efficiency and effectiveness of your personal portable storage?

   _____

   _____

   _____

   _____

ORGANIZATION AND STRESS

Disorganization—whether in the way you manage your time or the way you keep your work and storage areas—can create stress. Since stress is emotionally and physically draining, it makes sense to develop strategies that will help limit the stressors in your life.

Types of stress

Stress can compromise the integrity of your body. Although you have encountered stressors for your entire life, college has introduced some new ones (see chapter 1). When we refer to **stress,** we typically describe how our bodies react to external and internal pressures. Physiologically, stress represents a time of extreme arousal in the body. Blood pressure can rise, the heart and pulse beat more rapidly, the body can perspire, and clear thinking may become more difficult. Psychologists generally recognize two types of stress: distress and eustress.

Distress is what we usually refer to when using the word *stress.* It is considered "bad" stress or pressure. For instance:

> **You are walking across a dark parking lot after a night class. As you move toward your car, you hear footsteps behind you. The footsteps are quickly gaining on you; as you walk faster, so does the person behind you. Your heart beats so fast it feels as though it might jump through your chest.**

Eustress is positive, or "good," stress or pressure. For example:

> **A student has a date tonight with someone she has been interested in for a long time. She is excited and looking forward to the evening. As the hour of the date gets closer, she feels a bit flushed; "butterflies" are in her stomach. When her date knocks on the door, her heart beats with anticipation.**

Stress can move us to action. In our dark parking lot example, for instance, a fight-or-flight response can move the person to action to get out of harm's way. But continual exposure to stress

YOUR STRESS SIGNALS

1. How do you know when you are under stress? What signals does your body tend to give you? List them here.

_____

_____

_____

_____

_____

2. How do you listen to these signals? That is, what do you do when your body is "talking to you"?

_____

_____

_____

_____

_____

can lead to physical ailments or emotional trauma—both of which will compromise the integrity of your body.

Stress signals

Stressors differ from person to person. One student may be stressed to the point of tears before having to deliver a speech, while a second student is energized by the prospect of talking in front of an audience. Pay attention to your body; it will give clues when something is wrong. Some of the more common signals include the following:*

- Shallow or rapid breathing
- Sweating
- Increased heart rate
- Headache
- Muscle tension
- Grinding teeth
- Hunched shoulders
- Eye strain
- Hives or similar rash
- Change in appetite (loss or gain)
- Feeling anxious or depressed
- Short-tempered

*This list is not meant to be diagnostic. Seek professional assistance as needed. For additional information see the St. Vincent Catholic Medical Center Web site, http://www.svcmc.org/body.cfm?xyzpdqabc=0&id =841&action=detail&AEProductID=HW%5FCatholic&AEArticleID=rlxsk&AEArticleType=Brain%20and%20nerves.

- Angry
- Change in sleep patterns.

Stress-reducing suggestions

As with stress signals, stress-reducing strategies are individualistic. What works for one person may not work for another. The following list provides a few of the more common healthy and legal suggestions:[6]

- Limit caffeine (a stimulant) intake.
- Exercise regularly.
- Get a good night's sleep.
- Take a break and relax.
- Maintain realistic expectations.
- Reinterpret situations in a positive light (reframing).
- Examine your belief systems.
- Develop a support network.
- Maintain a sense of humor.
- Take breaks for peak performance.
- Learn to say "no" if saying "yes" will overwhelm you.

HOW DO YOU HANDLE STRESS?

Long before you arrived on this college campus, you encountered stress. You also handled that stress. You found ways to confront, avoid, or cope with the stressors in your life.

1. List the *healthy* strategies you have used to deal with stress.

   _____

   _____

   _____

2. Which strategy or strategies do you tend to use the most—and why?

   _____

   _____

   _____

3. If you have engaged in any *unhealthy* stress-reducing strategies, what can you do to replace those choices with *healthier* choices in the future?

   _____

   _____

   _____

- Engage in healthy recreation.

- Concentrate on your breath—slower, deeper and longer.

- Practice guided imagery.

- Meditate or pray.

- Talk with a trusted friend or mentor.

Some other strategies, while they may reduce stress in the short run, have long-term unhealthy consequences:

- Drinking alcohol to excess

- Abusing drugs

- Promiscuous sexual activity

- Chain smoking

- Binge eating

SUMMARY

ORGANIZATION: MAXIMIZING TIME AND SPACE WHILE LIMITING STRESS

Organized people respect their time. They know it is a precious commodity and they refuse to waste it. But organization refers to more than mere time management. An organized workspace will have a positive impact on personal time. Organization will help create a calmer more manageable environment. This in turn will reduce stressors.

As you apply the tools for managing your time and space outlined in this chapter, remember that life can have organization but still be adventuresome. Planning does not translate into rigidity. You can be efficient and effective—and still be spontaneous.

Before leaving this chapter, keep the following points in mind:

- You cannot control time. You cannot create time. *However,* you *can* effectively use time for your benefit.

- The more courses you take means more demand on your time. That sounds simplistic, but many students fail to look at the big picture when planning a semester.

- Without establishing priorities (an order of importance) you can easily end up spending time on minor tasks while ignoring the major projects that require immediate attention.

- Procrastination can rob your time and derail your best intentions.

- Organize your personal and portable spaces outside of the classroom.

- Organizing time and space will help to limit the chaos and stress in your life.

tuning your life-strings

the 4 Rs

self

change and personal growth

The following activities will allow you to reflect on the three levels of student success as they apply to the major concepts introduced in this chapter. Each activity will give you an opportunity to reflect and apply the chapter concepts in a way that is meaningful to you during this transitional phase of your life. Use this opportunity to apply newly acquired information and also keep an ongoing journal of growth in the various facets of your life.

The 4 Rs

Describe a personal example of how you used each of the 4 Rs as you considered your organizational challenges.

1. *Reflection* (Example: How have you evaluated your organizational skills?)_____
   _____
   _____

2. *Respect* (Example: How have you effectively managed time in the past?)_____
   _____
   _____

3. *Responsibility* (Example: Describe responsible steps you have taken to move toward more effective and efficient organization of time and space.) _____
   _____
   _____

4. *Renewal* (Example: In what ways have organizing your time and space reduced your stress level?)_____
   _____
   _____

The Change Cycle

For this activity, reflect on a change that you are currently considering concerning your organizational skills.

1. What is the situation that requires change?

   _____

   _____

2. What led you to recognize this?

   _____

   _____

3. What is (or will be) your plan to address this situation?

   _____

   _____

4. If you have put the plan into action (executed it), how are you progressing?

   _____

   _____

5. Once the plan has become a reality, how do you plan to enjoy this achievement? How will you reward yourself?

   _____

   _____

Tuning Your Life-Strings

Pause for a moment and reflect on the balance—or lack of balance—in your life at this point in the school term. As you fill in the table that follows, apply newly acquired information from this chapter to gauge the level of strength in the various facets of your life. You may wish to refer to your responses in previous chapters.

Life-string	Questions to ask yourself	What possible activities could help you tune this string?	Who can help you tune this string?
Social	• Does your social life interfere with the time you need to devote to your studies? • How do you schedule your social time?		
Occupational	• Have you scheduled time to gather information about possible majors?		
Spiritual	• Have you scheduled time during your week to quietly meditate or pray?		
Physical	• Have you made exercise, proper sleep, and relaxation a permanent part of your daily schedule?		
Intellectual	• How have you organized your space to help you study effectively and efficiently?		
Emotional	• In what ways has organization of your time and space had an impact on your college stressors?		

Rhythms of Reflection

To complete this chapter, please reflect on the following quotation:

> *The main thing is to keep the main thing the main thing*
>
> –Stephen Covey

Now, using the words above for inspiration, explain how you can use the strategies introduced in this chapter to "keep the main thing the main thing." Please write your thoughts here.

_____

_____

_____

_____

_____

_____

_____

_____

_____

_____

To further respond online, please go to the *Rhythms of Reflection* module in chapter 4 of the Companion Website.

ENDNOTES

1. Some of the material on time management can be found in Steve Piscitelli, *Study Skills: Do I Really Need This Stuff?* (Upper Saddle River, NJ: Prentice Hall, 2004), module four.
2. Lee Shulman, president of the Carnegie Foundation for the Advancement of Teaching, quoted in Ann R. Martin, "College Student Devotion to Homework Debated," *Chicago Tribune*, January 4, 2004, http://nsse.iub.edu/articles/Chicago_Tribune_1_4_2004.htm (accessed July 1, 2006). In the article, Shulman maintains, "How many hours they spend is irrelevant. It's what they spend their time doing."
3. Stephen Covey, A. Roger Merrill, and Rebecca R. Merrill, *First Things First* (New York: Simon & Schuster, 1994), is one of many, many examples. An Internet search will also bring up a number of sites with a variety of suggestions.
4. Piscitelli, *Study Skills*, 76.

5. From Linda Sapadin with Jack Maguire, *Beat Procrastination and Make the Grade: The Six Styles of Procrastination and How Students Can Overcome Them* (New York: Penguin Books, 1999), 15–16. See pages 10-20 for a quick overview of the different types of procrastination.

6. David B. Posen, "Stress Management for Patient and Physician," *Canadian Journal of Continuing Medical Education*, April 1995, http://www.mentalhealth.com/mag1/p51-str.html#Head_1 (accessed August 10, 2006). Also see St. Vincent Catholic Medical Centers, http://www.svcmc.org/body.cfm?xyzpdqabc=0&id=841&action=detail&AEProductID=HW%5FCatholic&AEArticleID=rlxsk&AEArticleType=Brain%20and%20nerves (accessed January 13, 2006).

PART TWO

ACADEMICS

WHAT'S ON YOUR MIND?

Thoughts from Fellow Students

The first few weeks of our college life were a blur. There were so many things to get used to. Yes, classes were important—but there was a lot to deal with emotionally and socially. We were not really worried about our studies. After all, we had been in school for most of our life—how much different could college really be? Then came the first round of quizzes and exams, and a new set of concerns presented themselves. Perhaps you have questions similar to these:

- How can I manage my time so that I'm not cramming at exam time? (chapter 8)
- In the past, all I had to do was memorize and repeat information on tests. That's not working for me now. How can I get a deeper understanding of the course material? (chapter 5)
- I never had to take class notes before, and some of the professors move through information way too fast. What is the best way to get the professor's important points? (chapter 6)
- What is the most effective way of taking notes from the text? (chapter 6)
- I'm used to working alone. Would a study group really help me study for tests and complete homework assignments? (chapter 6)
- I always thought I was a good writer. My professors think differently. What can I do to improve my writing skills? (chapter 7)
- Is there any way to know exactly what I should study? (chapter 8)
- I've always been pretty good with computers, chat rooms, and blogs. Now, some of my professors require online testing, as well as Internet research. Are there any strategies to help me with these cyberspace requirements? (chapter 9)

College classes will get progressively more difficult with each passing term. We know people who just threw up their hands and quit. You can do that, too—or you can use the skills you already have and recognize the skills you still need to build. You will not only survive—you will thrive!

By this time in the term you have confronted and navigated the various transitional and adjustment issues associated with the first year of college. Relationships have been forged and campus resources have been discovered. Now it's time to examine the academic skills you need to successfully complete your college course work. Let's take a quick look at what you will find in this part of *Rhythms of College Success: A Journey of Discovery, Change, and Mastery*.

- **Chapter 5: Critical Thinking.** Critical thinkers, problem solvers, and creative thinkers do more than memorize and repeat information. They reflect on the information before them—and then they demonstrate understanding by using the knowledge for practical purposes. You have a head start because you have used critical thinking skills to solve problems your entire life. Keep this question in mind as you read the chapter: *How will using higher-order thinking skills benefit you as a student—and as a critical thinker?*

- **Chapter 6: Becoming an Active Learner Inside the Classroom.** Active learning strategies can help you become a more effective student *inside* the classroom. To become an active learner you will need to forge productive working relationships with your classmates and your instructors. Keep this question in mind as you read the chapter: *How will you benefit from being an active learner?*

- **Chapter 7: Becoming an Active Learner Outside the Classroom.** You also need to use active engagement strategies *outside* the classroom to get the most from lectures, discussions, and student group work. In college you have more pages to read, more essays to write, more assignments and projects to juggle with other obligations, and very little hand-holding by your instructors. Keep this question in mind as you read the chapter: *How can you effectively use outside-of-class time to master your course work?*

- **Chapter 8: Test Performance and Memory Skills.** Successful test-taking is not a one-day event. It requires a plan. This chapter will help you develop a plan to improve your test performance and will also introduce strategies to help you develop your memory skills. Keep this question in mind as you read the chapter: *What do you need to do in order to improve your test performance?*

- **Chapter 9: Information Literacy.** Today we can get information from virtually anywhere in the world with a couple of keystrokes and a push of the Enter button. But the explosion of data does not necessarily equate to an explosion of credible knowledge. Once you locate information, you need to know how to evaluate it before you use it. Keep this question in mind as you read the chapter: *How will you benefit from knowing how to efficiently and effectively locate and evaluate information?*

You have reflected on your reasons for attending college and have established your goals. Now is the time to act on these thoughts. Please turn the page and continue that transitional ride that translates your musings into reality.

5

Critical Thinking
Creating Your Own Song

REFLECTIVE QUESTIONS

Keeping the following questions in mind will make this chapter more meaningful:

- Do you know what your learning style is?

- Are you an active learner taking control of your learning, or do you sit passively and wait for something to happen?

- Do you understand the difference between critical thinking, problem solving, and creative thinking?

- What specific strategy do you use to solve problems?

- How do you benefit by using higher-order thinking skills?

Key Terms

active learning

creative thinking

critical thinking

higher-order thinking skills

learning style

multiple intelligences

plus-minus-interesting (PMI)

problem solving

remembering

GUEST SPEAKER

MEET **QUENTIN HART**

Associate Director of Multicultural Affairs

Hawkeye Community College

Waterloo, Iowa

Every time I'm blessed with the opportunity to tell students about higher education, I start with the word *collage.* A collage is an artistic collection of shapes and images brought together to form a complete picture. Similarly, your mind is like a collage in that your ideas and thoughts come together to create a unique experience. This experience will differ depending on the choices made. Critical and creative thinking will inform your choices and create a meaningful educational experience.

It is important that you challenge your beliefs, thoughts, and understanding of society and your role as one of its most valuable resources. As a learner, you have the right to hold fast to your values and beliefs—but at the same time open your mind to new and exciting adventures. These opportunities are waiting for those who use their mind to critically think about what is happening in today's world, and why. Always remember that some people live to see what will happen, while others live to make things happen. Which are you?

My top three suggestions for thinking critically:

1. Ask questions when ideas or expressions are not familiar to you. A great mistake students make is not alerting instructors when they have questions.

2. When problem solving, remember to appreciate what you bring with you. No matter what your SAT or ACT scores were, your personal experiences and perspectives are just as important. Draw from these experiences and recognize they are valuable tools to your success.

3. Self-reflection is your opportunity to realize where you are now versus where you should be heading. Assess and understand your own learning style and the way in which you process information. Self-reflection is our checkpoint along the track toward increased knowledge.

INTRODUCTION

Even when a person seems to be absentmindedly performing a rote task, thinking occurs. If a student comes to class but has forgotten to bring the day's assignment, she might say, "Oh, I wasn't thinking when I left for class this morning." In reality she *was* thinking, but about other things. She may have been guilty of an oversight, but she *was* thinking.[1] Often, when students first arrive on campus, they do not know what they should know. That is, they may not be aware of all that will be demanded of them. But when deadlines, commitments, and expectations become realities, then—and only then—do many students start to examine their challenges and shortcomings. Compared to the beginning of the term, you probably have a better idea now of what works and what does not work for classroom success and interpersonal relations.

Perhaps you recognize that each assignment has a reason and a place in your instructor's grand scheme of things. (You might not know *exactly* what that scheme is, but you figure there is one.) Consider that recognition a personal success for yourself.

As you start to think more critically about your academic experiences, you will build habits that will make you a more successful student. More and more, you will think about your thinking—you will think about how you process information. (When you become more aware of how you are thinking, you engage in *metacognition*.[2])

This can be as simple—and effective—as knowing how you learn best. Do you have to *hear* an explanation, *see* a visual representation, or actually *hold* a model to understand a new concept? Do you understand the limits of what you can and cannot do (and therefore what you should work on improving)? As your experience grows this term, so will your insights about the thinking process.

POINTS TO CONSIDER

- **Why is it important to understand the way you think?** Once you are aware of your thought process, you will better understand how you can best complete a task. You will see how the individual assignments and concepts of a class connect to larger bodies of knowledge. As you complete this chapter, reflect on what helps you understand how small concepts fit into a bigger overall picture in a class.

- **What do you need to do in order to become a critical thinker?** Critical thinkers actively engage their environment. First they *notice* something, and then they *do* something with that information. In short, they examine or analyze it; they *use* the knowledge before them. What strategies do you have to help you become more actively engaged in your life?

- **How can you become a student who uses higher-order thinking skills?** Critical thinkers, problem solvers, and creative thinkers do more than memorize and repeat information. That is, they do more than merely reproduce a textbook definition or echo an instructor's lecture. They *reflect* on the information before them—and then they demonstrate understanding by using the knowledge for practical purposes. What higher-order thinking skills have you been able to use so far this term?

THINKING: HOW DO YOU PROCESS INFORMATION?

Your brain

Enclosed in your skull is a wrinkled three-pound lump of tissue and nerve impulses that never sees the light of day—yet it interprets all you experience. Long lists of words attempt to describe what the brain does. These tend to be action words such as *analyze, argue, compare, contrast, describe, deliberate, evaluate, fantasize, guess, solve,* and *understand*.[3]

Exploring in depth how the brain operates creates a set of challenges that are beyond the scope of this book. For our purposes, let's examine what a cognitive psychologist* would: how we

---

*Cognitive psychologists study how we come to know things.

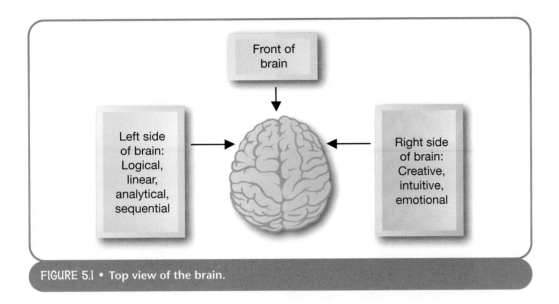

Left side of brain: Logical, linear, analytical, sequential

Front of brain

Right side of brain: Creative, intuitive, emotional

FIGURE 5.1 • Top view of the brain.

acquire knowledge (*learning*), how we remember that information (*memory*), and how we manipulate that information (*thinking*).[4]

Left-brain, right-brain, and whole-brain thinking

Each side of the brain has a different function (see Figure 5.1). In the most general terms, the left side of the brain has been associated with logical, analytical, linear, and sequential (step-by-step) thought processes. Studies have shown a "specialization of the left hemisphere for language."[5] It is the organized and fact-loving side of the brain. Methodically working through a math problem requires the sequential skills of the left side of the brain.

Whereas the left hemisphere is associated with verbal abilities, the right hemisphere is considered to be the home for nonverbal thinking processes and pattern recognition. From here the traits of creativity, intuition, and emotion spring into action. Molding a statue from a ball of clay relies on the right side of the brain.

There is also the argument that rather than right-brain/left-brain, we should consider the "whole-brain" model to understand the thinking process.[6] This model continues to recognize the distinct traits and abilities of the different sides of the brain, but maintains that the two must eventually work together. For instance, the right side of the brain might help a student arrive at a creative solution to a problem or see the "big picture" of a particular issue—but then the sequential, organized, and detailed-oriented left brain will put the creative solution into action. Have you ever known a creative person who had marvelous ideas yet never seemed able to apply them to the real world? His creative ideas needed a left-brained rational driver to carry them to reality.

Do you tend to be a methodical and organized learner? In the past, have you done better with teachers who clearly map the exact steps you must take to complete a task? Or have you been more comfortable with teachers who allowed you a great deal of flexibility in completing a project? Are you comfortable thinking about abstract ideas, or do you need concrete instructions and explanations? In short, what helps you understand your course material and assignments?

Learning styles

When students are engaged—taking an active part—in their course work, the chances for success increase significantly. One way to become an engaged student is to know as much as possible about the way you learn—and then apply that knowledge to your academic tasks.

Learning style refers to the manner in which individuals process information.* Although the material in this section just scratches the surface of a large body of research,[7] it will provide an opportunity to deepen your understanding of how you best process classroom information.

---

*For a quick, simple, and free online assessment that will provide information on how you process information, visit "VARK: A Guide to Learning Styles," http://vark-learn.com/english/page.asp?p=questionnaire.

© Stockdisc

© BananaStock Ltd.

Various factors—from the classroom environment to the manner of presentation by the teacher—will affect people differently, depending on their learning style. These factors include *environmental* influences (the impact of the physical surroundings on learning), *auditory* (the impact of hearing on learning), *visual* (the impact of seeing on learning), and *kinesthetic* (the impact of doing, touching, and moving on learning).

Environmental influences include such factors as food and drink (what we put into our bodies), light (how the room is illuminated), sound (how much silence or noise surrounds us), and temperature (how cool or hot the room is). Other environmental factors are comfort of furniture (how soft, hard, or firm the chair is), structure of time and/or task (how much time we have), ability to move about (how much movement we can have while working), and peer interaction (who we work best with or without when completing a task).

When it comes to teacher presentation, individual students typically have a particular style that helps them best understand the material being presented. For instance, some can *listen* to a verbal explanation of a task and then carry out the assignment successfully. These students receive *auditory* (oral) directions and translate them into a product.

Other students must *see* something before processing it effectively. For example, if such students had to assemble the components of a new desktop computer, it would be very helpful for them to have diagrammed instructions on what to do. *Visual* aids enhance their ability to learn; if they received only oral instructions, the process would be more difficult for them to complete. Similarly, some people must be able to *read* and *write* about a task in order to understand it.

Other people work best by *handling or manipulating* objects. A student who is better able to understand a biological principle by physically manipulating a laboratory experiment learns in a *kinesthetic* (or body movement) manner.

Difficulties in the classroom?

If you have difficulties in the classroom, they may not be due to a lack of effort on your part. The problem might be related to how you process information.

For instance,[8] let's assume you have to study for a quiz on the branches and functions of the nervous system. If your preferred method for learning is auditory, you could recite the information aloud to yourself in an attempt to hear and "burn" the concepts into your memory. If, however, you learn best visually, by seeing the material, you could read your class textbook and review your class notes. However, you could, just as well, draw up a diagram of the nervous system and physically label it as a warm-up activity for your in-class quiz. Such a study approach encourages the whole-brain model described earlier. Drawing a diagram (creativity) and then labeling the particular parts (organization) engages more of the brain than just staring at a piece of

HOW DO YOU LEARN BEST?

Reflect on the various ways you process information. Then answer the following questions.

1. *Auditory:* Describe a recent class situation in which you understood the material by *hearing* the explanation. You really "got it"! Rate how often this happens on a scale of 1 (almost never) to 5 (almost always). Explain why you think you got it or why you think you did *not* get it.

   Rating: _____

   Explanation: _____

   _____

2. *Visual:* Describe a recent class situation in which you understood the material by *seeing* the explanation. Maybe the instructor used pictures or a model. Whatever she used, you really "got it"! Rate how often this happens on a scale of 1 (almost never) to 5 (almost always). Explain why you think you got it or why you think you did *not* get it.

   Rating: _____

   Explanation: _____

   _____

3. *Kinesthetic:* Describe a recent class situation in which you understood the material by *physically doing something.* Maybe it was a science lab or maybe you constructed a model. Whatever happened, you really "got it"! Rate how often this happens on a scale of 1 (almost never) to 5 (almost always). Explain why you think you got it or why you think you did *not* get it.

   Rating: _____

   Explanation: _____

   _____

4. *Environment:* Describe the environment (climate, lighting, ventilation, sound) that helps you learn the best.

   _____

   _____

notebook paper with terms written on it. It also allows you to work kinesthetically (drawing and physically labeling the diagram) and visually (looking at the diagram and the labels).

It is one thing to *know* how you learn best but it is quite another to *use* the knowledge. When we actively learn we listen, view or manipulate information, *and* then we process that information. That is, we *use* it in some way.

Multiple intelligences

Whereas *learning style* looks at how we learn, *intelligence* refers to our ability to use information to solve problems. A great deal of research has been done in the area of **multiple intelligences.**[9] This theory addresses "the broad range of abilities that humans possess by grouping their capabilities into [multiple] comprehensive categories of intelligence."[10]

While nothing so profound is attempted here, a brief overview of this concept will prove helpful.

Howard Gardner, a Harvard professor, did the pioneering research in this area. He maintains that the traditional manner of measuring intelligence (IQ) with a single number is misleading. It leads us to believe that there is *one* intelligence. According to Gardner, there are actually eight in-telligences.[11] That is, we have eight different abilities to pick from when solving problems. Unfor-tunately, many of us have been trained to use only two or three of these. Just think of what you can do once you tap into as many of the eight intelligences as possible.*

The Eight Intelligences. Gardner maintains we all have at least a trace of each of the intelligences. Some may be highly developed and some a little less developed. Here is Gardner's list, with a brief explanation of each category:[12]

- **Linguistic intelligence ("word smart"):** You are good with the written word. You can express yourself with language. Occupations that might rely on this intelligence include writ-ers, speakers, lawyers, and teachers.

- **Logical-mathematical intelligence ("number smart"):** You can think abstractly and solve problems. Logic and order are strengths for you. You understand cause and effect. Manipulation of numbers comes easily. Occupations include scientists and mathematicians.

- **Spatial intelligence ("art smart"):** You can visually re-create your world. A sound sense of direction is involved, too. Occupations include sculptors, painters, and anatomy teachers.

- **Bodily-kinesthetic intelligence ("body smart"):** You have coordinated control of your own body. There is strong sense of learning by movement or action. You can effectively use your hands, fingers, and arms to make something. Occupations include athletes, actors, and dancers.

- **Musical intelligence ("music smart"):** You have the ability to use the major compo-nents of music (rhythm or pitch). You can recognize patterns and use them effectively. Occupations include musicians and dancers.

- **Interpersonal intelligence ("people smart"):** You have an understanding of the mood and motives of those with which you associate. If you are to effectively deal with other people you must be skilled in this intelligence. Occupations include teachers, politicians, and salespeople.

- **Intrapersonal intelligence ("me smart"):** You understand yourself and you can apply that knowledge in real-life situations to produce the best results. You understand what is good for you. You know who you are and what you can do. You know what to associate with and what to avoid. Occupations include independent-type work such as researchers, entrepreneurs, and ministers.

- **Naturalistic intelligence ("nature smart"):** You can understand, explain, and relate to things in the natural world around you. You have a unique ability to classify and separate items based on characteristics. Occupations include botanists, zoologists, archaeologists, and environmentalists.

OK. What Does All This Mean? If you can understand what your dominant intelli-gences are, you will be better equipped to tackle challenges—and this knowledge may even pro-vide a clue to future life choices. For instance, someone with a well-developed natural intelligence may excel at farming, zoo work, or wildlife management. A linguistically intelligent person may have a future as an attorney, author, or teacher. The logical-mathematical type may become a gifted scientist or astronomer. You get the idea.

The intent here is not to give you a rigid label. There will be times when you learn well by visual means, and times when auditory techniques are more productive. There will be times when your "word smart" intelligence stands out above all else, and other times when you will exhibit great spatial capabilities ("art smart"). Or perhaps individual work might be your normal routine, but a study group can be appropriate when trying to understand a troubling concept. The point is to understand what works best *most of the time.* Then, use that knowledge for your benefit.

For instance, a "word smart" person might take advantage of that talent and use the note-taking TSD strategy† described in chapter 7. A more visually oriented student with creative "art smart" intelligence, not tied to formal structure, might have more success with the informal flowchart for-mat of note-taking (described in chapter 6) than by using a traditional outline. And *all* students can

---

*A ninth intelligence is being investigated—spiritual. This intelligence refers to the ability to connect with nonphysical or metaphysical stimuli. For our purposes, however, we will look at the first eight.

†TSD stands for *title, summary, details.* It provides an active way to review class notes.

benefit from tapping into more than one intelligence when reviewing information. That means if you have a tendency to process your textbook readings or class lecture notes primarily through your linguistic intelligence, you may benefit by reprocessing the same information with your interpersonal or spatial intelligence. This helps your brain to develop a stronger connection with the information. Think of nursery rhymes that children learn. They usually internalize these by using more than one intelligence—reading, singing, movement, and interaction with others.[13]

MULTIPLE INTELLIGENCES, CAREERS, AND MAJORS

Selecting a major area of study will be one of your most important academic decisions. Chapter 12 will examine this topic in depth. For now, take a few moments to reflect on the connection between majors and careers. The middle column of the following chart correlates each multiple intelligence with a handful of associated careers. Complete the final column ("What Majors Will Prepare You for These Careers?"). Your college catalog will be one source of help to complete this assignment.[14]

Multiple intelligence	Possible careers (selected)	What majors will prepare you for these careers?
Linguistic intelligence ("word smart")	Writer, public speaker, lawyer, teacher, journalist, librarian, talk show host, tour guide	
Logical-mathematical intelligence ("number smart")	Scientist, mathematician, banker, investment broker, accountant, doctor	
Spatial intelligence ("art smart")	Sculptor, painter, anatomy teacher, architect, builder, photographer, urban planner, artist	
Bodily-kinesthetic intelligence ("body smart")	Athlete, actor, dancer, trainer, gymnast, thespian, massage therapist, model	
Musical intelligence ("music smart")	Musician, dancer, critic, music instructor, singer, record producer	
Interpersonal intelligence ("people smart")	Teacher, politician, salesperson, arbitrator, manager, human resources executive, psychologist, social worker, marriage counselor, coach	
Intrapersonal intelligence ("me smart")	Independent-type work, lifestyle coach, energy healer, clergy, philosopher, writer	
Naturalistic intelligence ("nature smart")	Botanist, zoologist, archaeologist, meteorologist, environmentalist, animal trainer, veterinarian	

Successful intelligence

Have you ever known a person who was a "genius" but seemed to lack basic common sense? Some folks might say your genius friend was book smart but not street smart.

Robert J. Sternberg addresses this seeming contradiction in his book *Successful Intelligence.*[15] Traditional intelligence tests, according to Sternberg, measure analytical abilities. Two other aspects of intelligence—creative intelligence and practical intelligence—cannot be measured by the typical pencil-and-paper multiple-choice tests.

The genius friend mentioned above would more than likely score high on an IQ test. This ranking, however, would not necessarily indicate success in the real world. Sternberg explains that successful intelligence

> involves analytical, creative and practical aspects. The analytical aspect is used to solve problems, the creative aspect to decide what problems to solve, and the practical aspect to make solutions effective. The three aspects are relatively independent of one another.[16]

There is a great deal more to intelligence than a single IQ number. Developing as many facets of intelligence as possible to learn and actively apply your education (book smarts) will help you to develop practical ways to succeed in life (street smarts).

HIGHER-ORDER THINKING SKILLS

In 1956, educational pioneer Benjamin Bloom developed a six-tier thinking skills model:[17]

1. *Knowledge:* Remembering facts, names, events; rote recall

2. *Comprehension:* Putting information into your own words

3. *Application:* Taking learned information and using it in a new situation

4. *Analysis:* Examining or breaking down the parts of information

5. *Synthesis:* Combining pieces of information to create a larger and newer piece of information

6. *Evaluation:* Assessing or judging the worth of information

The first level, *knowledge* or recall information—that is, **remembering** facts or names—is the lowest level of thinking. When you memorize a list of vocabulary words and then repeat those words on a classroom quiz, the information has been recalled from your memory. Do not, however, confuse "low level" with "unimportant"; this level is a basic building block in the learning process. Think of it as gathering the fundamental pieces of knowledge. This vital skill helps lay the foundation for the higher-order thinking skills—similar to a football receiver, who cannot be expected to catch a football successfully in a game unless he can first remember the pass pattern he needs to run.

The next level up on Bloom's list, *comprehension*, requires an understanding of the information presented. When you can read or hear something and then put it into your own words, there is an increased chance you will remember it. It may be only one step above recalling general knowledge, but comprehension indicates that the information has been interpreted for individual understanding.

The next four levels move your thinking into **higher-order thinking skills.**

Using higher-order thinking skills

To make the most appropriate use of the higher-order thinking skills described next, a person must master the smaller details noted in the preceding paragraphs. The effectiveness of critical thinking, problem solving, and creative thinking will be significantly reduced if the basics are not understood. A person may know the steps (the method) to solve a problem, but without an understanding of this knowledge, usefulness of the process will be diminished.

Critical thinking

Active learning involves many forms of thinking. You have no doubt been exposed to the terms *critical thinking, problem solving,* and *creative thinking* during your schooling. Some people use the terms interchangeably, freely substituting one term for the other.

A more precise view would be to think of each as a distinct thinking process; one leads to the other; one builds on the previous and uses deeper thinking skills.

One author believes that someone who engages in **critical thinking** "responds with awareness" and leads an "examined life."[18] Critical thinkers take time to reflect on the issue before them. They analyze what has happened and what is needed. Critical thinkers question assumptions; they do not passively accept other people's explanations. But this requires the use of higher-order thinking skills.

Obviously, the facts must be gathered about a particular situation, problem, or question. But knowing the facts is only the first step (lower-level thinking). The information must be seriously examined. For example, during the academic year campuses across the nation hold elections for student government offices. Student candidates place their names on ballots in hopes of winning a spot on the campus decision making team. A *noncritically thinking* voter may make a decision strictly based on name recognition (a fact): "I know that person from my history class. She seems nice. I'll vote for her." This is an example of a *noncritical review* of the candidate. Factual recall (the name and personality trait) does not mean an understanding of the issues.

The critical thinker will go through a deeper process by seriously examining the issues: "I recognize the name and I also have asked her about the parking problem on campus. She has a four-point plan to provide more space by the end of this term. The plan is reasonable and has a chance to work. I'll vote for her!" This would-be voter has critically analyzed the candidate according to a particular issue, evaluated the proposed solution, and then made a decision based on the analysis and evaluation. The critical thinking process is illustrated in Figure 5.2.

Reviewing Bloom's categories once again, note that the first two categories exhibit *noncritical thinking characteristics,* but the last four levels describe forms of critical thinking. Table 5.1 outlines Bloom's levels of critical thinking and suggests that a critical thinker is actively and deeply involved in processing information.

Problem solving

The next level of thinking, problem solving, uses critical thinking. Not all critical thinking is problem solving, but all problem solving requires critical thinking. **Problem solving,** in short, requires the use of thinking skills to examine a dilemma and then to propose a solution. The process is illustrated in Figure 5.3 (p. 105).

For an example, let's look at the issue of campus security. A critical thinker would gather reports on the number of assaults that have taken place on campus during the last twelve months. He would determine at what hours and in what parts of the campus most of the attacks have taken place. The response time of the security personnel might also be considered. All of this requires deep thinking and fact-finding. But if our critical thinker gathers the information, analyzes, and then submits a report *without a solution,* then the problem has not been solved.

The problem solver moves to the next level as he looks at the information *and then* begins to propose alternatives and answers.

Problem Solving Models. Two main points deserve emphasis:

1. You have confronted and solved problems your entire life.

2. Numerous models for problem solving exist.

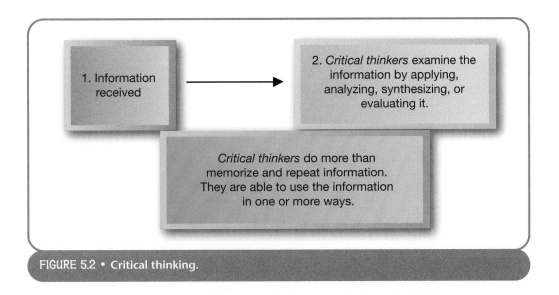

FIGURE 5.2 • **Critical thinking.**

Table 5.1
Bloom and critical thinking

Level of thinking	Characteristics	Is it critical thinking? Why?
Knowledge	Remembering facts, names, events; rote recall	*Noncritical thinking:* Surface learning only
Comprehension	Putting information into your own words	*Noncritical thinking:* Surface learning only
Application	Taking learned information and using it in a new situation	*Critical thinking:* The person understands the information and can use it in a new situation.
Analysis	Examining or breaking down the parts of information	*Critical thinking:* The person understands the information and demonstrates this understanding by separating or splitting the information into its pieces or parts.
Synthesis	Combining pieces of information to create a larger and newer piece of information	*Critical thinking:* The person understands the information and then brings pieces of the information together to form a big picture or new idea.
Evaluation	Assessing or judging the worth of information	*Critical thinking:* The person has the ability to judge or critique the value of the information.

While you examine the perspectives below, draw on your past experiences as well. Combining the new with the old will expand your collection of effective strategies. Whether you read a student success book such as this one or look at a book on conflict resolution, you will find they all share the following broad categorical strategies:

- Reflecting on the problem (What happened and why?)

- Brainstorming solutions (What can be done?)

- Choosing and implementing a solution (What steps will be taken?)

- Evaluating the chosen solutions (What happened as a result of the steps taken?)

For instance, notice how the above-mentioned strategies overlap with the six steps of the problem solving strategy known by the acronym SAC-SIP:[19]

1. *Stop:* Can you identify and define the problem? (Reflecting on the problem)

2. *Alternatives:* What options are available to solve the problem? (Brainstorming solutions)

3. *Consequences:* What results will occur for each alternative you have generated? (Reflecting on the alternatives)

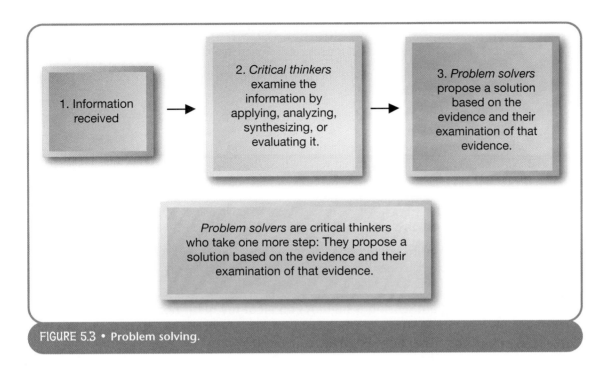

FIGURE 5.3 • Problem solving.

USING CRITICAL THINKING SKILLS TO SOLVE A PROBLEM

All college and university campuses have challenges facing them. Perhaps your campus has a parking problem—too many cars, not enough space. Or maybe students do not find the cafeteria satisfying. Or there might be a concern about the increasing costs of schooling.

Using the SAC-SIP model (or another model with which you are familiar), propose three solutions to a campus problem.

1. State the problem as clearly as you can.

_____

_____

_____

2. List potential solution #1. _____

_____

_____

3. List potential solution #2. _____

_____

_____

4. List potential solution #3. _____

_____

_____

4. *Select:* What alternative will you decide to try? (Choosing a solution)

5. *Implement:* How will you put the selected solution into practice? (Implementing a solution)

6. *Pause:* When will you pause and evaluate whether the chosen alternative is working? (Evaluating the chosen solution)

Regardless of the model used, problem solving requires a "will and a way" to improve. And effective problem solving involves a plan or a strategy. There must be a "set of ideas or insights that help [you] act smarter on hard problems, in a world of changing rules."[20] Thus, problem solving goes far beyond the classroom walls and campus grounds. It is a staple of everyday life— something that communities must continually address.

Visualizing the Problem Solving Process. No matter which model or strategy you choose, the problem solving process involves the following steps:

- **Problem identification:** Before a problem can be solved, the actual problem must be identified. How can you solve the problem if you have not clearly identified it? This sounds simple, but it is frequently overlooked.

  Example: "I am scoring B's and A's on all of my math homework assignments. My test grades have not been above a D. My problem: The effort I put into my studies does not match my test grades."

- **Vision of the solution:** Once the problem has been pinpointed, now identify where you would like to go. Where do you want to end up when the problem is solved?

  Example: "I want my math exam grades to reflect my homework grades. That is, I want to earn B's and A's on my math exams."

- **Problem analysis:** Welcome to the *real work* of problem solving. Put on your critical thinking hat and try and figure out *why* your problem exists. For instance, why is it that you do not perform as well on your math tests as you do on your math homework assignments?

  Example: "My homework is nonthreatening. I never feel rushed. I start to feel anxious about the math test two or three days before the exam. I stay up late the night before, trying to memorize everything in the chapter. When I walk into a math test I am stressed and tired."

- **Solution:** Once you have dissected this problem from various angles, it is time to come up with a solution. For instance, if you had used the SAC-SIP method you would now have a number of possible solutions. Pick the best one.*

- **Implementation:** It is time to put your plan (goal) into action. Remember, it's great to have dreams, but they are only fantasies if you are not breathing life into them.

This process is shown graphically in Figure 5.4.

The Problem Solving Trap. Whether a corporation looks at ways to increase its profit or a community agency examines how to meet the needs of the local citizens, a problem must be solved. People in all walks of life and business use various models to tackle problems. But there is a potential trap. Sometimes we can be blinded to *new* alternatives by becoming stuck in routine. Perhaps we continue to look at a particular problem from the same point of view. For example, if you earn poor grades your response may be, "I'll study harder!" Listen to the real communication here: "I'll continue to use the same study methods that have not worked—but I'll do them longer and with more effort." It does not appear practical when viewed from that perspective. It is limited because you have not been particularly creative in determining alternative routes.

---

*You can also use the plus-minus-interesting (PMI) strategy (discussed later in this chapter) as a way to come up with your best solution.

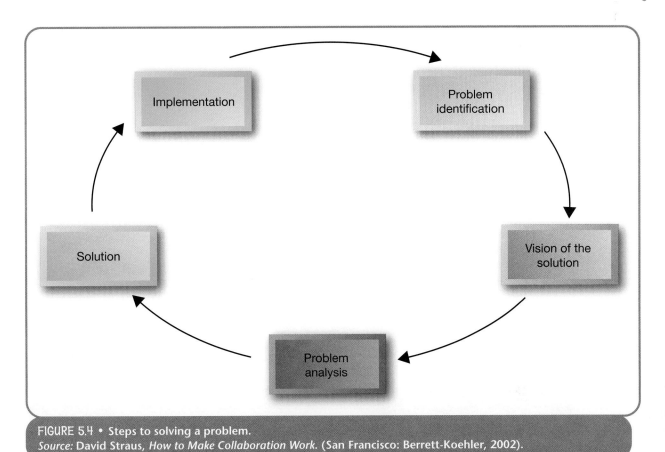

FIGURE 5.4 • Steps to solving a problem.
Source: David Straus, *How to Make Collaboration Work.* (San Francisco: Berrett-Koehler, 2002).

SOLUTION AND IMPLEMENTATION

You will notice in the description of the problem solving process that there are no examples for the Solution and the Implementation steps. Use this activity to identify a solution to the above-mentioned problem and then explain how you would implement that solution. Below is a review of the problem, the vision, and the analysis:

Problem identification: "I am scoring B's and A's on all of my math homework assignments. My test grades have not been above a D. My problem: The effort I put into my studies does not match my test grades."

Vision of the solution: "I want my math exam grades to reflect my homework grades. That is, I want to earn B's and A's on my math exams."

Problem analysis: "My homework is nonthreatening. I never feel rushed. I start to feel anxious about the math test two or three days before the exam. I stay up late the night before, trying to memorize everything in the chapter. When I walk into a math test I am stressed and tired."

1. Solution: _____

_____

_____

2. Implementation: _____

_____

_____

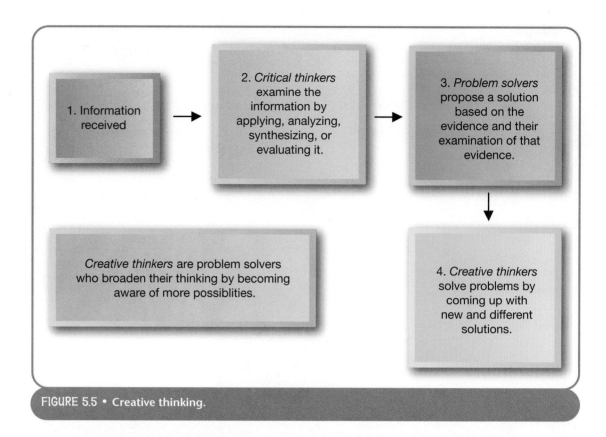

FIGURE 5.5 • Creative thinking.

Creative thinking: You have to do it differently if you want different results

Albert Einstein reportedly said, "The definition of insanity is doing the same thing over and over again and expecting different results." The same goes for your studies. If you have difficulties with your math exams, it would seem "insane" to continue preparing for the exams in the *same* manner you have in the past. Just because you put more effort into your preparation does not mean that you will see better results on the next exam. We use the term **creative thinking** to refer to thinking that develops (creates) a *new* or *different* product. It requires that we look at situations in new ways, from different angles or perspectives (see Figure 5.5).

Take another look at the example of a campus security concern described earlier in this chapter. Solutions might include hiring more security officers for the campus, improving lighting, or installing more emergency phones in high-risk areas on campus.

However, a *new* approach might be to explore the possibility of developing a campus "citizen watch program" in which student organizations work with campus security personnel to increase student confidence about campus safety.

By *creatively* tackling a problem, we become more aware of the greater number of possibilities. In fact, we will become better equipped to broaden our thinking and develop new patterns of problem solving.

Pros and Cons—With a Twist. We all have had the experience of facing a dilemma and trying to decide whether we should do one thing or another. Very possibly you pulled out a piece of paper in times like this, drew a line down the middle of the page, and then labeled the left column with a "+" and the right column with a "−". You then proceeded to list all the positive reasons for following a particular course of action in the left column and all the reasons for *not* doing a particular choice in the right column. The side of the paper with the most items guided your decision.

One method, developed by Edward de Bono,* who has written extensively about creative (or lateral) thinking and is recognized worldwide as *the* expert on how we think, takes this a step

---

*His models of creative thinking include the *6 Thinking Hats* strategy and *PMI*, introduced here. As stated on his Web site (http://www.edwdebono.com/debono/biograph.htm): "Dr. Edward de Bono is one of the very few people in history who can be said to have had a major impact on the way we think. In many ways he could be said to be the best known thinker internationally." An interesting side note: In 1996 de Bono had a planet (DE73) named for him—*Edebono*.

Table 5.2 Decisions: Examining plus-minus-interesting factors Problem: Whether to take a part-time job at the campus bookstore		
Plus (favorable considerations)	**Minus (unfavorable considerations)**	**Interesting (may be positive or may be negative, but at least something to consider)**
1. I need to earn extra money.	1. I'm already taking a full load of course work. This could overburden my schedule.	1. Bookstores always have a variety of different items on the shelves—there are more than books.
2. I will be able to meet new people since most students on campus come to the bookstore.	2. I'll have less time to spend with my friends outside of classes.	2. I've never worked an "inside" job before. All my past jobs have been outdoors.
3. The hours are flexible since the bookstore manager understands the realities of classes and college activities.	3. I'll need to either get up earlier before class or stay up later at night to complete my homework.	3. I don't know how I will react to customer complaints and demands.
4. The distance from class to work will be short—everything is on the same campus.	4. I'll end up being on campus 10 or 12 hours some days.	4. I'm not usually on campus after 5 p.m. I wonder what the night students are like?

further. The strategy is called **plus-minus-interesting (PMI).**[21] Using this approach, you would decide whether a given factor is favorable ("plus"), unfavorable ("minus"), or perhaps not immediately positive or negative but still something to consider ("interesting").

To illustrate this strategy, assume that you are trying to decide whether to take a part-time job at the campus bookstore that will require you to work fifteen hours a week. Table 5.2 outlines the PMI way to attack the problem.

SUMMARY

CRITICAL THINKING EXPANDS YOUR CONFIDENCE

In this chapter you have been asked to think about *how* you should think about *what* you think about. You have examined the importance of taking control of your learning process. As each week on campus passes, you will begin to notice what *is* working for you and what is *not*. You will know where your challenges lie and what strengths you can draw on to meet those challenges. Before moving on to the next chapter, take a moment to reflect on the following points:

• Understand how you think about your challenges. Identify and evaluate the strategies you are currently using to help you succeed in college.

• It is important to understand how you process information best. Are you an auditory learner, visual learner, hands-on learner—or some combination of the three?

USING PMI TO SOLVE ONE OF YOUR PROBLEMS

Pick a problem or challenge that is facing you right now. It may be a class that you have given thought to withdrawing from this term. Or maybe, as in our example, you too have been considering taking on a new job. Or maybe it is time to register for classes next term and you want to take a larger load of courses. Whatever it is, write the problem below.

1. The challenge I have to face at this time is _____

    _____

    _____

2. Now, use the PMI model to look at the different sides of the issue:

Plus (a favorable point)	Minus (an unfavorable point)	Interesting (may be positive or negative but at the least it is something to consider)
1.	1.	1.
2.	2.	2.
3.	3.	3.
4.	4.	4.

3. Finally, based on your entries in the chart, what decision have you arrived at—or are leaning toward—concerning this challenge? _____

    _____

    _____

    _____

- Do not just receive information. Grab it and use it in various ways. Actively apply your class notes and textbook reading in order to have a better understanding of course material.

- Critical thinking requires reflection and analysis of issues or events.

- Problem solving requires the use of critical thinking skills to examine a dilemma and then propose a solution.

- When solving a problem, use creative thinking strategies to look at multiple perspectives. This will help you see that problems and issues generally have more than two sides.

tuning your life-strings

the 4 Rs

self

change and personal growth

Your SELF: Personal growth and balance

The following activities will allow you to reflect on the three levels of student success as they apply to the major concepts introduced in this chapter. Each activity will give you an opportunity to reflect and apply the chapter concepts in a way that is meaningful to you during this transitional phase of your life. Use this opportunity to apply newly acquired information and also keep an ongoing journal of growth in the various facets of your life.

The 4 Rs

Describe a personal example as to how you used each of the 4 Rs to improve your thinking skills.

1. *Reflection* (Example: How have you examined your critical thinking strategies?)

   _____

   _____

2. *Respect* (Example: You have solved problems all of your life. What successful strategies can you now draw upon?)

   _____

   _____

3. *Responsibility* (Example: Describe responsible steps you have taken to solve a recent problem.)

   _____

   _____

4. *Renewal* (Example: How do you feel when you have successfully solved a problem?)

   _____

   _____

The Change Cycle

Critical thinking skills play a vital role in the change cycle. Each of the stages requires a critical evaluation of where you are and where you need to go. (Recall the four stages of the change cycle: *recognizing* the need for change, *planning* for the change, *executing* the plan, and *enjoying* the achieved goal.) For this activity, reflect on a change that you are currently confronting.

1. What is the situation that requires change?

   _____

   _____

2. What led you to recognize this?

   _____

   _____

3. What is (or will be) your plan to address this situation?

   _____

   _____

4. If you have put the plan into action (executed it), how are you progressing?

   _____

   _____

5. Once the plan has become a reality, how do you plan to enjoy this achievement? How will you reward yourself?

   _____

   _____

Tuning Your Life-Strings

Pause for a moment and reflect on the balance—or lack of balance—in your life at this point in the school term. Use this activity to apply newly acquired information from this chapter to gauge the level of strength in the various facets of your life. You may wish to refer to your responses in previous chapters.

Life-string	Questions to ask yourself	What possible activities could help you tune this string?	Who can help you tune this string?
Social	• Have you had to confront a troubling issue or solve a problem concerning a friend or family member?		
Occupational	• How have you made decisions that will impact your major or career interests?		
Spiritual	• What types of explorations have you been involved in that have helped you examine the deeper meanings of life—and your purpose in this life?		
Physical	• Have you participated in any recreational activities this week? • What can you do creatively to find more time to exercise and relax?		
Intellectual	• What did you do this week that involved critical thinking, problem solving, or creative thinking? • How did this expand your knowledge and/or skill base?		
Emotional	• What strategies have you used to effectively deal with your college stressors?		

Rhythms of Reflection

To complete this chapter, please reflect on the following words:

The illiterate of the 21st century will not be those who cannot read and write, but those who cannot learn, unlearn, and relearn.

–Alvin Toffler

As a result of reading this chapter, explain one thing you have *learned* (or need to learn), one thing you have *unlearned* (or need to unlearn), and one thing you have *relearned* (or need to relearn). Please write your thoughts here.

_____

_____

_____

_____

_____

 To further respond online, please go to the *Rhythms of Reflection* module in chapter 5 of the Companion Website.

ENDNOTES

1. Frank Smith, *To Think* (New York: Teachers College Press, 1990), 1–10.
2. See Scott W. VanderStoep and Paul R. Pintrich, *Learning to Learn: The Skill and Will of College Success* (Upper Saddle River, NJ: Prentice Hall, 2003), 121–124, for a discussion of metacognition.
3. See Smith, *To Think,* chapter 1, for Smith's list titled "Thinking in Seventy-seven Words."
4. Smith, *To Think,* 12.
5. Arthur W. Toga and Paul M. Thompson, "Mapping Brain Asymmetry," *Nature Reviews: Neuroscience 4* (January 2003): 37.
6. See Ned Herrmann, "Is it true that creativity resides in the right hemisphere of the brain?," *Scientific American,* January 26, 1998, http://scientificamerican.com/askexpert_question.cfm?articleID= 00049843-7DBA-1C71-9EB7809EC588F2D7&catID=3&topicID=12 (accessed July 20, 2006); and "Ned Herrmann's Whole Brain Model," Kheper.net, http://www.kheper.net/topics/intelligence/Herrmann.htm (accessed September 17, 2005). Also see John McCrone, "Right Brain or Left Brain—Myth or Reality?" *New Scientist* 163 (July 3, 1999): 26ff.
7. This information on learning styles comes from Steve Piscitelli, *Study Skills: Do I Really Need This Stuff?* (Upper Saddle River, NJ: Prentice Hall, 2004). A great deal has been written about learning styles. My intent here is to provide a brief overview. For more information, see Nancy Lightfoot Matte and Susan Hillary Henderson, *Success, Your Style: Right- and Left-Brain Techniques for Learning* (Belmont, CA: Wadsworth, 1995); Rita Dunn and Kenneth Dunn, *Teaching Students Through Their Individual Learning Styles: A Practical Approach* (Reston, VA: Reston, 1978); Roger G. Swartz, *Accelerated Learning: How You Learn Determines What You Learn* (Durant, OK: EMIS, 1991); James Keefe, *Learning Style Handbook: II. Accommodating Perceptual, Study and Instructional Preferences* (Reston, VA: National Association of Secondary School Principals, n.d.); and David Lazear, *Seven Ways of Knowing: Teaching for Multiple Intelligences* (Palatine, IL: Skylight, 1991).
8. John Wall, professor of psychology at Florida Community College at Jacksonville, provided the inspiration for this example.
9. Some material for this section came from Piscitelli, *Study Skills,* 37–43.

10. Thomas Armstrong, *Multiple Intelligences in the Classroom* (Alexandria, VA: Association for Supervision and Curriculum Development, 1994), 2. Armstrong, in a very straightforward manner, describes and analyzes the first seven intelligences identified by Howard Gardner. The descriptions of the intelligences contained here come from an interview of Howard Gardner found in Kathy Checkley, "The First Seven . . . and the Eighth: A Conversation with Howard Gardner," *Educational Leadership* 55, September 1997, Association for Supervision and Curriculum and Development, http://www.ascd.org/portal/site/ascd/ template.MAXIMIZE/menuitem.459dee008f99653fb85516f762108a0c/?javax.portlet.tpst =d5b9c0fa1a493266805516f762108a0c_ws_MX&javax.portlet.prp_d5b9c0fa1a493266805516f762108a0c _journaltypeheaderimage=%2FASCD%2Fimages%2Fmultifiles%2Fpublications%2Felmast.gif&javax.portlet.prp _d5b9c0fa1a493266805516f762108a0c_viewID=article_view&javax.portlet.prp_d5b9c0fa1a4932668055 16f762108a0c_journalmoid=7f33c29725eaff00VgnVCM1000003d01a8c0RCRD&javax.portlet.prp _d5b9c0fa1a493266805516f762108a0c_articlemoid=7563c29725eaff00VgnVCM1000003d01a8c0RCR D&javax.portlet.prp_d5b9c0fa1a493266805516f762108a0c_journalTypePersonalization =ASCD_EL&javax.portlet.begCacheTok=token&javax.portlet.endCacheTok=token) (accessed May 20, 2002).

11. Gardner's groundbreaking book is *Frames of Mind: The Theory of Multiple Intelligences* (New York: Basic Books, 1983).

12. See Armstrong, *Multiple Intelligences in the Classroom,* for more detailed information.

13. Thanks again to John Wall for reminding me of the importance of staying in touch with our inner child. Personal correspondence, October 27, 2005.

14. For an in-depth review of multiple intelligences (MI) and the practical applications, including a list of occupation–MI connections, see Clifford Morris, "Linking Most General of Occupations to Multiple Intelligences," 2004, http://www.igs.net/~cmorris/smo_comments.html (accessed August 10, 2005).

15. Robert Sternberg, *Successful Intelligence: How Practical and Creative Intelligence Determine Success in Life* (New York: Plume, 1997).

16. Sternberg, *Successful Intelligence,* 47.

17. For additional information and resources, see Benjamin Bloom, "Major Categories in the Taxonomy of Educational Objectives," 1956, http://faculty.washington.edu/krumme/guides/bloom1.html (accessed July 18, 2006).

18. Elaine Gray, *Conscious Choices: A Model for Self-Directed Learning* (Upper Saddle River, NJ: Prentice Hall, 2004), 26–34.

19. Piscitelli, *Study Skills,* 13–15.

20. "Strategy for a Changing World," 2003–2005, Community Problem Solving, http://www.community-problem-solving.net/cms/ (accessed May 30, 2006).

21. See de Bono's groundbreaking book, *New Think: The Use of Lateral Thinking in the Generation of New Ideas* (New York: Basic Books, 1968). Also see Scott W. VanderStoep and Paul R. Pintrich, *Learning to Learn: The Skill and Will of College Success* (Upper Saddle River, NJ: Prentice Hall, 2003), 215–216.

6

Becoming an Active Learner Inside the Classroom

Lessons from the Maestro

REFLECTIVE QUESTIONS

Keeping the following questions in mind will make this chapter more meaningful:

- How can you build productive and supportive relationships with your instructors and classmates?

- What do you do to remain focused and engaged in each class?

- Are your notes logical, understandable, and useful?

- What skills and strategies do you have that will help you to be successful inside the classroom?

KEY TERMS

active learning
classroom success
instructor styles
note-taking styles
office hours
online classes
peer study partner

GUEST SPEAKER

MEET **MICHAEL HOLTFRERICH**

Author of the textbook *College Algebra* **and Chair of the Math/ Computer Science Department**

Glendale Community College

Glendale, Arizona

Your success in any classroom is dependent, in large part, on the amount of effort you devote to the course. If you will expend the necessary effort to be in class on time and ready to learn, participate in classroom discussions, ask questions whenever you do not understand, and find help outside of class when needed, you will pass the course with a good grade. Whether the subject matter is something you like or not, take pride in doing the best job you can. I can tell you as an instructor and a department chair—students who do all of the work asked of them, who interact with their instructors, and who show a willingness to work hard will almost always find their instructors to be more understanding, caring, and willing to help students achieve their goals.

My top three suggestions to successfully learn in the college classroom:

1. Always come to class ready to engage in the discussions. Be involved and known by the instructor.

2. Do all of the work asked of you. Turn in all assignments on time.

3. Don't hesitate to ask and get help. Ultimately your success in a course is your responsibility!

117

INTRODUCTION

The road to **classroom success** presents twists, turns, detours, and potholes. There is, however, a destination—a journey's end that is wonderful and fulfilling. No doubt, you have experienced transitional and adjustment issues that tested your abilities to cope with college life. But you have *brought skills with you* that will help you to succeed. Let's work from your strengths in order to address any weaknesses you may have. Accentuate the positive; do not dwell on the shortcomings (though you will need to work on these eventually).

After all, it's not like you *never* stepped into a classroom before. *You know* what strategies have worked well, which ones just helped you get by, and those that were less than successful.

POINTS TO CONSIDER

- **Why is sitting in your classrooms important to your overall goal as a student?** Do you understand the purpose of your courses, the meaning of the lectures, the connection of the readings to class activities, and the objectives for the term? This goes beyond saying, "I'm in the classroom because the professor takes attendance and expects me here." That is a good start (understanding what the instructor requires), but can you go further? What does this course (and any course, for that matter) have to do with your overall college experience?

- **How will you be successful in class?** Once you understand why you are in the classroom, it is time to look at what you need to do in order to be successful. Does the instructor's teaching style create any challenges for you? For instance, does the course require class participation based on homework assignments? Are you expected to sit quietly and write pages of notes? Or will you be expected to work in groups to complete assignments? Whatever the instructor's approach and course requirements, you will need the necessary skills, attitude, and motivation to successfully meet your goals for the course.

- **How will you know if you have chosen the correct road to travel?** As you have read in earlier chapters, periodic progress checks help you to recognize the need for adjustments. Your classes will require you to work cooperatively with classmates, take notes in class, and interact with your professors. How will you know if you need to adjust the way in which you work inside your classrooms? If you do need to change, what can you do to make the adjustment?

LEARNING HOW TO BE AN ACTIVE LEARNER INSIDE THE CLASSROOM

Students are expected to remember, comprehend, and apply a great deal of information. In some cases, the information is quite complex. If you passively sit in class acting as a receptacle for your instructor's notes or, worse yet, if you *simply sit there* and *not take notes,* you will have completed only one piece of the learning process—the listening part. However, students need to become involved, to engage in **active learning** both inside and outside the classroom. Meaningful involvement requires two broad steps:

1. Taking in the information

2. Manipulating or using the information

This chapter describes strategies that will help you become more active and effective *inside* your classroom. Chapter 7 will examine the issue of active engagement *outside* the classroom, helping you build on class lectures, discussions, and student group work once you leave the classroom.

WHAT HAS SURPRISED YOU?

Take a moment and reflect on a few of the major surprises you have encountered with your classes this term. For instance, were you surprised by the amount of work required, the size of your classes, or the manner in which professors interacted with students? Or maybe the first test result was not what you expected, or your study group did not prove to be very productive. You may not know when your professors hold office hours; you might not even know where their offices are located. Write your response below. Be as specific as you can.

1. What has surprised you about your courses this term?

_____

_____

2. What changes have you made (or do you plan to make) to address the above reflections?

_____

_____

You may find after careful reflection that you need to make a few changes to enhance your potential for success. Whether the adjustments involve your relationship with classmates or the manner in which you take notes, this is a good time to build on the skills you have and accept the responsibility to make corrections that will benefit you.

BUILDING RELATIONSHIPS IN THE CLASSROOM: THE C.A.P. PRINCIPLE REVISITED

The term to this point in time

Maybe in past school experiences, a little last-minute studying or paper writing helped you complete assignments. But now, after you have completed your first two or three weeks of college, a new reality may be coming into focus. A great deal is expected of you—more pages to read than you are used to, more essays to write than you ever attempted before, more assignments and projects to juggle with your other obligations, and very little hand-holding by your instructors.

You are *expected* to complete quality work—and to complete it on time.

Chapter 1 introduced the C.A.P. principle. As you recall, the three most important people to establish a supportive relationship with are a classmate, an advisor, and a professor. For the purposes of this chapter, let's concentrate on the classmate and the professor. Support from your advisor will be covered in chapter 12.

Do you need a study partner or group?

An old saying says that misery loves company. A more positive approach holds that success loves *good* company!

The importance of a strong support network to help you develop your intellectual skills cannot be overemphasized. Students who feel connected to their classes and their campus have a better chance to experience success. This support system can be as simple as a compatible roommate, as socially dynamic as a study group, or as effective as a good mentor.

A **peer study partner** (or a study group) can help you with the following:

- Making sense of those crazy scribblings you call notes

- Understanding lengthy and confusing reading assignments

- Seeing different perspectives (interpretations) of the course material

© Eyewire, Inc.

- Choosing a topic for the term research paper
- Preparing for an upcoming exam
- Understanding a difficult concept
- Coping with classroom failures
- Celebrating classroom successes

A study partner may be one of the most important people you will meet. He or she can be the beginning of a larger support group. A major reason students leave college (especially within their first year) is because they do not feel a part of the college community. As one professor noted:

> Support is a condition for student learning. . . . Least [*sic*] we forget the first year is a period of becoming, a period of transition. . . . Without academic and social support some students are unable to make that transition.[1]

Your study partner is a small step toward building a much larger network of support. Study partners can be helpful outside of the classroom (see chapter 7) as well as in the classroom during group discussions.

Sometimes, however, working with study partners or study groups can seem like a nightmare that never ends. If you function better without a group, then you may wish to pursue another course of action. Your campus may have peer tutors or other types of academic support services that can provide valuable resources on an as-needed basis.

There will be times your instructors will assign group work. For instance, an in-class activity might require a group product. Generally, you will not have much control in choosing these groups, although sometimes you will be able to choose your own partners. (Chapter 10 will provide suggestions to make any group experience a positive one.)

Do unto others: Creating a working relationship with your instructors

Perhaps you have heard the expression, "Do unto others as you would have them do unto you." When dealing with your professors, remember to treat them as you want to be treated yourself. Paying tuition does not entitle a student to treat *any* college employee (or classmate) in a rude, disrespectful, or demanding manner. Nor does college enrollment entitle students to immediate and around-the-clock access to their instructors. Whether you are in the classroom, visiting your instructor during **office hours,** or corresponding by e-mail, remember two things:

1. You are interacting with a fellow human being. Be courteous and respectful.

2. Your professors have the authority and professional obligation to require you to do work and have it in by a certain time. You can expect first-class teaching and appropriate feedback, but professors are not there to respond to your every demand.[2]

Concentrate on behavior that will build a strong foundation of support, encouragement, and respect.

Instructor Style and Emphasis. In chapter 5 you read about the importance of learning styles. You have a particular way to process information that works best for you. Instructors have their own unique teaching styles as well.[3] These **instructor styles** may range from lecture, to question-and-answer, to group work, to lab work, to discussion, to seat work. Regardless of the method of presentation, each instructor has a set of expectations for student performance. Some emphasize minute details; others seek broad generalizations for application to new situations. One may require you to "take ownership" of the class by being actively involved, while the next instructor wants you to be a passive receptacle, diligently copying her words of wisdom.

HOW DO YOU KNOW WHO WOULD MAKE GOOD STUDY PARTNERS?

Let's assume you have to find a study partner by the end of this week. When buying a car or renting an apartment or securing a job, you establish certain criteria to help you make the decision. After all, you want the very best for yourself. The same rigor should hold for locating a study partner. For this activity, pick one of your courses in which a study partner may be of assistance.

1. List the strengths (attitude, skills, content knowledge) that you want your study partner to have. Be as specific as you can.

   _____

   _____

   _____

2. List at least three students you consider to be good candidates for your peer study partner this term.

   Student #1: _____

   Student #2: _____

   Student #3: _____

3. For each of your choices, list at least one strength that person would bring to a study group. Be as specific as you can.

   Student #1 (strength): _____

   Student #2 (strength): _____

   Student #3 (strength): _____

4. What steps will you take to approach these people to be your peer study partners? When will you do it?

   _____

   _____

5. Finally, for any strategy to be successful, the person using it must see a benefit in the strategy. What benefit does a study partner or group bring to you? What benefit do you bring to the partner or group?

   _____

   _____

   _____

If you are aware of your teachers' styles, expectations, and emphases, preparation for the class can be more focused and anxiety should lessen. Knowledge of teacher methodology can become a vital consideration in determining what courses you wish to schedule for the next term. If you learn best from *lecturing* instructors, then you might want to steer clear from those who rely heavily on interactive work. Obviously, the reverse holds true, also. This little bit of knowledge allows you to be more proactive in determining your class schedule.

HOW EFFECTIVE AND BENEFICIAL HAS YOUR STUDY GROUP BEEN?

Save this activity until you have met with your study partner or group at least three times. Reflect on the experience and then evaluate the benefit of the partner or group. Be as specific as you can.

1. If you think there has been a benefit, explain what the benefit or benefits have been.

   _____

   _____

   _____

2. If you believe there has been *no* benefit, explain what has happened or not happened.

   _____

   _____

   _____

3. Do you believe forming a study partnership has been the right choice for you—and will you continue working with one? Why or why not?

   _____

   _____

   _____

THE BASICS ABOUT ACTIVE LEARNING

The key to success inside the classroom is *participation*.[4] If you can discuss a concept, you have a much better chance of understanding it. If your teacher's style does not lend itself to

© BananaStock Ltd.

class discussion, you can still be actively involved by anticipating the teacher's lecture (based on reading assignments *outside* of the classroom and past class sessions), asking questions of yourself, and so forth. Do what you can to maintain focus. If you understand the teacher's style (how he emphasizes important information) and the teacher's expectations (often found in the syllabus), you will be able to identify the important class material. Understanding the major points of a lesson makes note-taking easier and more streamlined; you will not need to write down every word spoken by the instructor. However, although class notes provide an excellent review guide, wordy or extensive notes can have a downside: The more you write in your notes, the more you have to wade through to get ready for an exam.

IDENTIFYING INSTRUCTOR STYLES AND EXPECTATIONS

Here is a sampling of instructor styles and expectations. Check the ones that apply to the instructors you currently have.

1. I have instructors who:

    _____ Give lecture after lecture
    _____ Expect students to participate in class
    _____ Concentrate on group work
    _____ Concentrate on in-class seat work
    _____ Are sticklers for details like dates, formulas, and classifications
    _____ Pay close attention to grammar and writing skills
    _____ Very seldom assign a writing assignment
    _____ Are very serious and do not allow any joking in class
    _____ Are very serious but do allow for lighthearted moments
    _____ Never accept an assignment late
    _____ Accept assignments late, but with a penalty
    _____ Do not seem to care about punctuality
    _____ Seem to always go off on a tangent
    _____ Are always on target, seldom straying from the topic at hand

2. Of the foregoing, which styles help you to perform the best? In your past schooling experiences, which teacher style or styles increased your chances of success in a classroom?

    _____

    _____

    _____

    _____

3. Two last reflective questions: Why do you think the styles you identified in the section above work best for you? How can this information be of help to you?

    _____

    _____

    _____

Active learning strategies help to manipulate class material in as many ways as possible to suit your learning style. Even if your teacher is a "straight lecturer," you can still find ways to actively engage the material. For instance, consider a biology class in which the professor lectures for the entire class period. The following questions will help the student become involved with the material—even when class discussion is absent. Note that each of the examples will be completed *outside* the classroom, further showing the connection between what you do during class and after class (see chapter 7 for detailed strategies).

- Can you read about what the instructor lectured on for seventy-five minutes? (You probably can in your textbook.)

- Can you write about it? (More than likely you could do this by summarizing your notes. See the TSD strategy in chapter 7.)

- Are you able to talk about the topic? (This could be something for your study group to tackle.)

WHAT DOES MY INSTRUCTOR EXPECT FROM ME?

For the moment, let's consider the instructors you currently have. Complete this activity for each class you have this term, and place them in your notebook or study area so you will always be reminded of these important expectations.

Course title: _____

Instructor's name: _____

1. What are the requirements of the course? (These are typically found in the course syllabus and/or in the instructor's oral instructions.) Do you have to maintain a notebook? Read a textbook? Complete written assignments? Participate in group work?

   _____

   _____

   _____

   _____

2. Which of the course requirements might give you some difficulties? What can you do to ease those difficulties?

   _____

   _____

   _____

   _____

3. How will the instructor evaluate you? That is, on what is your grade based in this class? Is it based on reading quizzes, notes quizzes, major exams, projects, group work, or some other measure?

   _____

   _____

   _____

   _____

4. How does your instructor conduct the class? Is most of the work done in groups? Or does this instructor lecture each class? Will you be expected to participate by answering questions or

A friendly reminder of what you already know: Seven steps to classroom success

You know the importance of being in class—that is not new information. But every so often you can find wisdom in reminders of past lessons. Think of the following checklist as providing basic strategies that will move you toward a more active and successful term.[5]

1. *Do you come to class?* Be serious about your education. The instructor has class expectations. It is difficult to meet those expectations if you are sitting in the student lounge during class time or asleep in your bed. Tuition is costly. Be sure to get your money's worth by being in class every possible minute.

engaging in class discussions? Do you need to complete activities based on textbook assignments? What else do you know about how this class will be conducted?

_____

_____

_____

_____

5. What kind of tests will the instructor use during this term? Will there be multiple-choice questions, fill-in-the-blank items, matching exercises, true-false statements, short-answer definitions, or lengthy essay exams? Some tests use a combination of these formats. What will this instructor's tests be like?

_____

_____

_____

_____

6. Based on what you know about this instructor's expectations, what do you think your biggest challenges will be in this course? (For this section, you may wish to review your answers in the previous sections of this activity.)

_____

_____

_____

_____

7. Finally, what can *you* do (now) to help *you* succeed in this course?

_____

_____

_____

_____

2. *Do you bring all you need for class?* This is not the time to be without paper, pen, or textbook. A baseball player would not take the field without a glove. You, too, need to have your proper tools of the trade.

3. *Do you arrive on time?* Punctuality is important. The classroom is not a bus stop where if you miss one, there's always another time you can show up. Many instructors carefully orchestrate each moment of class. There may be a review of the last class at the very beginning of the current class. Perhaps the instructor will announce a new test date—you most definitely do not want to miss that important nugget of information. And remember that latecomers are almost always a distraction to the instructor and to the class.

4. *Do you sit where you will benefit the most?* To minimize distractions, you may wish to sit close to where the instructor is standing. To see the PowerPoint presentation well, jockey for

a good seat close to the screen. Practice your manners—don't slouch, and, for goodness sake, don't put your head down for a quick nap. (The snoring will annoy the student next to you.)

5. *Do you carry your passion with you?* Be excited! That can be difficult for some classes but it is something that will pay dividends. Practice your active listening skills. Listen intently; ask questions; be involved.

6. *Do you remain actively engaged?* The class period has a recognized starting and ending time. Respect those times. Just as it is important to be punctual, plan on remaining for the entire class period. Think of a movie. If you come in late or leave early you will miss critical scenes that will hinder your understanding of the entire film. Please, do not pack up your books before the end of class.

7. *Do you review your class notes as soon as possible?* If you have the time, complete this review before you leave the room. Remain in your seat for a few moments and quickly note if you have any questions or confusion about the day's material. If the instructor has already left the room, this may be a perfect opportunity to visit his or her office. Of course, many times you will need to leave the room quickly for another class or appointment. In those cases, find a quiet place as soon as possible to complete your review (see chapter 7).

Staying actively engaged as an online student

Online classes have witnessed explosive growth within the last few years. Technology has extended the classroom beyond the campus. Students can now complete coursework without ever sitting in a classroom. The obvious advantage is flexibility—you can complete the course from (virtually) anyplace in the world. Online education, however, is not for all students. It requires a great deal of responsibility and self-discipline. Here are a few tips to help you successfully complete an online class:

- Know how to use a computer. This sounds so obvious, but sometimes the obvious is missed. Know how to create, save, and send document files.

- You need computer access. Having your own computer—with unencumbered access to it—will make life as an online student much easier. You can use a computer lab or a library, but sometimes those facilities will not allow you to download files or programs you may need for your course, or a computer may not be available when you need to use it.

- You will need an e-mail address and Internet service provider so that you can send and receive communication.

- If there is an orientation for the course, find a way to attend (or read it online). This is when you will receive hands-on instruction about where to view assignments and how to submit work. Your instructor may use a platform such as Black Board. Practice navigating the site; click on buttons and links; know where everything is on the site. Be proactive and learn as much about the site as you can—as soon as you can.

- Back up all of your computer work—and back it up on a regular basis. (This tip proves helpful as well for students taking the more traditional in-the-classroom course.)

- Just as for an on-campus class, you will need to turn in assignments according to the class schedule. Find an effective way to remind yourself of these dates. Probably the simplest advice from past online students has been to "stay current with all work."

- Remember to practice good "netiquette" (online etiquette). Some people may use the anonymity of a computer to insult others. Keep your discourse civil. Once you send an e-mail or post it on a discussion board, it is out there for the class to see.

- Online courses may be flexible, but they still require a large quantity of time. *Flexibility* should not be confused with *rigor*. An effective online course will require as much—if not more—time to successfully complete as an on-campus class.

- Ask for help as soon as you recognize there may be a problem with content, timing, or technological glitches.

- Ask a current online student for advice. Or perhaps you have already completed an online class. If so, you may be able to act as a mentor for students new to this form of course delivery.

Note-taking skills: An active learning strategy

Whatever your instructor's teaching style, a great deal of information is presented each class session. But knowledge and insights do not come only from the front of the room. Group work, class discussions, video presentation, or an Internet site can add to the lesson for the day. One way to engage your mind and focus on the class is to take notes. Writing the notes will help you stay connected to the class presentation. Your notes will also prove valuable *outside* of class when it comes time to review for an exam (see chapter 7).

Organized class notes will help you focus on teacher expectations and emphasis. For instance, if you have followed the seven steps to classroom success listed earlier in this chapter, your notes will have the teacher's preview points and review points—points that can, and probably will, appear again on a quiz or test.

What Is Your Note-Taking Style? Even if you have not had formal note-taking instruction, there is a good chance you already have a style—even if it defies all logic—that works for you. If it does work, keep it.

The **note-taking style**[6] you choose is really a very personal thing. Whatever style you choose, however, make an effort to *consistently* use it, reflect on its effectiveness, and make necessary changes for improvement.

Let's review three of the many note-taking styles: the traditional outline, flowchart notes, and notes with a study guide.

If you are a very organized and linear thinker, the *traditional outline* format shown in Figure 6.1 might work best for you. It is structured. You can easily see what comes first, second, and so on.

If you tend to be more of a visual thinker—more creative and less bound to formal structure—something like the *flowchart* shown in Figure 6.2 might be more fitting for you.

Figure 6.3 is an adaptation of the Cornell Note-Taking System.[7] You will notice there is an expanded margin on the left side of the page for student questions or other organizing comments. This model is more linear than the flowchart model, but not quite as structured as the outline model.

You can easily revise these note-taking styles to come up with your own. Examine the notes you take in class now. Do they resemble one of the foregoing examples? Is there *any* organization to your notes? If so, great. If not, make some adjustments; maybe your study partner or tutor could help.

Even if a class is "easy" and you feel notes are not needed, consider taking them anyway. This will help in three ways:

1. Practicing note-taking will help make the habit permanent.

2. Writing notes helps you stay focused on the class and the material.

3. Writing will help you translate oral information to visual information, thereby using two types of learning styles to help you remember the material.

Regardless of your technique, consider using short phrases rather than full sentences; by using this type of shorthand, there will be less chance of your getting lost while trying to write every word the professor speaks. Be sure to write down any key phrases or words the instructor emphasizes. And try to write legibly; eventually you will need to review this material for a quiz or exam. Your class notes are an important aid in learning and remembering the course concepts.

Note-Taking: The Traditional Outline

I. Main topic #1

    A. Subtopic

        1. important detail

        2. important detail

    B. Subtopic

        1. important detail

        2. important detail

II. Main topic #2

    A. Subtopic

        1. important detail

        2. important detail

    B. Subtopic

        1. important detail

        2. important detail

III. Main topic #3

    A. Subtopic

        1. important detail

        2. important detail

    B. Subtopic

        1. important detail

        2. important detail

FIGURE 6.1 • Traditional outline.

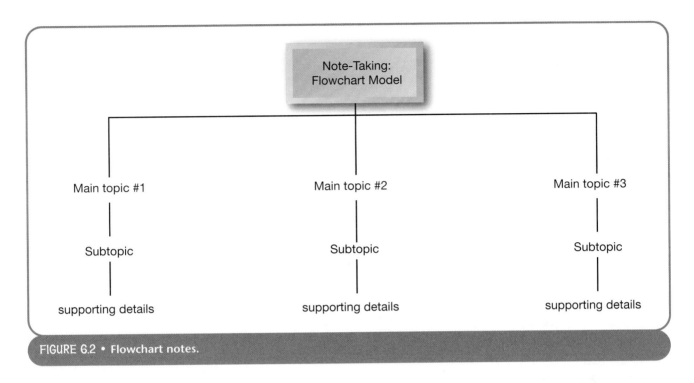

FIGURE 6.2 • Flowchart notes.

HOW DO YOU KNOW YOUR NOTES ARE EFFECTIVE?

Take a moment to reflect on your class notes.

1. Do you tend to write everything the instructors say, or just a few words? In what way is your current note-taking style effective? If it is effective, congratulations! You have developed a successful strategy. If not, how can you adjust your style to focus on the key words and topics of the lesson?

   _____

   _____

   _____

2. Does the instructor seem to speak faster than a sprinting track star, causing you to miss major parts of the lecture because you are still writing when new information is introduced? How have you been able to cope with this?

   _____

   _____

   _____

3. If you are not satisfied with your notes, what can you do to make them more effective? When will you start this new approach?

   _____

   _____

   _____

Personal		Date
Study Guide	**Class Notes**	

Write a question you might have about topic #1 or any of its subtopics. Comment on an important detail the instructor emphasized.	I. Main topic #1
	
	    A. Sub-topic
	
	        1. important detail
	
	        2. important detail	

Write a question you might have about topic #2 or any of its subtopics. Comment on an important detail the instructor emphasized.	II. Main topic #2
	
	    A. Sub-topic
	
	        1. important detail
	
	        2. important detail	

Write a question you might have about topic #3 or any of its subtopics. Comment on an important detail the instructor emphasized.	III. Main topic #3
	
	    A. Sub-topic
	
	        1. important detail
	
	        2. important detail	

FIGURE 6.3 • Notes with a study guide.

Managing your studies with a notebook

A well-organized notebook facilitates studying for final course tests, national certification exams, or future courses.[8] Great notes are useless if you cannot find them once you get *outside* the classroom. A notebook will also allow you to quickly find handouts or past notes that may prove helpful during a class discussion or group activity.

Perhaps you already use a notebook for your classes. If so, you know that your notebook can, and should, be a vital learning tool for you. The key, however, is found in one word—*organization*. Think twice about using those "stuff-it-in-the-pocket" folders. They may have a place every so often, but they tend to be agents of chaos more times than not. The following are some pointers students have found helpful about notebooks:

- Have a separate three-ring binder for each class. Nothing can be more frustrating than finding English class notes buried in the midst of information on the life of the Roman emperors.

- Place the course name, classroom number, time of class, and your name on the front cover.
- The first section of the notebook should include all general, yet important, handouts. This may include a course description, a listing of term assignments, and/or a class schedule of homework.
- Have a separate section for each unit. It may be helpful to divide the units with tab dividers so that it will be easy to find the material. Each unit may include something like the following items:
  - A summary outline or study guide for the entire unit
  - Daily notes with the date of each class (place this in the upper right-hand corner)
  - Handouts that pertain specifically to that unit
  - Quizzes and other graded assignments
  - The unit exam
- File all papers appropriately—do not simply stick papers in the notebook or your textbook. There should always be an established order to follow.
- Keep a grade sheet. This can take on a very simple three-column format:

<u>Assignment</u>   <u>Points Earned</u>   <u>Points Possible</u>

With this score sheet you will always know your grade. This is important for two reasons:

1. There will be no surprises about your grade. You know all along how well or poorly you are doing. Just because you "turn in" all the assignments does not mean you will pass the course. Understand your instructor's grading scale, your grade, and what your average is at all times in the term.
2. Sometimes the instructor may make an error in grade calculation. If you have retained all your graded assignments (similar to holding on to receipts from a store purchase) and have kept an ongoing record, you will have a much sounder way to challenge an error.

Make the notebook work for you. Keep it current and review it every night. An orderly notebook says something about a student's seriousness and dedication to the course. It also helps you to prepare daily for your next exam. This in turn will help reduce test anxiety.

What happens if you don't follow all of the basics?

If some of the active learning basics pass you by, consider the suggestions in Table 6.1.

Can you think like the teacher?

To play great golf, some golfers say they must "be the ball." Another way to actively engage your course material is to "be the course." If you are sitting in a history class, don't just learn about history—*be the historian*. Don't just complete your science lab experiment—*be the mad scientist*

HOW DO YOU KNOW THAT YOUR NOTEBOOK IS WORKING FOR YOU?

ACTIVITY 6.7

List three specific examples of how your notebook has helped you so far this term in one of your classes.

1. _____

2. _____

3. _____

Table 6.1

Strategies for when you miss the basics

The basics	Oops! I missed the basics. What can I do now?
Take notes diligently each class session.	If you happen to miss class, leave space in your notebook as a reminder to get those notes from a classmate, or visit the instructor as soon as possible.
Be punctual for each class.	Car trouble, a cantankerous alarm, or a late night out can be the reason for even the best student to be tardy. If you arrive late to class, enter the room quietly. Hold the door so it does not slam, and quickly find a seat. And have your cell phone in the *off* position. Also, remember that your lateness is not the fault of your instructor. His or her expectations for punctuality and attendance still stand.
Come to class each day with your notebook and a fresh supply of writing paper.	Maybe you dashed out to class and left your class notes behind. As soon as you discover this, borrow some paper quickly and quietly. You can transfer these notes to your class notebook later in the day. Maybe you could have an extra pad of paper and a few extra pens tucked in one of the pockets of your book bag for such emergencies.
Be ready—each day—to be actively involved with the class discussion and group activities.	More and more students complain of boredom. Yes, the instructor might be a challenge to follow; or the material might be more effective than a sleeping pill. But *you* still need to focus on the material. This will require more effort on your part, but it is something you need to monitor and discipline yourself to do. Find a way to actively engage yourself.
Make sure you focus on the important points in each class. Write these in your notebook.	Sometimes you may not know what is important. Maybe your study partner can help by comparing notes. You may wish to visit your instructor during office hours and ask if your notes are capturing the main points of the lesson. Does the instructor have any suggestions for you?
If the class is one hour long, "keep your head in the class" for the entire hour. If it is a longer class (perhaps one that meets only once per week), you still need to stay focused. A wise student does not stop listening and participating before the class has been completed.	The classroom clock may be moving slower than molasses in wintertime and the last 10 minutes of each class may seem like a whole semester. Fight the urge to pack up. Shoving your books and papers into your backpack early is rude, at the very least. It also signals a student who is not fully committed. Remember, the instructor assigns final grades; impressions can be important—and perceptions can become realities.
Review your day's notes immediately after class—before you leave the classroom if at all possible.	Sometimes you need to get to another class or an appointment immediately and, thus, may have to leave the classroom hurriedly at the conclusion of the lesson. Make a commitment to review your notes as soon as possible later that day. Contact your study partner if you have one; it will be a great way to review notes.

(with all safety precautions of course!). The point is to *think like the course*—and think like your teacher. Ask the types of questions the subject discipline asks. Although this may be hard to do while you are trying to keep up with the professor's lecture, you can accomplish it later when reviewing your notes or reading your textbook. Formulate some questions. You can also practice this approach when reading your assignments. Consider the following:

- In a history class, think about cause and effect, turning points, and the impact of decisions on the people of a nation.

- Science classes may need you to think about how different items are classified or grouped together.

- Your literature instructor will want you to understand tone, character development, and plot.

Actively use the course material, preferably while you are sitting in the classroom and hearing the material. At the very least, apply the concepts of the subject matter while you are reviewing your notes (see chapter 7).

SUMMARY

IF THE WORK STARTS HERE . . . EVERYTHING ELSE WILL FALL INTO PLACE!

The road to classroom success will have some obstacles along the way. But if you remember the following points, you can skillfully navigate the journey:

- Whether it is a reliable roommate, a dependable study partner, or a larger study group, develop a strong network of supportive relationships.

- Develop a respectful relationship with your instructors.

- Identify and understand the style, emphasis, and expectations of each instructor you have this term. Clarifying *their* expectations will point you toward achieving *your* academic goals.

- Be an active learner by showing up to class, bringing all you need, arriving on time, sitting where you will benefit the most, getting excited about the class, remaining actively engaged, and reviewing your notes as soon as possible.

- Pick an effective note-taking style—and use it consistently.

You have been expected to adjust to many new challenges during this term. Your strategies grow in number with each passing week. As we move to the next chapter, consider how you can build on these strategies and expand your thinking in order to increase your competence and mastery of class material. This in turn will build confidence.

Your SELF:
Personal growth
and balance

The following activities will allow you to reflect on the three levels of student success as they apply to the major concepts introduced in this chapter. Use this opportunity to apply newly acquired information and also keep an ongoing journal of growth in the various facets of your life.

The 4 Rs

Describe a personal example as to how you have used each of the 4 Rs as they relate to active learning.

1. *Reflection* (Example: What thoughts do you have about your classroom relationships?)

_____

_____

2. *Respect* (Example: What skills do you bring to the classroom?)

_____

_____

3. *Responsibility* (Example: Describe responsible steps you have taken to make adjustments in your classroom strategies.)

_____

_____

4. *Renewal* (Example: How have active and engaged learning strategies helped you better enjoy your classes?)

_____

_____

The Change Cycle

Reflect on one of your classroom challenges. What can you do (or have you done) to change this from a challenge to a strength?

1. What is the challenge? Be specific.

    _____

    _____

    _____

    _____

2. What led you to recognize that this was a challenge for you?

    _____

    _____

    _____

    _____

3. What is (or will be) your plan to address this challenge?

    _____

    _____

    _____

    _____

    _____

4. If you have put the plan into action (executed it), how are you progressing?

    _____

    _____

    _____

    _____

5. Once the challenge has become a strength, how do you plan to enjoy this achievement? How will you reward yourself?

    _____

    _____

    _____

    _____

Tuning Your Life-Strings

Pause and reflect on the balance—or lack of balance—in your life at this point in the semester. Use this activity to apply newly acquired information from this chapter to gauge the level of strength in the various facets of your life.

Life-string	Questions to ask yourself	What possible activities could help you tune this string?	Who can help you tune this string?
Social	• Is there a mentor in your college life? • Have you become part of a study group? • Have you visited your instructors?		
Occupational	• Have you found a particular class or course more interesting than the others you are enrolled in this term?		
Spiritual	• Have class discussions with your instructor and/or classmates had an impact on your spirituality?		
Physical	• What kind of an exercise schedule do you maintain? • Have you taken a few moments for yourself to relax? • Do you feel rested each morning when you awaken?		
Intellectual	• What did you do this week that involved critical thinking? • How did this expand your knowledge and/or skill base? • How have you expanded your knowledge about classroom success strategies?		
Emotional	• What strategies have you used to effectively deal with your college stressors?		

Rhythms of Reflection

To complete this chapter, please reflect on the following words:

> *We are what we repeatedly do.*
> *Excellence then is not an act, but a habit.*
>
> *–Aristotle*

Now, using these words for inspiration, explain how you will apply the knowledge you have gained with this chapter to create a "habit of excellence" in the classroom. Please write your thoughts here.

_____

_____

_____

_____

_____

To further respond online, please go to the *Rhythms of Reflection* module in chapter 6 of the Companion Website.

ENDNOTES

1. Vincent Tinto, "Taking Student Learning Seriously," keynote address to the Southwest Regional Learning Communities Conference, Tempe, AZ, February 28–March 1, 2002, http://www.mcli.dist.maricopa.edu/events/lcc02/presents/tinto.html (accessed March 29, 2004).
2. For a look at how e-mail has impacted the professor–student relationship, see Jonathan D. Glater, "To: Professor@University.edu Subject: Why It's All About Me," *New York Times,* February 21, 2006, http://www.nytimes.com/2006/02/21/education/21professors.html?ex=1298178000&en=361f9efce267b517&ei=5090&partner=rssuserland&emc=rss (accessed April 22, 2006).
3. Information in this section is adapted from Steve Piscitelli, *Study Skills: Do I Really Need This Stuff?* (Upper Saddle River, NJ: Prentice Hall, 2004), 94–98.
4. Information in this section is adapted from Piscitelli, *Study Skills,* 102–103.
5. Even though this list provides fairly basic and common points, I would like to thank Joseph B. Cuseo, professor of psychology and director of Freshman Seminar at Marymount College, for helping to focus these thoughts. He facilitated a session at the 2004 Conference on the First Year Experience (Dallas, Texas) that addressed many of these issues.
6. This section on note-taking styles is adapted from Piscitelli, *Study Skills,* 104.
7. Walter Pauk, *How to Study in College,* 5th ed. (Boston: Houghton Mifflin, 1993), 110–114. Also see Nancy Lightfoot Matte and Susan Hillary Henderson, *Success, Your Style: Right- and Left-Brain Techniques for Learning* (Belmont, CA: Wadsworth, 1995), 78–82.
8. This section on notebook strategies was previously published in Piscitelli, *Study Skills,* 113.

7 Becoming an Active Learner Outside the Classroom

Rehearsing for the Performance

REFLECTIVE QUESTIONS

Keeping the following questions in mind will make this chapter more meaningful:

- How can you actively review class notes?
- What is the most effective and efficient way to read a textbook?
- How can you apply your critical thinking skills to textbook reading?
- How can you effectively organize a writing assignment?
- How can you avoid plagiarism?

KEY TERMS

academic integrity

5 × 5 writing formula

key words

plagiarism

prompt

reading purpose

SQ3R

TSD strategy

writer's block

writing purpose

GUEST SPEAKER

MEET **BRUCE J. DIERENFIELD**

Director of the All-College Honors Program

Canisius College

Buffalo, New York

College courses usually do not meet every day, so more preparation outside of class is necessary than students may be used to. Study the course syllabus regularly in order to know what is coming next and to have time to present your best work. You can become a better student if you attend every class, ask questions as needed, and study consistently hard—outside of class as well as in it.

My top three suggestions to become an active learner outside the classroom:

1. For better comprehension, rewrite or type your notes more fully after each class and review them prior to the next class. A few days before a quiz or test, reread your entire set of notes several times, preferably aloud.

2. Before a reading assignment is due, read the material carefully, take notes, and read your notes. A lecture or class discussion will make much more sense if you do the required reading beforehand.

3. Writing requires rewriting. Compose your next paper several days before it is due, have someone else read and comment on your work, study your previous academic papers for instructors' suggestions, and then edit your paper before submitting it.

INTRODUCTION

In the preceding chapter you examined how to sharpen your classroom focus, take effective notes, and build relationships with instructors and classmates. But if your diligent work *inside* the classroom is not complemented by follow-up activities *outside* the classroom, you will not enjoy maximum return on your investment of time. This chapter will introduce learning strategies to enhance your outside-the-classroom study skills.

POINTS TO CONSIDER

- **Once you have your notes, do you know what to do with them?** Writing effective notes is an active learning strategy for inside the classroom. Knowing what to do with them outside of the classroom is just as important. Do you know how to actively review and use your class notes?

- **What is the best way to read and understand a textbook?** Do you wander through your reading assignments with the only goal to finish the reading as soon as possible? Active learning, as the name implies, requires the student to become engaged in the academic subject matter. To get the most from your reading requires three steps: preparation for the reading, the actual reading, and a review of the reading.

- **How can you improve your writing skills?** Before writing, you need to know why you are writing. How do you know exactly what your instructor expects on a writing assignment? Any assignment must reflect a high level of academic integrity. Do you know how effective writing strategies can help you to avoid plagiarism?

USING YOUR NOTES TO UNDERSTAND THE BIG PICTURE

Now that you have your notes, what should you do next? Time for reflection

Taking clear notes in class moves you another step closer to becoming a successful student—but more needs to be done. *Studying* truly begins the next time you look at those notes. The "Seven Steps to Classroom Success" (see chapter 6) recommend reviewing your notes as soon as possible after the class. For this review to truly be active and engaging, you want to do more than passively read the notes. A simple three-step strategy—*review, relate,* and *reorganize*—will help you understand the class material, cut down on last-minute test preparation, and be ready for your next test-day performance.[1]

Review. As soon as possible after class, look at the class notes you wrote earlier in the day. Read them and highlight what you consider to be the important information. Is there anything that is not clear? Do you understand all principles, generalizations, and theories?

If you have questions, put an asterisk or question mark in the margin of your notes. This should be your first question at the beginning of the next class meeting—or when you visit the instructor during office hours. If you wait until the night before the unit exam, it becomes rather difficult to get a clarification from the instructor. In addition, by asking the question in class, you are actively participating—which is, coincidentally, another success strategy. Reviewing notes should be an important nightly activity.

Relate. Too many times, students attempt to memorize isolated pieces of information. This is a daunting and boring task. As an alternative, look at the previous day's notes and reading assignments and ask yourself the following questions:

- Are there any connections?

- Do you see emerging trends or patterns?

REVIEW, RELATE, AND REORGANIZE

Choose the notes from one of your classes this term. They could come from this class, your history class, psychology class, math class, science class, computer class, or foreign language class. It might be best to pick the class where you are having the most difficulty. In your notebook (or in a computer document file) practice the method just described.

- Are you still confused and need clarification?

- Can you fill in your notes with any of the information from the textbook?

Once you start seeing this big picture, the material will make sense and will be easier to remember.

Reorganize. As you look over your notes, try to see if there is a clearer way in which to understand the message of the lesson. Sometimes an instructor will present material out of order, or go off on tangents. Reshuffle your notes so they make sense *to you*. You may wish to write a brief outline in the margin of the notes.

What should you do if you still don't get the big picture?

Even the best note-taker can be overwhelmed by a mountain of information and miss the overall meaning of a lesson. Two strategies that you can use in conjunction with the *review, relate, reorganize* strategy are TSDs and exit slips.

Title/Summary/Details (TSD). You will have a better chance of understanding class notes if you put the material into your own words. Copying word-for-word from the board, overhead transparencies, or PowerPoint presentations will not be useful if you cannot explain the material in your language.

Try the **TSD strategy,** an *active* review strategy that consists of three simple steps:

T: Start by giving the notes a *title*. What is the big picture? Try to come up with your own title that effectively captures the day's notes.

S: Write a one- or two-sentence *summary*. How would you summarize the notes, in your words, in a sentence or two? What was the central theme or main point? If you can do this, you understand the overall thrust of the instructor's lesson.

D: List three *details* that would support your summary. What do you see as the major details in the lecture? What questions might the instructor pose on the exam?

Once written (or typed and saved in a computer file), the review should be no more than about a quarter of a page in length. Quick, easy, and efficient.

Continue to review, relate, and reorganize each night in this manner. Keep your TSDs at the beginning of your unit material (or in a computer document file). Add to them each day. By test time, you will have several pages of review notes to serve as a practical study guide. *You have developed an ongoing study guide based on your class notes.* No more cramming for the exam.

Exit Slips. Another review strategy is the *exit slip* concept employed by some classroom instructors. Before students exit the class at the end of the class period, they write a sentence or two about what they learned from the lesson. A variation asks the students to write about the most

PRACTICING A TSD

Go back to the notes you used for Activity 7.1 and complete a TSD for that lesson. Remember to use *your own words*.

Title: _____

Summary: _____

_____

Details:

1. _____

2. _____

3. _____

confusing point in the lesson. You can do the same thing to determine your level of understanding of the day's notes, as follows:

- After reviewing your notes, write (or highlight) *three new* things you learned in the lesson.

- Now write *two* items from the lesson that you found to be the most *interesting*.

- Finally, what is the *one* thing you found the most *confusing*.

You can adjust these steps to fit the particular class. For instance, in a computer class you may find it helpful to list two new strategies that you can apply immediately to help organize your computer files.

Have you created working relationships with your instructors?

If, after a careful review of your notes and use of the foregoing strategies, you are still confused, consider a visit to your instructor's office. Instructors typically post the office hours they are available to students. You can find this information in the syllabus and/or on the instructor's office door. The department office can provide the information as well. If you still cannot locate the office hours, you can send a quick e-mail to the instructor. Whatever it takes, find the office, know the office hours, and make it a goal to visit your instructors this term.

Use these hours as the valuable resource they are. When you enter your professor's office, you can:

- Obtain clarification on class notes.

- Seek assistance on a particularly troubling lesson.

- Ask to review the last exam or quiz to learn from any mistakes you may have made.

- Obtain clarification on future assignments.

- Start to develop a face-name relationship, as your instructor will likely remember you as a student who has taken the time to seek help and clarification of course material.

- Discuss challenges you are experiencing in the class.

- Seek advice about future courses.

FINDING YOUR INSTRUCTORS

On the chart that follows, write the name of each instructor you have this term. Next to the name, write the professor's office hours and where the office is located. Make a note of the last time you visited this instructor and when you will visit the instructor next. Finally, what classroom issues or questions will you bring to the office visit? If you know what you need to discuss with your professor before you walk in the door, chances for a positive meeting (and relationship) will increase dramatically.

Hint: When you visit an instructor with a problem, be as specific as you possibly can. Starting your visit with "I'm lost" or "I don't understand this book" or "I don't do math" does not give the instructor much to work with. You may, in fact, be lost—but start your conversation by telling the instructor what *you do know.* For instance, you may start a math office visit with, "I can get up to the point where I try to find a reciprocal fraction—and then I'm totally flummoxed." Now, at least there is a place to start. (By the way, "flummoxed" is a way of saying "I'm really confused!")

Instructor's name	Office hours	Office location	Last visited	When will you visit next?	What topic or question will you bring to the office visit? That is, what will be the purpose of your visit?
1.					
2.					
3.					
4.					
5.					

GETTING THE MOST FROM YOUR TEXTBOOK

This section[2] will not provide tips on how to "get the most" money from the bookstore during book buyback time. Rather it will provide simple and effective strategies to help you focus, understand, and apply your textbook readings.

More than five decades ago, F. P. Robinson developed a reading strategy that has been duplicated ever since. The technique, known as **SQ3R** (survey, question, read, review, recite), is the basis for the following plan. Most student success books have some variation of this plan. Call it what you will, there are essentially three stages to the plan: pre-read, read, and post-read.

Pre-read

You Have to Know the Purpose. To start, establish your **reading purpose.** Do you know what you are looking for in the reading assignment? If you understand why the instructor assigned the chapter, there will be a better chance of focusing on the important information. Try to find a connection with what the instructor is concentrating on in class. Or, try to anticipate test questions that may come from the reading.

Warm Up Your Intellectual Muscles. Establishing a purpose is essential. Now, stretch those mind muscles. You need to actively prepare to read. To accomplish this, do the following:

- Sit in a comfortable but not sleep-inducing position.

- Quickly review in your mind (or by opening your class notes) what you have covered in class to date on the topic covered in the text.

- Relate as best you can, before you start reading, how this material might connect to the overall emphasis in the classroom. In other words, you should warm up by using past knowledge to ground you in the reading *and* to establish memory hooks for this new material. (See the information presented earlier on reviewing notes.)

Skim. Send yourself on a fact-finding mission. What is the important information? Use all clues that have been provided. If you have been given a study guide, use it. Still warming up, quickly flip through the pages of the assignment. Skimming provides a quick feel for the big picture of the chapter. What you want is a general sense of the assignment. Read the introduction and the summary of the chapter. If you have to accomplish a certain outcome by the end of your reading—say, answer teacher-provided questions—then skim the material with that particular purpose in mind.

Skimming includes the following steps:

- Read the chapter headings/subheadings. Form questions from the headings. These questions will give you a purpose for reading. You will be actively looking for information.

- Look at all pictures, graphics and captions.

- Look at boldfaced, italicized, and underlined terms.

- Look at the end-of-chapter terms and/or questions (if available).

- Read the chapter's introductory and summary sections. Unlike a good mystery novel, you want to know where this reading is going to lead you.

Read

Now, you are ready to read. Refer to the questions you posed when you were skimming. As you read, look for the answers.

If you have difficulty understanding the central idea of an assignment, read one section at a time. Stop after each section and write a brief summary. Start with one paragraph, and move on to longer sections as you become more skilled. Yes, this initially will add time to your assignment—but think of how much time you will waste if you read the entire assignment without understanding any of it. You may even decide to clump two or more headings together in order to develop relationships.

Mortimer J. Adler and Charles Van Doren, in their classic work *How to Read a Book*, advise readers to pay particular attention to the words that give them trouble. These words may be the ones the author uses for a significant reason. As Adler and Van Doren say, "From your point of view as a reader, therefore, the most important words are *those that give you trouble*" (authors' emphasis).[3] In other words, if a word appears awkward, unusual, or strange within the context, there is a good likelihood that it is an important term. This is not foolproof, but if you pay attention to the context of the paragraph, you will have a better chance of picking out the main point.

Keep a dictionary handy. This will slow the reading pace at first, but if you do not know the words, it is difficult to understand the meaning.

Don't forget your English training, either. Look for the topic sentence of each paragraph. Let this guide your reading notes. Remember, the topic sentence can be in the beginning, middle, or end of a paragraph.

A word about highlighting: If you choose to highlight or underline in your text, be careful. You want to highlight the major points. Too many students highlight every word. This is useless. Taking notes on the reading may be more effective because it forces you to write the material in your own words. If you can do this, you *understand* it.

Post-read

Don't shut that book yet. When you have completed the reading, immediately take five or ten minutes and study the notes you just wrote. Organize your notes according to theories, trends, people, issues, or some other categorical grouping. What is the big picture? Can you hook this new knowledge to previously learned material? Can you see any relationships emerging? If you have any confusion about the reading, bring your question(s) to the next class.

What do I do with my reading notes?

Now that you have mastered this reading assignment, bring the reading notes to class. Using reading notes in class serves a variety of purposes, including the following:

- Serving as a guide for discussion

- Helping you answer teacher-posed questions

- Reminding you to ask clarifying questions

- Allowing you to focus on the important points the teacher is making

If you are familiar with the material the instructor presents, taking class notes will be that much easier to accomplish. You will be more prepared to listen and participate actively. And since you will be looking at the reading material for (at least) the second time, you are now studying on the instructor's time. Now, that's efficient!

© BananaStock Ltd.

Putting critical thinking to work for you and your reading assignment

Active learning, as the name implies, requires the student to become engaged in the academic subject matter. In some cases, classroom instructors arrange their lessons so that the students must wrestle with an issue or engage in a group discussion, or do some other type of hands-on activity. This gives the student opportunities to problem-solve and/or apply newly learned material to new situations.

In those classrooms where the teacher does not provide such a hands-on environment, try the following active learning strategy that you can implement immediately to kick your learning into a higher gear. It will work with a textbook assignment, class notes, or a study group, and consists of these five steps:

- **Review.** Before beginning a reading assignment, review what you already know about the topic. For instance, if you are about to read a textbook chapter comparing the economic systems of capitalism and socialism, you might want to quickly review in your mind the major points you know about each system. Ask yourself a few questions. For instance: What are the benefits of each economic system? Are there any drawbacks in each economic system? This type of review will remind you of what you know *and* what you do not know. Do this according to your learning style (see chapter 5): Say it aloud, write key words into your notebook, or perhaps diagram your thoughts.

- **Reinforce.** Once you tackle the assignment at hand (read the textbook, listen to a lecture, or participate in a study group), note all of the information that reinforces what you thought you already knew about the subject. Using the preceding example, did the information support your preexisting knowledge of the two economic systems? This step can be invigorating, as it lets you know how much you actually *do* know.

- **Refute.** This is the opposite of the previous step. Did you read anything in the assignment that contradicted what you thought? Staying with our example, did you learn about any benefits or drawbacks of capitalism and socialism that you did not think of initially?

- **Replenish.** Look at your initial review of the material, the information that supported your beliefs, and the additional material that brought new perspectives. Is a new picture of the issue emerging?

- **Revise.** Based on the preceding four steps, do you need to revise your initial thoughts on the subject? Finishing with our example of comparative economic systems, do you have any different thoughts now on whether capitalism or socialism presents a more effective economic system?

Applying the strategy to study groups

The preceding strategy can be effectively used in a study group. As you may have experienced already this term, study groups can be either extremely effective or a huge waste of time. Students come together to review notes, clarify an assignment, or provide moral support for classmates before an exam. Many times such encounters lack a clear direction. At best they provide an opportunity to generally review notes; at worst the groups can degenerate into a gripe session about the course or instructor. Little positive is accomplished—and your precious time has been squandered.

This approach, in its simplest application, becomes a way for students to come to the group with different perspectives about a class topic or exam essay. At first this does not have to be particularly deep; but it can grow into more meaningful applications with practice. For instance, if your instructor has presented four causes for the Great Depression, your group members might try to isolate the *main* reason—and then make an argument why it is *more important* than the other three.

Here is another example that would require more preparation. (You might even say this is "pie-in-the-sky"—but it can be a model for which to aim.) Let's say your group is studying for a unit exam in psychology. The instructor has given the class a study guide that includes five possible essays for the in-class exam. Before the study group meets, each member must *review* the possible essay prompts and bring an outline to the group. During the group meeting each person will present his or her outline, listen to the other group members, and then discuss what *reinforces* and what *refutes* the initial thoughts on the subject. After *replenishing* their outlines with the new information, the group as a whole can agree on the *revised* essay outlines.

EFFECTIVE WRITING

Your out-of-class writing assignments can range from a short essay to a major term paper. Whether you write effortlessly or struggle over every sentence, a few strategies will help you become more effective and efficient.[4]

Writing purpose

Before you start writing, you need to know your **writing purpose**—*why* you are writing. What does your instructor expect from your efforts?

There are various types and styles of writing assignments. You will, at one point or another in your classroom career, be asked to create essays that are descriptive, narrative, comparative, or persuasive. Some essays focus on how to do something, while others are more interested in describing cause and effect. (This section will not cover each type of writing. Rather, it will examine basic strategies designed to get you *started* writing.)

First, before you begin, plan your response. Always make sure you know what your instructor wants before you start writing. Read the instructions *aloud* (when appropriate). Make sure you *hear* what you are to do. A quick and effective method is to "mark up the prompt." (The **prompt** is a term for the actual assignment—the essay question or term paper topic, for instance.) Develop a series of symbols: The tasks (what you are to do) could be underlined, the key issues circled, and other important guidelines boxed.

APPLYING THE REVIEW STRATEGY

Look at your course assignments for the coming week. Pick one and apply the above model. It can be a textbook reading, an upcoming exam essay, a research topic, a book review, a class debate, or a study group topic. Complete the following steps:

1. *Review.*   Look at the topic you have chosen. What information do you already know about this subject?

   _____

   _____

   _____

2. *Reinforce.*   Once you have read the assignment or conducted further research, what new information do you have that supports your initial review of the material?

   _____

   _____

   _____

3. *Refute.*   Once you have read the assignment or conducted further research, what new information do you have that disagrees with your initial review of the material?

   _____

   _____

   _____

4. *Replenish.*   Based on the new information you have, are you starting to see the issue or topic differently? How accurate was your initial review?

   _____

   _____

   _____

5. *Revise.*   Based on the four steps above, write a revised view of the topic.

   _____

   _____

   _____

Writing decisions

Some of the basic decisions that a writer must make (for either a short essay or longer term paper) include determinations about the following:

- The topic

- An opinion on the topic

- Supporting evidence for the opinion

- The audience for whom the writing is intended (for our purposes, the instructor)

MARKING UP A PROMPT

Pick an essay or term paper prompt from a previous class exam, a current assignment, or one you have developed from your notes. Underline, circle, and box as appropriate. Once you have done that, complete the following items:

1. What tasks do you have to complete? Do you have to evaluate something, describe an event, or analyze an issue?

   _____

   _____

   _____

2. What key issues must you address? Do you have to examine the causes of an event, the results of an experiment, or the operation of a process? Be specific.

   _____

   _____

   _____

3. Are there any important guidelines? For instance, are you restricted to a specific time period, a certain group of people, or a particular issue?

   _____

   _____

   _____

- The organization of the paper

- The individual who will proofread the essay (besides you)

Most instructor-assigned papers require a string of related paragraphs that explain, analyze, argue, or persuade the reader about a particular topic. For example sake, let's assume your history syllabus states the following about a term paper:

> **One of the requirements in this history class is to write a ten-page paper identifying and explaining five major consequences of World War II. The sources you use must include at least five books, three periodicals, and two nonprint sources. The paper is due two weeks before the final exam. The paper will be worth 25 percent of the final course grade.**

How would you approach this? (Running for the door is not an option!)

The first step requires that you *understand* what you need to do—the purpose. The guiding words of this sample assignment have been highlighted :

> **One of the requirements in this history class is to <u>write a ten-page paper identifying and explaining</u> five major consequences of World War II. The sources you use must include at least five books, three periodicals, and two nonprint sources. The paper is due two weeks before the final exam. The paper will be worth 25 percent of the final course grade.**

Whether you highlight, underline, box, or circle the words, make sure they stand out and that you *understand what you need to do.* It may be helpful to answer the following questions:

- What do I need to do?

  - *Write a 10-page paper*

- What is the topic?
  - *Identify and explain five consequences of World War II*
- What types of source material must be used?
  - *At least five books*
  - *At least three periodicals*
  - *At least two nonprint sources*
- When is the paper due?
  - *Two weeks before the end of the term* (You can enter this on your calendar; see chapter 4.)
- How much is this assignment worth?
  - *25 percent of the final course grade* (In other words, this is a *major* part of your grade for the entire term.)

These initial steps require a relatively small investment of time and energy that will maximize your efforts to efficiently find appropriate source material. The flowchart in Figure 7.1 graphically outlines the steps for effective writing.

Key words

As you tackle more and more assignments, you will notice certain **key words** appearing with frequency. The list below[5] provides a partial glimpse of words you are most likely to find in essay prompts and assignment notices. It may prove helpful to know these words.

analyze: to divide a topic or issue into its parts, showing the relation of one part to another

apply: to use your knowledge in a new or different situation

assess: to judge the merits of some issue; to evaluate

classify: to put things into categories

compare: to provide similarities, differences, consequences (see *analyze*)

consequences: the results produced by an act or set of conditions

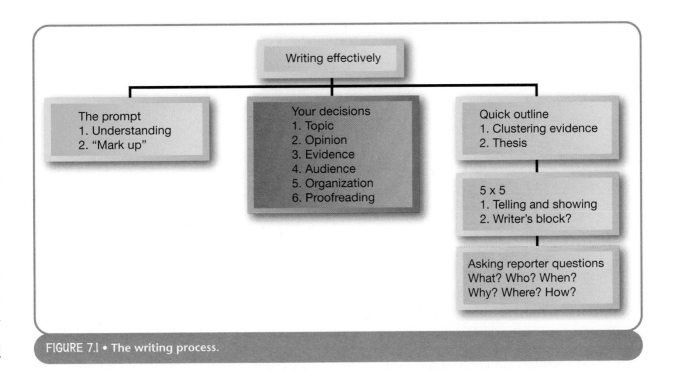

FIGURE 7.1 • The writing process.

contrast: to provide differences

criticize: to judge critically

defend: to argue for a particular issue

describe: to explain an event, issue, or topic, particularly the main characteristics

discuss: to explain in detail, beyond mere description

evaluate: to judge, criticize, establish standards

explain: to describe an event, issue, or topic

identify: to show how something is unique or individual

illustrate: to provide examples

interpret: to describe the meaning of an issue

motivations: what caused something to happen

relative importance: how two or more factors compare to one another

summarize: to restate briefly

trace: to provide an order or sequence of events

Make sure you understand these words. Do what the assignment calls for. If you are asked to *describe* the *consequences* of World War II, do not *assess* the *motivations* for going to war.

General steps for organizing and writing a paper

After you determine the purpose of a particular writing assignment and make decisions as to the topic and the approach you will take, it's time to start organizing. Here are some basic guidelines:[6]

- "Say it. Support it. Conclude it." In other words, make sure you have a clear introduction to your presentation; provide an overview of the evidence that will support your thesis; and tie the presentation together at the end.

- One simple formula—the **5 × 5 writing formula**—calls for an essay to have five paragraphs and each paragraph should have five sentences.* (See Activity 7.6.)

- Logically develop your presentation. Stay focused.

- Content is important, but so is how you present your argument. Pay attention to grammar, diction, syntax, and typing. Avoid verbosity. Get to the point. Remember the KISS principle: "Keep It Simple, Scholar."

- Before you write the paper, take a moment to plan. Jot down a brief outline. Do not go off wildly into a writing frenzy. Take a deep breath, think—and then write.

Other helpful guidelines for writing a paper include the following:

- Remember to use citations to give the proper and required credit to your sources. (There will be more on this topic toward the end of the chapter.)

- Schedule enough time so that you can write, proofread, edit, and revise at least one time before completing the final version of your paper.

- If the due date for the paper is the 30th of the month, make every effort to have your paper completed by the 28th of the month. This two-day cushion gives you a little breathing room in case unforeseen events present themselves.

---

*There is a point, however, at which the five-paragraph format is inappropriate, rigid, and restrictive. Don't get caught in the mind-set that you can write *only* five paragraphs. Some prompts might actually ask you to address four or five points. Your essay could easily be longer than five paragraphs.

A 5 × 5 ESSAY

For this activity, choose a topic from one of your classes and outline an essay using the 5 × 5 writing formula.

Paragraph 1: The Thesis or Introduction

1. State your opinion about the topic:

   _____

   _____

2. What specific topic will support your opinion?

   _____

3. What second specific topic will support your opinion?

   _____

4. What third specific topic will support your opinion?

   _____

5. Write a concluding or transition sentence:

   _____

   _____

Paragraph 2: Support

1. Write the paragraph's topic sentence regarding the first specific topic (listed in paragraph 1):

   _____

   _____

2. What is one fact that supports the topic sentence?

   _____

3. What is a second fact that supports the topic sentence?

   _____

4. What is a third fact that supports the topic sentence?

   _____

5. Write a concluding or transition sentence:

   _____

   _____

Paragraph 3: Support

1. Write the paragraph's topic sentence regarding the second specific topic:

   _____

   _____

(*continued*)

A 5 × 5 ESSAY (continued)

2. What is one fact that supports the topic sentence?

   _____

3. What is a second fact that supports the topic sentence?

   _____

4. What is a third fact that supports the topic sentence?

   _____

5. Write a concluding or transition sentence:

   _____

   _____

Paragraph 4: Support

1. Write the paragraph's topic sentence regarding the third specific topic:

   _____

   _____

2. What is one fact that supports the topic sentence?

   _____

3. What is a second fact that supports the topic sentence?

   _____

4. What is a third fact that supports the topic sentence?

   _____

What do I do about writer's block?

Almost everyone encounters **writer's block** sooner or later. Even the best-prepared student will "come up empty" at times. You have all your tools, but you just cannot get moving. Even a well-tuned car with all the options won't leave the driveway unless the battery is cranking.

When your "writing battery" is drained ask yourself the following questions to get moving again:

- Can I relate this (the topic) to anything else?

- Are there any groupings or connections I can make?

- What are the consequences of this issue?

- Is this good/positive or bad/negative?

- Do others really care about it? Who?

- How do I feel about it?

- Is this an absolute, or are there counterexamples?

- How does this fit with a bigger picture?

5. Write a concluding or transition sentence:

_____

_____

Paragraph 5: Conclusion

1. Write the paragraph's topic sentence:

_____

_____

2. Summarize paragraph 2 above:

_____

_____

3. Summarize paragraph 3 above:

_____

_____

4. Summarize paragraph 4 above:

_____

_____

5. Write the concluding sentence:

_____

_____

Activity 7.6

ACADEMIC INTEGRITY

When students submit their papers, they expect to receive a fair review. They have invested many hours in finding, evaluating, and crafting information into a completed paper. In short, they want their work to be respected.

Students—all researchers and authors for that matter—have a similar obligation to respect the sources used in their research. Researchers must adhere to a code of **academic integrity.**[8] Whether you conduct research to write a book or complete an English class assignment, certain standards of behavior are expected. For students, this means providing credit when using the words and ideas of other authors. Anything short of that is the theft of another person's intellectual property.

If you walked into your room at the end of the day to find that your computer had been stolen, what would you do? After the initial feeling of being violated, a call to the police would follow. The computer was your property—and you want it returned. The same holds for the property of one's intellect. When a writer, researcher, or student takes another's words or ideas and does not give credit to the author, a theft has been committed.

POST-WRITING ASSESSMENT: A CHECKLIST

Your paper is finally completed. You feel good and are ready to get it out of your book bag and into the hands of your instructor. Before you give yourself that final pat on the back, however, do one final check of your paper. Find a quiet spot where you can reflect on your work, and use the following checklist to assess your writing:[7]

_____ 1. Did you correctly interpret the instructions? Did you understand each key word in the prompt?

_____ 2. Does your paper have a clear introduction (main idea)?

     _____ a. Is there a topic?

     _____ b. Is there an opinion presented?

     _____ c. Did you present a brief "road map" of how you will prove your argument or present your case?

_____ 3. Is all of your support relevant to the topic and the opinion? Always ask yourself: Why is this fact or paragraph important? How does it support the purpose of your paper?

_____ 4. Is your evidence based on support—or is the essay full of unsubstantiated glittering generalities? For instance, rather than saying "Lots of things happened as a result of World War II," be more specific: "World War II brought about the Cold War, increased military spending, and an economic boom for the United States."

_____ 5. Does the paper follow a logical path?

_____ 6. Have you checked your grammar and sentence structure? Do subjects and verbs agree? Are you using the correct words to express your thoughts?

_____ 7. Is your writing style and wording appropriate for your audience? That is, is the presentation suitable for the person(s) who will read the essay? As a rule, most school assignments should not use slang.

_____ 8. Have you cited all of your sources?

_____ 9. Is the essay neat? (Typing format, errors neatly corrected, and so forth.)

_____ 10. Have you read your paper aloud? *Listen* to your words and sentences. Do they flow? Do they make sense? An even better strategy is to have a study partner review your paper. A new set of eyeballs on the paper will provide a much needed new perspective.

_____ 11. And in the category of "simple things often overlooked," make sure your name is on the paper.

Congratulations! You have completed a thorough and well-prepared paper.

Consider this example. After many hours of research, writing, and rewriting, you finally have finished your term paper. You have poured a piece of your life into this project. The night before the assignment is due a friend asks if she can read your paper. Feeling proud of your work, you hand it to her. Unbeknownst to you, this friend copies major portions of your paper and then hands it in as her work. How do you feel?

Besides the fact that the professor will possibly fail both of you for the assignment, this friend has committed a violation of academic integrity. She has taken the work of another person and presented it as her work.

UNDERSTANDING ACADEMIC INTEGRITY

You may wish to collaborate with a classmate to complete this activity. For each term listed below, write what you consider to be the best definition.

1. academic integrity _____

   _____

2. cheating _____

   a. For this item, provide an example of cheating:

   _____

3. citation _____

   _____

4. copyright _____

   _____

5. paper mills _____

   _____

6. paraphrase _____

   _____

7. plagiarism _____

   _____

   a. For this item, provide an example of plagiarism:

   _____

8. public domain _____

   _____

9. recycled papers _____

   _____

Academic integrity must be demanded of both students and faculty members. It has to be an essential expectation. One professor states the expectation like this:

> Integrity is an essential part of any true educational experience, integrity on my part as a faculty member and integrity on your part as a student.[9]

Avoiding plagiarism

The best way to avoid charges of **plagiarism**[10] is to take careful notes when doing research. Be sure to write all of the appropriate bibliographic data of your source. This includes the title, author, publisher and place of publication, copyright date, and page number of the information. If the material has come from an Internet site you will need to provide the Web address of the site and the date you accessed the information on that site.

When instructors assign work, whether it is a term paper or nightly math problems, the purpose is for the students to grapple with the concepts and show their own thinking and understanding of the topic. Plagiarism is a violation of academic integrity precisely because it is a dishonest representation of someone else's work as your own. When writing a paper and submitting work, it is your responsibility to provide appropriate citations to your sources. Here are some basic guidelines to avoid plagiarism:

- Whether you use another person's exact words or just her ideas, give credit. Do this as soon as you use the words or ideas. Even a paraphrase of a work must be cited. Remember that quotation marks must be used when using another person's words.

- When in doubt, cite!

- Cite specific facts that you use to support an argument.

- Common knowledge does not need to be cited. This includes statements such as "George Washington was our first president"; "Pearl Harbor was bombed by the Japanese"; and "Mickey Mantle played center field for the New York Yankees."

- Cite the opinions of others you use to build your own argument. Don't pass off someone else's opinion as your own.

- While doing research, be sure to include all necessary bibliographic data in your notes.

- Check with your professors about the appropriate citation (documentation) style to use.

SUMMARY

ACTIVE LEARNING DOES NOT STOP WHEN YOU LEAVE THE CLASSROOM

Before leaving this chapter, keep the following points in mind:

- As soon as possible after class, review your day's notes by using an active learning strategy such as the TSD method.

- Before reading, you need to know why you are reading.

- Before writing, you need to know why you are writing.

- Plagiarism is a violation of academic integrity precisely because it is a dishonest representation of someone else's work as your own.

- Academic integrity must be demanded of both students and faculty members. It has to be an essential expectation.

tuning your life-strings

the 4 Rs

self

change and personal growth

Your SELF:
Personal growth and balance

The following activities will allow you to reflect on the three levels of student success as they apply to the major concepts introduced in this chapter. Each activity will give you an opportunity to reflect and apply the chapter concepts in a way that is meaningful to you. Use this opportunity to apply newly acquired information and also keep an ongoing journal of growth in the various facets of your life.

The 4 Rs

Describe a personal example of how you used each of the 4 Rs when you studied outside of the classroom.

1. *Reflection* (Example: What new information have you learned as a result of reading this chapter?) _____

_____

_____

2. *Respect* (Example: What do your past experiences say about your reading skills?) _____

_____

_____

3. *Responsibility* (Example: Describe responsible steps you can take to improve your writing skills.) _____

_____

_____

4. *Renewal* (Example: How can knowing this information make your college experience more enjoyable?) _____

_____

_____

The Change Cycle

For this activity, reflect on a change that you are currently considering concerning your outside-the-classroom study skills.

1. What is the situation that requires change? _____

_____

_____

_____

2. What led you to recognize this? _____

_____

_____

_____

3. What is (or will be) your plan to address this situation? _____

_____

_____

_____

_____

4. If you have put the plan into action (executed it), how are you progressing? _____

_____

_____

_____

5. Once the plan has become a reality, how do you plan to enjoy this achievement? How will you reward yourself?

_____

_____

_____

_____

Tuning Your Life-Strings

Pause for a moment and reflect on the balance—or lack of balance—in your life at this point in the school term. Use this activity to apply newly acquired information from this chapter to gauge the level of strength in the various facets of your life.

Life-string	Questions to ask yourself	What possible activities could help you tune this string?	Who can help you tune this string?
Social	• Do you have a study partner or study group who might be able to help you with your reading and writing skills?		
Occupational	• How will reading and writing skills be important to your major and career choice?		
Spiritual	• What types of books or articles have you read that have helped you examine the deeper meanings of life—and your purpose in this life?		
Physical	• Do you take breaks from your reading or writing to stretch and give your eyes a rest?		
Intellectual	• How can you make sure that you maintain a high level of academic integrity when submitting papers?		
Emotional	• What strategies have you used to effectively deal with your college stressors?		

Rhythms of Reflection

To complete this chapter, please reflect on the following quotation:

> *Learn as much by writing as by reading.*
>
> *–Lord Acton, historian*

Now, using these words for inspiration, explain how you learn by writing *and* reading. Please write your thoughts here.

_____

_____

_____

_____

_____

_____

_____

_____

_____

_____

_____

_____

_____

_____

_____

 To further respond online, please go to the *Rhythms of Reflection* module in chapter 7 of the Companion Website.

ENDNOTES

1. Material in this discussion is adapted from Steve Piscitelli, *Study Skills: Do I Really Need This Stuff?* (Upper Saddle River, NJ: Prentice Hall, 2004), 108–109.
2. Adapted from Piscitelli, *Study Skills*, 123–140.
3. Mortimer J. Adler and Charles Van Doren, *How to Read a Book* (New York: Simon & Schuster, 1972), 102.
4. Material in this discussion is adapted from Piscitelli, *Study Skills*, 141–174.
5. Lists such as this can be found in many sources. This particular list comes from Piscitelli, *Study Skills*, 152, 154.
6. This information is adapted from Piscitelli, *Study Skills*, 154.
7. This information is adapted from Piscitelli, *Study Skills*, 159.
8. I would like to thank Amy Baldwin of Pulaski Technical College in Little Rock, AR, for comments she made during her presentation, "Preventing Plagiarism, Advocating the Art of Scholarship, and Strengthening the Culture of Academic Integrity" (Pearson Prentice Hall Symposium on Student Success, Chicago, IL, November 4, 2005).
9. Bill Taylor, "Integrity: Academic and Political. A Letter to My Students," 1, http://www.academicintegrity.org/pdf/Letter_To_My_Students.pdf (accessed December 17, 2005).
10. Information for this section comes from Margaret Procter, "How Not to Plagiarize," Writing at the University of Toronto, 2006, http://www.utoronto.ca/writing/plagsep.html (accessed January 15, 2006).

8

Test Performance and Memory Skills
Avoiding Stage Fright

REFLECTIVE QUESTIONS

Keeping the following questions in mind will make this chapter more meaningful:

- What positive test-taking experiences have you had as a student?

- How do you explain the reasons for test anxiety?

- What study skills strategies can you use to improve or maintain your level of test performance?

- What factors have had an impact on your test performance in the past?

- How can you improve your memory to help you with test performance?

KEY TERMS

active listening
emergency studying
forgetting
memory blocks
post-exam analysis
problem solving
test anxiety
test-taking strategies
types of exams

GUEST SPEAKER

MEET **JANN MacINNES**

Instructor of Statistics
University of North Florida
Jacksonville, Florida

Tests come with college life. They provide an opportunity for you to demonstrate that you understand the course material and can perform required skills. Because your classroom success partially depends upon the grades you receive on tests, it is important that you begin to prepare the day you enter a class. In order to score high marks on tests, you need to participate in class discussions, complete course assignments, and review course materials on a regular basis. However, no matter how hard you study, you cannot do your best if you do not know how to prepare for and take a test.

My top three suggestions for preparing for and taking a test:

1. Start your test review early. If possible, begin studying at least three days before test day. Avoid an all-night cram session the night before the test.

2. Organize both your study materials and study time. You may find it helpful to make a study schedule. Break up your study time into meaningful segments of approximately one hour.

3. Arrive early on the day of the test. Give yourself time to relax before the test begins. Come prepared to take the test. Make sure you bring extra pens or pencils, and any other materials you might need, such as a calculator.

INTRODUCTION

As you study this chapter, remember that you have been confronted with tests, in one form or another, your entire life. Granted, the tests described in this chapter are of the academic nature, but don't lose sight of the fact that you have taken these types of tests often in your career as a student. Whether your transcript reflects a test-savvy student or a person who freezes at the thought of an examination, one commonality remains: You have been down this road many times before. The content and the courses may have changed, but you already have test-taking strategies. Remember them; learn from them; and move to a higher level of competence and success.

POINTS TO CONSIDER

- **What skills do you already have that will help you with test performance?** Draw on those experiences. Keep the good practices, modify the questionable practices, and get rid of those practices that have been holding you back. In keeping with the themes of this book, reflect on your past experiences, respect the skills you have, and take responsibility for the changes you need to make.

- **What causes test anxiety—and what can you do about it?** Anyone who has taken an exam has experienced, at one time or another, some form of apprehension. As you will see in this chapter, sometimes test anxiety can actually be beneficial. It can keep you alert and ready to perform. At the same time, text anxiety can be paralyzing. Even if you do not experience test anxiety, a general review of strategies will help to maintain a healthy level of confidence prior to an exam.

- **What do you need to do in order to improve your test-taking skills?** From diet to sleep to emotional readiness to study skills, many factors influence test performance. Your life-strings, once again, will have an impact on how well you score on exams. Each of the six dimensions—social, occupational, spiritual, physical, intellectual, and emotional—contributes to your success. So, while the intellectual skills of study strategies, note-taking, time management, and memory techniques are critical, so too are your physical conditioning and your emotional well-being. A tired, sick, or stressed student will have greater difficulty successfully completing an exam than a rested, alert, and calm student.

WHAT DO YOU BRING TO THE TEST-TAKING TABLE?

Whether you attended school last year or twenty years ago, you still have testing experience as part of your background. Although you took many of those exams in classroom situations, you may have also taken tests in the workplace—in order to be considered for a job, to be eligible for a promotion, or to attain certification in your profession. If you were to add together all of the tests you have ever taken, you would be surprised to see you have been in hundreds and hundreds of exam situations. Whatever your background or age, you bring positive experiences and, perhaps, a few challenges to your college exams.

TEST ANXIETY

Anxiety is a general feeling of unease, uncertainty, anticipation, and even fear about an event. The resulting stress may be positive, helping you "stay on your toes" and perform well, or it may be so debilitating that it causes you to "freeze up." As you read in chapter 4, stress exists on two levels: positive stress and negative stress. Both create a physical arousal of the body. Positive stress helps a

WHAT TEST-TAKING SKILLS DO YOU HAVE RIGHT NOW?

Reflect on your past test-taking experiences. Try to think about the "big picture." That is, don't just concentrate on an exam you completed last week. Try not to concentrate on only the good experiences or only the poor grades. Rather, think about your testing experiences in general as you complete this activity.

1. *Preparation.*   What have you done to prepare for exams? Check any of the following items that apply to you:

    _____ I used instructor study guides when provided.

    _____ I reviewed my notes nightly.

    _____ I participated in a study group.

    _____ I asked the instructor if there were old tests I might be able to use for practice.

    _____ When available, I used the textbook publisher's companion Web site to review chapter objectives and take practice quizzes and tests.

    _____ I used a tutor.

    _____ I visited my instructor's office for content clarification.

    _____ I very seldom did any preparation for a test.

    _____ Other methods of test preparation I tried included these:

    _____

    _____

2. *Timing.*   Generally speaking, when did you start preparing for an exam? Check any of the following items that apply to you:

    _____ At the beginning of a new unit of material, I would study my class notes nightly.

    _____ I would start reviewing my notes and readings at least three or four days prior to the examination.

    _____ I waited until the night before the exam.

    _____ I only looked over my notes the morning of the exam.

    _____ Generally speaking, I never did study for exams.

    _____ Is there any other way to describe when you started to prepare for exams?

    _____

    _____

3. *Good results.*   What test-preparation strategies have *worked well* for you in the past? Describe them below.

    _____

    _____

    _____

(continued)

WHAT TEST-TAKING SKILLS DO YOU HAVE RIGHT NOW? (continued)

4. *Poor results.* What test-preparation strategies *did not work well* for you in the past? Describe them below.

_____

_____

_____

5. *Best practice.* Based on your past test-taking success, which strategies do you believe will continue to work for you in school? Explain how you know this is a beneficial strategy.

_____

_____

_____

_____

_____

6. *Questionable practice.* Based on your past test-taking success, which strategy or strategies will you need to *discontinue*? Explain how you know this is *not* a beneficial test-taking strategy.

_____

_____

_____

_____

_____

person to remain focused and move toward a goal. This may be similar to having "butterflies in your stomach," but your heightened sense of awareness allows you to perform at a higher level of competence. Negative stress goes beyond a few butterflies; you may actually feel as though a boulder is crushing your chest and breathing becomes difficult. The fight-or-flight response may be triggered.

The same kinds of feelings can occur on test day, resulting in **test anxiety.** A reasonable amount of uncertainty is bound to be present in most students. They wish to perform well, score high, maintain a respectable GPA, and feel good about their efforts. Even when well prepared, there may still be nagging doubts: "Did I study the correct material?" "Maybe I should have looked at my notes one more time." "I wonder if a study group or a visit to the professor's office would have been helpful?" "Maybe the instructor will be ill and the test canceled!" Whatever may have caused the anxiety, these students make their way to the class, complete the test successfully, and move on to the next unit of material.

Other students can become so paralyzed by thoughts of an examination that they make themselves ill with worry. One unsuccessful testing experience leads to another, which leads to another, and a self-fulfilling prophecy is born: "I never do well on tests!"

How does test anxiety happen?

One source maintains that "20 percent of U.S. college students experience symptoms of test anxiety and most athletes and artists experience performance anxiety at some point in their careers."[1] But why does this happen? Among the reasons are fear, feelings of inadequacy, and lack of preparation.

Fear. The consequences of the test or performance may be so great as to cause an unhealthy physical or emotional response. For instance, if one test result would determine whether you get into the school of your choice, your level of anxiety may increase due to the fear of losing your dream. This form of high-stakes testing heightens your physical and emotional arousal.

Feelings of Inadequacy. You believe that no matter what you do, your lack of ability (perceived or real) will be the rea-

© Stockdisc

son you cannot perform to an acceptable standard. This may be the case, for instance, when a student auditions for a play with a number of talented actors.

Lack of Preparation. The final exam is in one hour—and you have not read the assigned readings, not looked at your notes, nor reviewed the instructor-provided study guide. No wonder your blood pressure is elevated, your hands are sweating, and your mouth is a little dry!

Improving test performance with strategies you already know

Let's take a moment and review some of the major concepts introduced earlier in this book. Table 8.1 suggests how to apply these previously learned strategies to address test performance challenges.

As you read in chapter 5, *identification* of a problem, while important, represents only the first step in the problem solving process. Figure 8.1 provides a graphic reminder of the problem solving steps.

I CAN'T REMEMBER A THING ON TEST DAY!

Why do I forget—and what can I do about it?[2]

Forgetting is the failure of a previously *learned* behavior to appear. If you haven't learned it, you cannot possibly forget it. People forget for a variety of reasons, including these:

- They fail to use what they have learned.

- The reward they received for learning is no longer present.

- A previously learned behavior interferes with a newly learned behavior.

- A newly learned behavior interferes with a previously learned behavior.

WHAT IS YOUR LEVEL OF TEST ANXIETY?

How often do you experience test anxiety? For each of the following items, rate yourself on a scale from 0 (not at all) to 5 (all the time). Circle the numbers that most closely apply to you.

1. When you look back on your test performance this term (or over a number of years if you so desire), how often do you experience the following?[3]

Symptom	Frequency (0 = not at all, 5 = all the time)
Headaches	0—1—2—3— 4—5
Nausea	0—1—2—3— 4—5
Vomiting	0—1—2—3— 4—5
Diarrhea	0—1—2—3— 4—5
Sweating	0—1—2—3— 4—5
Increased heartbeat	0—1—2—3— 4—5
Shortness of breath	0—1—2—3— 4—5
Dizziness	0—1—2—3— 4—5
Crying	0—1—2—3— 4—5
My mind "goes blank"	0—1—2—3— 4—5

2. Add your ratings and divide by 10. On a scale from 0 to 5, you have rated your level of test anxiety to be _____. (A score of 4 or higher indicates that testing situations create high levels of apprehension for you.)

3. Reflect on your score in item 2. Why do you think you have come to respond to tests in the manner you do? What insights can you draw from this exercise?

_____

_____

_____

_____

- The situation in which the new behavior must occur is different from the one in which the behavior was learned.

- Something blocks the learned behavior from reappearing.

Memory blocks

It has happened to most students at one time or another. They have prepared for an exam, they know the material, but they "freeze" on test day. Why? One explanation can be found in **memory blocks.**

Emotional Memory Blocks. Some students are afraid to challenge themselves. Whether it is a fear of failure or the memory of some distressing prior experience, they cannot (or will not) perform.

IDENTIFYING YOUR SOURCES OF TEST ANXIETY

Identifying stressors is the first step in learning to overcome them. What are *your* sources of test anxiety?

1. Do you tend to be anxious about exams due to any of the following? Check all that apply to you.

   _____ Lack of appropriate effort on my part

   _____ Lack of ability (course material beyond my capabilities)

   _____ Negative self-talk (convinced myself I would do poorly)

   _____ Not studying

   _____ Fear of how others may judge me

   _____ Listening to classmates complain about the difficulty of exams

   _____ Poor previous testing experiences

   _____ Panic brought on by timed situations

   _____ Focusing on the effect the test grade would have on my GPA

   _____ Comparing my performance to other students

   _____ Pressuring myself to get nothing but an A

   _____ Other sources:

   _____

   _____

   _____

2. Share your answers with a classmate. Brainstorm ideas to lessen your test anxiety. Write your answers here.

   _____

   _____

   _____

Physical Memory Blocks. Perhaps you decided to study late into the evening prior to an exam. You reviewed everything—textbook, notes, study guides. Once you get to the class, however, everything is a jumbled mess. You are so tired, you cannot think straight. A physical memory block can result from lack of sleep as well as an inappropriate diet. If you eat too much—or too little—right before an exam, focusing may become more difficult.

Mechanical Blocks. You have put a lot of time into your studies but you cannot seem to recall the data during the exam. This is usually an indication of some retrieval difficulty. The "file cabinet" in your brain holds the information; however, perhaps you have just thrown the information into the "drawers" without labeling. As a result, you cannot find what you need to answer an exam question.

Table 8.1
Test-performance strategies:
Building on previous skills and strategies

Student success strategy	Application to successful test-performance strategies
Attitude (chapter 2)	When you examine why you have difficulty with tests (in general or in a particular course), do you use self-defeating words, or positive words? • Self-defeating: *What should I expect? I never have done well on math exams. There is no reason to expect that will change this term. I'll hope for the best.* • Positive: *My experience with math has been a troubled one at best. I might not earn an "A" in this course but I do know that by using the campus resources available to me I will do better this term than I have ever done before.*
Intrinsic and extrinsic motivators (chapter 2)	Find a motivator that will help to move you through the test challenge you have been experiencing. Whether intrinsic or extrinsic, look for incentives that will prove motivating enough for you to meet and defeat your challenge. • Intrinsic: *I know what I need to do in order to achieve favorable test results. I've worked hard and owe it to myself to do the very best I can.* • Extrinsic: *Regardless of what I have done in the past, my financial aid depends on passing all my courses. Doing well on tests will not only prepare me for other course work but it will allow me to continue receiving the funding I need for school.*
Critical thinking (chapter 5)	Take time to reflect and analyze the reasons why you have difficulty with tests. Go beyond a superficial explanation; move into a deeper examination of the factors that have an impact on your test performance. • Visit your professors during office hours and ask for their input. • Perhaps a tutor would provide some additional insights about your challenges.
Problem solving (chapter 5)	Using your critical thinking skills, can you propose a solution to improve test performance? Review the following examples: • Based on the information received from your review of previous exams, your instructor's input, and a tutor's opinion, you decide that you will begin a new studying program that will set aside time to visit your professor once a week with specific questions about new material covered in class. • You will consider working with a study group. • At the very least, you decide to write a TSD for each day's notes (refer to chapter 7). This ten-minute exercise will be the beginning of a nightly review of your notes.

Table 8.1
(continued)

Student success strategy	Application to successful test-performance strategies
Creative thinking (chapter 5)	Sometimes desperate measures require desperate actions. Maybe you feel that you have tried absolutely everything to turn around your test performance—but nothing seems to work. The frustration mounts. Time for creative— outside-the-box, outside-the-lines, novel— thinking. For instance: • You recognize that you have not been exercising as you once did. You feel sluggish most of the time. Combining physical activity with intellectual stimulation, you decide to engage in a yoga class once a week. You believe yoga's meditative emphasis will help calm and focus your mind.
Review the review: Knowing the topic, summary, and details (TSDs) (chapter 7)	The TSD strategy allows for nightly reflection of class work through a brief writing activity. Try the following: • Maintain an ongoing file of your TSDs. Perhaps creating a computer folder labeled "TSDs" will make it easier to organize and keep up with your daily reviews. Over the course of a unit's material, you will build a comprehensive study guide. Reviewing your TSDs will help prepare you for the coming exam.
Study groups and study partners (chapter 6)	Whenever possible, maximize the benefits of relationships with your classmates. • Review Activities 6.2 and 6.3 to assess the effectiveness of your study group. How do you know participation in this group is beneficial to your test performance? • Maybe you do not wish to be a member of a study group. Is there someone in class you may feel comfortable asking for clarification about items you find confusing? Maybe you could approach someone with whom you have worked when the instructor has assigned in-class group work.

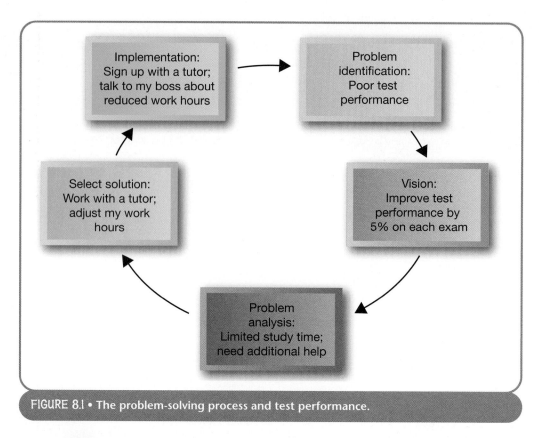

FIGURE 8.1 • The problem-solving process and test performance.

© Stockbyte

Strategies to minimize memory problems

Forgetting can occur for a number of reasons, but there *is* something you can do about it. Several strategies to overcome forgetting are presented here. All have implications for improving your memory in academic, social, and professional settings—and when practiced regularly they have the potential to improve test performance.

Organize the Information. The better your mental "filing system," the better your ability to find the data you are looking for. Poor labeling creates confusion. What would happen if you just threw pieces of paper into the file cabinet drawer without any order whatsoever? It is obvious that you would have a difficult time finding material. Yet this is what a lot of us do with vital information.

Therefore, just as you would store valuables carefully, do the same with the facts, concepts, and generalizations from your classes. Organize the "cabinet." Label the drawers, the files, and the folders. When you learn a new piece of information, place it in the proper mental "file folder." Now you know where it is—and you will be able to pull it up when you need it.

Remember the suggestion to review your notes nightly? The strategy described in chapter 7—*review, relate, reorganize*—will help you "file" information more efficiently. Developing connections is the best way to fight against improper filing. The *TSD* strategy described in chapter 7 will also help make the connections more permanent.

Use the Information. Just as with your muscles, if you do not use information, you will more than likely lose it. If you hear information about quadratic equations in class but do not review and use the material soon after, you increase your chances of forgetting the appropriate steps.

A nightly review of your notes (alone or with a study group) can help. If you tend to be a bodily-kinesthetic learner (see chapter 5), you may wish to use flash cards on a regular basis.

Look for Intrinsic Rewards. Our schools are based on a series of rewards. These incentives vary, but range from a compliment to grades to awards for high GPA. Many students have been conditioned by these *extrinsic* rewards—that is, those given to us by someone else (see chapter 2). The grade, for instance, becomes the overriding reason for performance. Once the reward (grade) is removed, the incentive to continue working with the material is removed. No reward, no effort—and no retention. Finding an *intrinsic* satisfaction from learning, on the other hand, provides motivation and improves your chances of remembering the material.

However, the reality remains that for most students many of the required courses hold little interest. Someone with a deep passion for English literature may find it difficult to stay focused in a history course. Perhaps the best advice is to remember that these prerequisites serve as "gate-keepers." You must pass through them successfully in order to move into the course work that really interests you. Once you successfully navigate these early courses, you will be able to concentrate on those subject areas that hold intrinsic motivation for you.

Perhaps you could reframe the way you view the courses that do not hold interest for you. Make a short-term goal to find in the instructor's lesson at least two items of interest each day you go to class. Perhaps you could go a step further and search for a connection between the course and your passion (or eventual major). If that proves difficult or impossible to do, then use that as a reason to visit your instructor's office. For instance: "I love science and do very well in those courses. Could you help me find a connection between your United States history course and science? Do they have anything in common?" Such questions let the instructor know of your passion and your interest to do well in the course—and they help build or maintain an important relationship (refer to the C.A.P. principle discussed in chapters 1 and 6).

Practice Situational Variation. Practicing a skill—whether it is athletic, artistic, or academic—in one situation and then performing it in a different situation can be intimidating to some people. Consider this a form of *stage fright.* A performing artist, for instance, may be able to recite lines or play an instrument flawlessly during rehearsal, but may "freeze" or stammer in a public performance. The practice occurred in one environment, but had to be performed in a quite different situation. The same can happen on exams. You may study in the cozy comfort of your room, iPod playing in your ears, but when it comes to test day you must "perform" in the sterile atmosphere of classroom.

Practice the material in various situations. Maybe your study group (if you choose to be part of one) can meet one day in the actual classroom in which you will sit for the exam. Does your textbook have a companion Web site (most do) that provides practice questions? If it does, use it regularly. If your instructor will allow fifty minutes for the test, practice in fifty-minute blocks of time. Prepare for the content as well as for the timed situation. Do as many practice tests as you can in a test-like environment. Depending on how much of a concern this is for you, you may give thought to actually doing a practice test, in the classroom, for the specified period of time.

Refer to the Basics. In some cases poor test performance does not reflect a problem with memory but rather a failure to remember the instructor's expectations. Activity 6.5 (in chapter 6) allowed you to review instructor expectations for a particular course. Understanding the requirements of the course and the manner in which the instructor conducts his or her class provides clues as to what may be on the next exam.

Improve Memory Through Active Listening. One way to improve your memory for information is through **active listening.** Here are some active listening techniques to help you remember more of what you hear:

- **Focus.** Pay attention to the speaker, whether he is your boss, your instructor, friend, or parent. If you *choose* not to concentrate, there is little reason to be surprised when you cannot remember a thing. Make a conscious effort to pay attention. Put aside other distractions. Focus on the words and meanings. Practice courtesy and you will retain more.

- **Find relevance.** You will not find every instructor to be exciting. Try to find something in the class presentation and focus on it. Find a relationship to something you already know or in which you have an interest.

SEARCHING FOR TEST CLUES

Select one of your courses for this term, and complete this activity to help you determine potential exam questions.

Course Title: _____

Instructor: _____

1. *What kind of tests will your instructor use during this term?*   Your instructor may present you with multiple-choice questions, fill-in-the-blank items, matching exercises, true-false statements, short-answer definitions, or lengthy essay exams. Some tests use a combination of these formats. What will your teacher use this term?

    _____

    _____

2. *What does the instructor do in class to emphasize key points?*   Does she write on the board, provide PowerPoint slides, or emphasize points with her voice?

    _____

    _____

3. *Did the instructor provide a study guide?*   Perhaps there is a study guide in your syllabus or maybe one was distributed at a study session.

    _____

4. *Does your school provide supplemental instruction?** *   If so, where and when is it held?

    _____

    _____

*More and more colleges provide some form of supplemental instruction (SI). It typically takes the form of an additional session per week in which the participating students use their notes and class discussions to better understand the course content and prepare for exams. See your instructor or learning resource center to find out if such a program is available on your campus.

- **Listen with your ears—not your mouth.** Too many people mentally phrase their response while the speaker is still speaking. You cannot understand the speaker fully (if at all) if you are just waiting to jump in and give your opinion. If you "listen" in this manner, you are creating your own distraction.

- **Participate.** Once your instructor has finished, rephrase what was said. If you can explain, in your own words, what has just been presented, you will have a better chance of retention. By paraphrasing you are, in effect, rehearsing the new material. Practice leads to understanding.

- **Ask questions.** This is part of a class participation strategy. Ask for clarification, relationships, or the significance of the topic at hand. You are not only drilling the information, but also doing it in the context of the big picture of the presentation. This will help you develop memory hooks.

- **Offer another explanation or another application.** This is a particularly effective strategy in discussion or seminar-style classes. As you process the new information, try to present another side of the issue. This should not be done in a combative manner, of course. Rather, attempt to understand other aspects of the topic. This allows for analysis, and consequently better understanding.

ADDITIONAL TEST-TAKING ISSUES

Test anxiety or inefficient test-taking strategies?

Some students are not anxious about exams. They are prepared and comfortable on test day. But they still perform at a less than satisfactory level. One reason may be time—they usually run out of it. Effective test preparation can be hampered by inefficient behaviors during the test. If this is your problem, try the following **test-taking strategies:**[4]

- **Review the entire exam.** Before you begin writing your exam answers, review all items. Get a "feel" for the test. How long will you need to do page 1? Page 2? In other words, establish a pace for yourself.

- **Keep track of time.** Wear a watch.

- **Do the easy items first.** If you do run out of time, you don't want to miss the easy points. "Easy" in this case refers to content as well as item type. Obviously, make sure you answer all the questions you *know*. You may wish to do the types of questions you are most comfortable with before you tackle the more challenging ones. If matching is easy for you, do it first.

- **Watch for trigger words.** Don't get an item wrong because you failed to see a trigger (important) word. Underline, circle and/or box key words.

- **Block your test paper.** If your eyes tend to drift from one item to another during an exam, a blocking technique will help you focus. Using two blank pieces of paper, cover the item above the problem you are working on with one piece and cover the succeeding item with the other. For example, if you are working on problem 3, "block out" problems 2 and 4. You force your eyes to focus on only one item.

- **Remove yourself from distraction.** If possible, sit as far away from any distractions as possible. Get away from windows, open doors, noisy students, and the like. In large lecture halls this may be difficult, but your instructor may be able to suggest some alternatives.

- **Become familiar with format.** Ask the instructor if he or she has past exam versions to review. By becoming familiar with the teacher's particular format, you are also mastering the content.

- **Consider tutoring.** If you have been diligent with your studies but still have difficulties with the subject matter, you may wish to seek help from the instructor or a student-tutor. Your academic advisor should have information on peer tutors.

- **Know your material.** The more comfortable you become with the course content, the more confident you will be on the exam. Timely and organized studying (see chapters 4 and 7) will help you become comfortable, confident, and successful.

- **Find out if "props" are allowed.** If you have a math test requiring many formulas, can you write the formulas on an index card and use it during the exam? How about your notes? Will the instructor allow their use during the exam?

- **Ask your instructor about an alternative testing environment.** If distractions are really a problem, perhaps the instructor will allow you to complete the exam in the campus testing and assessment center. If you have a documented disability, the student services office may be able to assist with specific accommodations.

Test-taking: Some general suggestions

There are several **types of exams**—multiple-choice, true-false, matching, essay, and so forth—but no matter what type of test you are taking, some general suggestions apply.[5] Perhaps the most basic is to get a good night's sleep prior to the exam. Give your brain a rest and do something nonacademic before going to bed—otherwise, you might wake up feeling like you have not had a break. Also, depending on the time of the exam, eat a meal that is appropriate for you.

Have all your tools with you (see the Test-Preparation Checklist in Activity 8.5).

Read *all* instructions carefully: Do *not* start until you know what you are expected to do. More than likely, the wording on the exam will be different from what you found in your book, or what the teacher said in class. That is why it is important to *know* your material. Do not just memorize. Relate to the big picture. Review the strategies in chapter 7.

As you prepare for the exam, be kind to yourself. Don't sit there saying you are going to fail. Respect your skills, talents, and past experiences.

Multiple-Choice Tests. If you are taking a multiple-choice test, the following suggestions can help improve your performance.

- Read carefully. Look for words like *not, except, which is incorrect, best, all, always, never,* and *none.*

- Cover all the answer choices before you look at them. Treat the item like a fill-in-the-blank question. Come up with an answer before you look at the choices.

- If you are not sure of an answer, use the process of elimination to arrive at the correct answer—or at least to narrow your options so you can make an educated guess.

- Answer the easy questions first. Save the tough ones for the end.

- Underline key words (if you are allowed to write on the exam) to help you focus.

- If you are using an answer sheet, make sure you transfer your answers to the correct number on the answer sheet.

Matching Tests. Keep the following suggestions in mind when you take a matching test:

- Read all the answer choices first.

- Cross out the items you pick (if you are allowed to write on the exam).

- Are you allowed to use an answer more than once?

- Answer the easy items first. Save the tough ones for the end.

Essay Tests. Essay tests require both a knowledge of the material and the ability to communicate it. The following suggestions can help you improve your answers to essay questions:

- Read the question carefully so you know exactly what you are being asked. Refer to the list of key words in chapter 7 (pp. 149–150).

- Develop a main idea (thesis) and follow it through.

- Support your thesis with substantial facts; avoid "fluff."

- Pay attention to grammar and sentence structure.

- Never leave an essay item blank. Make an educated attempt—you might get some credit.

Test performance and academic integrity

As you will see in much greater detail in chapter 11, behaving with *integrity* means to conduct oneself in an honest, responsible, and respectful manner. When it comes to testing situations, this means doing and submitting your own work without any unauthorized assistance. Any violation on exams is broadly classified as cheating and will be punished according to specific guidelines laid out by the school. Unless approved by the instructor prior to the exam, the following examples are violations of academic integrity during an exam:

- Copying from a classmate's paper
- Using "cheat sheets"
- Using class notes and/or the textbook and/or any other supplemental source
- Receiving assistance from or giving assistance to another student
- Accessing text messaging from a cell phone
- Listening to recorded material
- Using a laptop computer to access information
- Looking at or otherwise using stolen copies of exams

Colleges and universities publish academic integrity policies and consequences for violations of those policies. They expect that students be responsible for completing their work in an honest manner that is respectful of their fellow students and instructors.

THE FINAL CHECKLIST

Effective test preparation requires continual review and practice. Successful students have a plan—so as the big day approaches, establish a plan. Use the checklist in Activity 8.5 to get organized, reduce your levels of anxiety—and do well on your latest opportunity.

Post-exam analysis

A common reaction by many students following the completion of an exam is to forget it and concentrate on the next opportunity. Although this is an understandable reaction, pause—even if momentarily—and reflect on the exam.

Look once again at the checklist in Activity 8.5. Notice that the last portion is a **post-exam analysis.** This type of activity accomplishes a couple of things. While the material is still fresh in your mind, content review is critical. There is a good chance you will see some of this information again on a midterm or final examination (or in another course). Make sure you have it correct now. Don't get it wrong again. From a process point of view, it is important to understand what worked and what did not work for you. Why not use this time to identify your challenges and strengths? Set a goal for the next exam.

Assessment of strengths and weaknesses

Academic progress is not a one-time event. It requires a great deal of energy and time. But it will be easier to achieve if you apply the principles and strategies of the previous chapters. Throughout this book, the concepts of reflection, respect, and responsibility have been used as organizing principles for student success. Let's take a moment and apply that knowledge to test performance. The post-exam analysis provides a useful tool at this point.

Figure 8.2 shows the following connections:

- Step 1 requires *reflection* on what you would like to achieve. A well-planned goal, as you read in chapter 2, requires thought about what you want to achieve, how you will achieve it, and why you wish to achieve it.

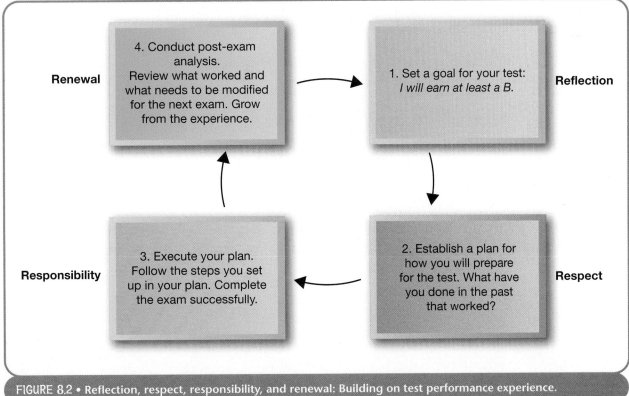

FIGURE 8.2 • Reflection, respect, responsibility, and renewal: Building on test performance experience.

TEST-PREPARATION CHECKLIST (✓)

Select one of the courses you are taking this term, and complete the following check-list[6] to evaluate your preparation for the next exam.

Class: _____

Instructor: _____

Test date, location, and time: _____

1. Type of exam:
    - ☐ Multiple-choice
    - ☐ True-false
    - ☐ Matching
    - ☐ Completion
    - ☐ Identification
    - ☐ Essay
    - ☐ Lab work
    - ☐ Problems
    - ☐ Other _____

2. What I need when I study:
    - ☐ Textbook
    - ☐ Notes
    - ☐ Teacher's study guide
    - ☐ Worksheets
    - ☐ Past exams (these can be very helpful)
    - ☐ Supplemental readings
    - ☐ Calculator
    - ☐ Pens, pencils, paper
    - ☐ Other _____

3. Will I study alone or with a study group?   ☐ Alone   ☐ Study group

    (To get the most from a study group you may wish to set an agenda before the meeting.)

4. Will the teacher lead any study sessions before or after class?   ☐ Yes   ☐ No

    If "yes", when? _____

5. When will I study? Make a plan—and stick to it.

    Date/time: _____

    Date/time: _____

    Date/time: _____

    (Put these dates on your calendar.)

6. Prioritization: What topics will the exam cover?

Topic	I really know this stuff	I am not too sure about this stuff	I have no clue about this stuff	Topic reviewed at least once
1.				
2.				
3.				
4.				

7. Predict some test questions.

8. Things I need for test day:
☐ Pens, pencils, paper, bluebook
☐ Calculator
☐ Notes (if I can use my notes during the test)
☐ Textbook (if the test is open-book)
☐ Ruler
☐ Wristwatch
☐ Other _____

Test preparation does *not* end when you hand in your test. Start preparing for your next exam by doing a post-exam analysis:

9. I was *most prepared* for _____

10. I was *not well prepared* for _____
    Why? _____

11. The biggest help was:
☐ My notes
☐ My homework
☐ Tutoring sessions
☐ My study schedule
☐ My study group
☐ My study environment
☐ Meeting with my instructor outside of class
☐ Other _____

12. My major weakness(es):
☐ Ran out of time during the test
☐ Did not expect this type of test
☐ Studied the wrong material
☐ Did not start studying early enough
☐ Other _____

(*continued*)

TEST-PREPARATION CHECKLIST (✓) (continued)

8.5
ACTIVITY

13. Grade I *realistically* expect to receive: _____ Grade I received: _____

14. My *realistic* plan to improve for the next exam:

_____

_____

- Step 2 incorporates *reflection* and *respect*. Here you think about and identify what you have done successfully in the past to prepare for exams. Establish a plan based on your previous experiences.

- Step 3 requires you to *responsibly* implement your plan. The success of your goal will depend upon the effort you put into its fulfillment.

- Step 4 provides the feedback you need to begin preparing for the next exam. Here you *reflect* upon what worked or did not work. By recognizing your successes and shortcomings, you can assume the *responsibility* to change as needed to improve for the next exam. This will help you renew your commitment to academic success—and grow as a student.

Emergency studying

"OK," you say. "Organization is great—but what do I do if I have not kept up? What do I do to survive a test when I'm down to the night before—and I am not ready?" Here are some pointers for **emergency studying.**[7] This is not a desirable situation—but if it's all you have, then get the most from it.

- *Do not* be tempted to read quickly everything you have not read yet. If you read large quantities of knowledge too fast, you will have poor recall.

- *Do not* panic. OK, so you did not study as you wish you had. Test day is no time to panic.

- *Do not* give up. Especially on essay exams—never leave the item blank. You surely can come up with something to write.

- *Do* accept the fact you will not be able to study everything.

- *Do* relax as best you can. Admittedly, this may be difficult but panic should not be an option.

- *Do* start by anticipating your teacher. What type of questions will the teacher ask? What types of content and/or skills will be tested? Refer to Activities 8.4 and 8.5.

- *Do* use your notes and text to find the most important material. Clues to guide you: chapter titles and subtitles; major emphasis in class discussions and lectures; relationships with past material; chapter summaries.

- *Do* try to find and study some important information from every chapter that was assigned.

When you find important information, do the following:

- Read it.

- Ask yourself a question for which the information is an answer.

- Say the information to yourself.

- Check to see if you were correct.

- Do it until you get it correct twice.

Improving test performance is an exercise in problem solving. You examine what went right, what could have gone better—and then you make a plan to improve performance on the next exam.

SUMMARY

TEST-TAKING IS NOT A ONE-DAY EVENT

Effective test preparation starts at the completion of the most recent exam. Before you leave this chapter, keep the following points in mind:

- Whatever your background, you bring positive experiences and, perhaps, a few challenges to the table. Recognize and build upon these experiences.

- Test anxiety is common. Even when well prepared, you may still have doubts. Recognize them but don't let them paralyze you.

- Strategies introduced earlier in this book can be applied to address test-performance challenges.

- Take time to analyze the reasons why you have difficulty with tests. Go beyond a superficial explanation; move into a deeper examination of the factors that have an impact on your test performance.

- Active listening can improve memory and test performance.

- Effective test preparation can be hampered by inefficient actions during the test.

Your SELF:
Personal growth and balance

The following activities will allow you to reflect on the three levels of student success as they apply to the major concepts introduced in this chapter. Each activity will give you an opportunity to reflect and apply the chapter concepts in a way that is meaningful to you. Use this opportunity to apply newly acquired information and also keep an ongoing journal of growth in the various facets of your life.

The 4 Rs

Describe a personal example of how you used each of the 4 Rs to effectively handle a testing or memory issue thus far in your college term.

1. *Reflection*   (Example: Perhaps you reviewed the errors you made on previous exams.)

_____

_____

_____

_____

2. *Respect*   (Example: To calm your test anxiety, you reminded yourself of the test successes you have had this term.)

_____

_____

_____

_____

3. *Responsibility*   (Example: You realized your past test preparation was not working well, so you made an appointment to speak with your professor.)

_____

_____

_____

_____

4. *Renewal*   (Example: After successfully completing an exam, you rewarded yourself.)

_____

_____

_____

_____

The Change Cycle

Reflect on one of your test performance challenges. What can you do (or have you done) to change this from a challenge to a strength?

1. What challenge have you identified as the biggest?

   _____

   _____

   _____

2. What led you to recognize that this challenge needed to be addressed? _____

   _____

   _____

   _____

3. What was (or will be) your plan to make the change a reality? _____

   _____

   _____

   _____

4. If you have put the plan into action (executed it), how are you progressing? If not, how will you begin to execute your plan? _____

   _____

   _____

   _____

5. Once the change has become a reality, how do you plan to enjoy this achievement? _____

   _____

   _____

   _____

Tuning Your Life-Strings

Before you move on to chapter 9, pause for a moment and reflect on the balance—or lack of balance—in your life at this point in the school term. Use this activity to apply newly acquired information from this chapter to gauge the level of strength in the various facets of your life. You may wish to refer to your responses in previous chapters.

Life-string	Questions to ask yourself	What possible activities could help you tune this string?	Who can help you tune this string?
Social	• Do you participate in a study group to help prepare for exams?		
Occupational	• Will you need to take entrance exams, or certification or licensing tests, in order to pursue your major or career choice?		
Spiritual	• Prior to an exam, do you seek out quiet time to meditate and quiet your inner self-talk?		
Physical	• Are you well rested when you take your exams? • Do you take stretch breaks frequently when engaged in study periods?		
Intellectual	• Have you created computer folders to organize review information? • Can you use your information literacy skills to assist you in test performance?		
Emotional	• What strategies have you used to effectively deal with test-day stressors?		

Rhythms of Reflection

To complete this chapter, please reflect on the following words:

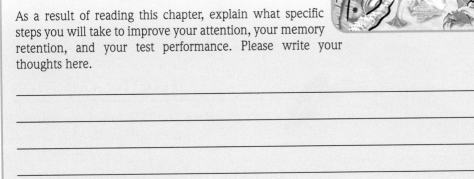

> *The secret of a good memory is attention, and attention to a subject depends upon our interest in it. We rarely forget that which has made a deep impression on our minds.*
>
> –*Tryon Edwards, theologian and author*

As a result of reading this chapter, explain what specific steps you will take to improve your attention, your memory retention, and your test performance. Please write your thoughts here.

_____

_____

_____

_____

_____

_____

_____

 To further respond online, please go to the *Rhythms of Reflection* module in chapter 8 of the Companion Website.

ENDNOTES

1. From "Test and Performance Anxieties," Campus Blues, 2002–2004, http://www.campusblues.com/test.asp (accessed February 24, 2006). This article provides a breakdown of physical, emotional, behavioral, cognitive indicators of test anxiety.
2. Some of the information for this section on memory can be found in Steve Piscitelli, *Study Skills: Do I Really Need This Stuff?* (Upper Saddle River, NJ, Prentice Hall, 2004), module 8.
3. Ibid.
4. Piscitelli, *Study Skills*, 198–199.
5. From Piscitelli, *Study Skills*, 206–207.
6. From Piscitelli, *Study Skills*, 202–204.
7. From Piscitelli, *Study Skills*, 205–206.

Information Literacy
Hip-Hop, Rock, Jazz, Blues — Which Is Best?

REFLECTIVE QUESTIONS

Keeping the following questions in mind will make this chapter more meaningful:

- What information literacy skills do you already possess?

- What resources does your school have to help students become information literate?

- Does your school require students to enroll in and pass an information literacy course?

- How do you know if a source is credible?

- What responsibilities do you have when sending e-mails?

academic integrity
information literacy
keyword search
reference librarian
search engines
World Wide Web

GUEST SPEAKER

MEET **AMY BALDWIN**

English Instructor and Author of *The Community College Experience PLUS*

Pulaski Technical College

North Little Rock, Arkansas

Information literacy is not just an academic skill; it is an essential skill for life in the information age. Because there is an abundance of information out there (thanks to the World Wide Web and an increase in published books), you need to know how to find the information you need, evaluate it, and use it in an ethical manner. You can't—and probably shouldn't—take for granted what "experts" say. Instead, be curious enough to learn more and critical enough to examine and assess what you read, see, and hear. Whether you're making important health decisions or deciding what peanut butter is the best, information literacy skills are among the most important you can learn in college.

My top three suggestions concerning information literacy:

1. Get to know the library staff at your college. They can be your lifesavers when you need information or need help finding it.

2. Be curious—being curious about life will make learning so much more enjoyable.

3. Question everything you read, see, and hear.

INTRODUCTION

Have you ever considered how much information is produced *worldwide* in one year? One study[1] discovered the following intriguing facts:

- "A half a million new libraries the size of the Library of Congress print collections" would be needed to hold *just* the new information produced in 2002.

- There is enough new information produced annually to require a thirty-foot-high pile of books for *each person* in the world.

- Ninety-two percent of this information is not in print form. Most of it can be found on hard disks. Paper only accounts for 0.01 percent of the new information.

- Even though paper accounts for a minimal amount of the stored information, it takes 786 million trees to produce the paper the world needs in *one year.* In the United States, that equates to almost twelve thousand sheets per person per year—or about thirty-two sheets of paper per person per day.

- The amount of stored information on disks, film, and paper *doubled* from 1999 to 2002. In less time than it would take a student to master course material for one undergraduate degree, the amount of available information worldwide increased by 100 percent!

Because there does not appear to be any slowdown in this phenomenal explosion of information, a number of challenges present themselves. For instance, just because information is increasing in volume does not mean that it is increasing in quality. How can you discern the credible from the absurd? Sometimes having too much information can be overwhelming. What should be done when you find hundreds—or thousands—of possible sources? How will you know which have the best information? Or, more practically, what is the most effective way to trim the vast numbers to a workable few?

This chapter will explore strategies that will help you efficiently and effectively locate, evaluate, and use this vast storehouse of information.

POINTS TO CONSIDER

- **What does it mean to be information literate today?** Twenty years ago, an information literate student knew how to find source information in the library's card catalog, locate bound books on the shelves in the library's reference room, and operate a microfilm or microfiche machine in the documents room. Although these resources are still available and valuable, as a student of the twenty-first century you need to know more than how to find a book at the library: You need to know how to navigate through hundreds, thousands, and even millions of pages of bound *and* digital resource material. But the explosion of data does not necessarily equate to an explosion of credible knowledge—so once the information has been found, you need to know how to evaluate it before you decide whether to use it.

- **What do you need to do to become an information literate individual?** People who do not know how to access (or who choose not to access) the incredibly rich storehouse of Internet resources put themselves at a great disadvantage. At the very least, students will need an adequate working knowledge of computers, e-mail accounts, and how to connect to the Internet. If cost creates barriers, find the computer lab on your campus and ask how you can get a free e-mail account and Internet access. More and more colleges and universities offer courses to assist students to effectively access and use information. Some schools offer online tutorials to instruct students how to make sense of the maze of available information. Does your school offer an information literacy course? Since you have been on campus, what have you done to learn how to access, evaluate, and use information?

- **How will you benefit from knowing how to efficiently and effectively locate and use information?** The obvious answer to this question is that being information literate will help you to successfully complete the requirements for your degree or certification.

But there is more—so much more. On the way to your diploma, you will become exposed to viewpoints that will challenge your currently held beliefs and values (see chapter 2). Where will you find the information to support *your* viewpoints? How will you know if a classmate or an instructor is presenting accurate conclusions? And once you leave your current school and enter the world of work, will you know how to access, judge, and use information to help you advance in your chosen career field? Yes, there is more information today than there was five years ago—but if you do not know how to use it effectively its effectiveness diminishes. In effect, you will be an illiterate standing alongside the information highway, as those who know how to use the tools pass you by at a rapid pace.

WELCOME TO THE INFORMATION AGE

What is information literacy?

As noted in the chapter introduction, the amount of available information has exploded—and all indications point to the explosion continuing well into the future. Not only is there an abundance of information, but there are a variety of locations in which to find the information. Libraries, blogs, commercial Web sites, government publications, service organizations, political action committees, and professional organizations are but a few of the disseminators of information.

This complex informational system creates challenges. If you were looking for information and did not care about its quality, but only wanted to find something *fast,* then a dizzying array of information is quickly available with a few clicks of a computer mouse. But ease does not always equate with quality. The key is to know not just *where* to look for information, but also *how* to separate the good from the bad, the informative from the misleading. An information literate person can "recognize when information is needed and [has] the ability to locate, evaluate, and use effectively the needed information."[2] These four facets of **information literacy**—knowing what information you need, where to find it, how to evaluate it, and how to use it properly—are shown in Figure 9.1.

While the thought of information literacy may be intimidating at first glance, consider that you have been doing this sort of thing for years. Activity 9.1 asks you to use the information literacy skills you currently have.

There is more than one type of information to access

Whether you are searching for a new cell phone or researching a term paper, you will be able to unearth a variety of pertinent sources. You can read a newspaper, listen to a radio advertisement,

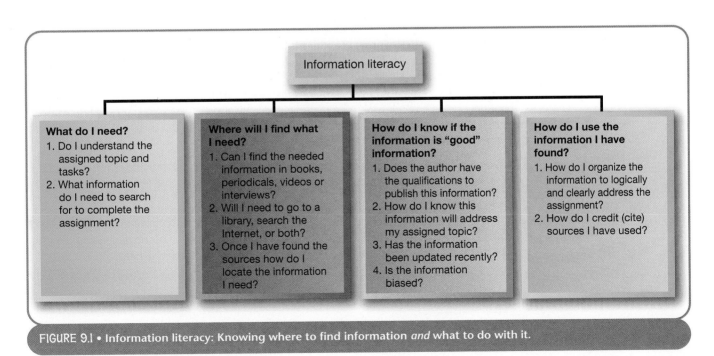

FIGURE 9.1 • Information literacy: Knowing where to find information *and* what to do with it.

BUILDING ON YOUR INFORMATION LITERACY SKILLS

Think of a time when you bought a piece of technology. It might have been a cell phone, a television, a laptop computer, or perhaps a personal portable digital audio player. For the purposes of this exercise, let's assume you want to purchase a new cell phone. You would like one that provides reliable service for a reasonable price, but you are confused as to which phone represents the best purchase. Applying the four basic facets of information literacy, answer the following questions:

1. What information do you need to know before you can buy a new cell phone?

   _____

   _____

2. How will you find the information you need?

   _____

   _____

3. How will you evaluate the information you found? That is, how will you know a "reliable and reasonably priced product" when you see it?

   _____

   _____

4. Once you have evaluated all of the literature about cell phones, how will you use the information?

   _____

   _____

or hear the opinion of classmates. Each of these represents a specific manner in which information can be relayed. Information formats include visuals, print or electronic media, and databases.[3]

Visuals. These are photos and illustrations including graphs, charts, tables, and maps. Visuals will not only help you understand the material, but may also suggest a way for you to effectively present your information in a term paper. These visuals can be found in books, periodicals, advertisement brochures, or on Internet sites.

- *Example:* Maps comparing nationwide cell phone coverage may provide information that is the deciding factor determining which phone to purchase.

Media. Electronic media include video clips (on tape or DVD) and CD recordings, which present information in visual and/or oral format. Print media that can provide information about the topic you are researching include books, magazines, journal articles, and newspapers.

- *Example:* An article in a magazine such as *Consumer Reports* will provide lab-tested reliability results. You might even find an article that compares cost of cell phones and cost of phone service.

- *Example:* If one of the requirements for a term paper is to use a nonprint source, the library's video collection may hold the film or documentary that you need.

Databases. These hold a great deal of information in computer-based indexes. You can find periodicals (newspapers, journals, magazines, research abstracts) in databases. Since some may require a password to enter, ask your reference librarian for assistance. Besides holding a wealth of information, databases have another benefit for the user: The information published in a database has typically been professionally reviewed. Whether evaluated by an editor or a professional reviewer, these articles carry more credibility than information simply posted to the Internet by individuals without a review process. If your professor has required that you use an Internet source, make sure that a database will meet that requirement.

- *Example:* Perhaps an English assignment requires you to find and compare literary reviews of a novel. Your library's collection of *Book Review Digest* will provide that information. Depending on the library, this resource could be found in book-bound form or in an electronic database.

FOUR STEPS TO COMPLETING AN ASSIGNMENT IN AN INFORMATION LITERATE MANNER

In its simplest form, information literacy engages a person on four different levels, as mentioned earlier in this chapter:

1. *Knowing what information is needed:* This requires reflection before starting your search.

2. *Accessing the needed information:* This requires time to responsibly seek out pertinent information.

3. *Evaluating the information that is located:* This requires responsible action to judge the effectiveness of the information found.

4. *Using the information that has been found and evaluated:* This requires time to reflect on the appropriate use of the information retrieved.

Each step builds upon the previous step. Miss one step, and the information gathered can be seriously flawed. Chapter 7 provided a detailed overview of the steps to complete a paper. As we move through this section, you will notice that a close connection exists between information literacy and a research paper; you really can't complete one without the other.

Step 1: Knowing what information is needed

This is a basic but often rushed step. Before digging through the library or surfing the Internet, be sure you understand what information you need. Chapter 7 used the following example from a history syllabus:

> **One of the requirements in this history class is to write a ten-page paper identifying and explaining five major consequences of World War II. The sources you use must include at least five books, three periodicals and two non-print sources. The paper is due two weeks before the final exam. The paper will be worth 25 percent of the final course grade.**

By asking yourself a few simple questions, the nature of the assignment became clearer:

- What do I need to do?
  - *Write a 10-page paper*
- What is the topic?
  - *Identify and explain five consequences of World War II*
- What types of source material must be used?
  - *At least five books*
  - *At least three periodicals*
  - *At least two nonprint sources*

- When is the paper due?
    - *Two weeks before the end of the term* (You can enter this on your calendar; see chapter 4.)
- How much is this assignment worth?
    - *25 percent of the final course grade* (In other words, this is a *major* part of your grade for the entire term.)

Step 2: Accessing the needed information

Once you know what topic you will research, the time has arrived to find pertinent information. One question guides this part of the process: Where can you locate the source material?

Taking a Trip to the Library: The Traditional Human-Touch Method. Ease and accessibility make the Internet a remarkable tool. It can be accessed from virtually anywhere, and it connects to millions of sites. There may be times, however, when you need to or wish to do

WHAT'S THE ASSIGNMENT?
PRACTICAL APPLICATION

Using an assignment from another class, answer the following questions. These initial steps require a relatively small investment of time and energy and will help maximize your efforts to efficiently find appropriate source material.

1. What is the *exact* wording of the instructor's assignment? Write that here and then highlight the key words in the assignment.

   _____

   _____

2. What task(s) do you have to complete? Is there a required length and format specified?

   _____

   _____

3. What is the exact topic? Can you state specifically what you need to write or speak about? This is *critical,* as it will guide you in the step of finding the needed information.

   _____

   _____

4. What types of sources are specifically called for? Are you required to use class notes, the textbook, databases, the Internet, or other sources?

   _____

   _____

5. When is the paper due? How much time do you have to complete this assignment? (Put it on your personal planning calendar.) _____

6. How much is the assignment worth? Is this a major portion of your grade for the course?

   _____

it the traditional and time-tested way—by walking into a library and using the reference material there. Once you enter your campus (or community) library, you will find the following:

© BananaStock Ltd.

- **Online catalogs.** The old "card catalog" is a thing of the past. Most libraries now have electronic catalogs of their holdings—often called OPAC (Online Public Access Catalog) or WebPAC. These can be accessed in much the same manner as when you use a search engine; Boolean searches will work here. (Boolean logic will be covered more fully a little later in the chapter, in the discussion of keyword searches.) Once you find the call numbers you can physically examine the books, photos, charts, and videos that are on the library shelves.

- **Reserve.** This material is usually held on a shelf behind the circulation desk. This is where an instructor might place a copy of an article he wants the class to read.

- **Reference librarian.** Sometimes there is nothing that can replace real human contact. The **reference librarian** will help you navigate successfully through the library's holdings. If you are having a difficult time getting started—knowing what keywords to use, for instance—this person will be ready to introduce you to various search strategies and direct you to the most appropriate databases.

- **Interlibrary loans.** Perhaps you have found a book that would be a perfect source for your term paper—but it is located in a university library on the other side of the state or nation. Librarians can arrange for the book to be sent to your campus library. Once your request is received by the library, the interlibrary loan will arrive on your campus within a matter of days.

- **Databases, indexes, and e-books.** As stated earlier, databases hold a large amount of material. Libraries typically subscribe to a number of these. Usually, a password is required to access a library's database. Once again, the reference librarian will prove invaluable by helping you obtain the password and also recommending the best databases to use based on your topic.

Taking a Trip on the World Wide Web: The Modern High-Tech Method. Perhaps you are a bibliophobe* and the thought of searching through endless stacks of books brings perspiration to your brow. Twenty years ago you would have been out of luck. Either you used the library or you depended on the personal collection of books you may have had. If all you had was an ancient encyclopedia set—and you did not wish to go to the library—you were doomed!

Today you have the option of being able to search a collection that is far more immense than any single library. The **World Wide Web** provides an entry point to a vast array of books, articles, nonprint sources, and personal communications that until recently were considered out of the reach of the common person. When accessed effectively, this information brings power to the hands of the users; unfocused use of this vast storehouse, however, will result in a huge waste of time.

Knowing How and Why to Use the Internet. Some have labeled the Internet as "the most important technology innovation of our generation."[4] Once connected to the Internet, your computer can access the World Wide Web (the *www.* found in most Internet addresses is the accepted abbreviation), which facilitates the connection between computer resources around the world. This is what most of us are familiar with when we "surf the Web." The amount of information is virtually endless. You could sit at a computer for hours, days, or even months and not exhaust the information available. Therein lays a potential calamity for the uninformed or unfocused user.

---

* One who fears books.

"Surfing the Web," in its popular usage, has come to describe an aimless ride through cyberspace, following one link to another without much thought or direction. Although this can be entertaining, it does not help a college student who has four or five classes and a like number of research papers to complete in a short span of time. Time becomes a critical resource that must be managed carefully. Step 1—knowing what information is needed—helps to limit wasted time. You can then effectively use the Internet rather than drifting from link to link.

Not all information on the Internet is created equally. Some Web sites provide expert and scholarly analysis, while others post inflammatory personal opinions with little substance. Other sites promote particular products, services, or causes. In short, there are various types of Web sites[5] that the casual user will encounter. At the very least, be aware of what the sites represent and how their information will affect your research. (Step 3 will provide more on evaluating information.)

A Web site address (also called a *URL*, the acronym for "uniform resource locator") will usually end with *.com, .net, .gov, .org,* or *.edu.* This suffix can indicate whether the site is trying to peddle a product or service commercially (*.com or .net*), advance the cause of an organization (*.org*), provide information from government agencies (*.gov*), or present information from an educational institution (*.edu*). While this description is an oversimplification, paying attention to the end of the address will provide a clue about the objectivity of a site.

WEB ADDRESSES

9.3 ACTIVITY

Using a search engine (Google, for instance), type in the following address suffixes one at a time and hit the Enter key.

1. Type *.com.* Explore a few of the links that appear. Do you find any similarities between sites that end with *.com?*

_____

_____

_____

2. Type *.net.* Explore a few of the links that appear. Do you find any similarities between sites that end with *.net?*

_____

_____

_____

3. Type *.org.* Explore a few of the links that appear. Do you find any similarities between sites that end with *.org?*

_____

_____

_____

4. Type *.edu.* Explore a few of the links that appear. Do you find any similarities between sites that end with *.edu?*

_____

_____

_____

In recent years, the Web has seen an explosion of Web log sites known as *blogs.* In some cases, these sites may be used internally by an organization to disseminate information and generate discussion. More often, a blog will post personal opinions by anyone who wishes to have his or her opinion on the Web.[6] Approach the information on such sites with a "user beware" mind-set. Traditional publishing (especially scholarly journals, books, and textbooks) requires that other professionals in the field review a manuscript for credibility and accuracy. There is no such requirement for a blog. A blogger can immediately post any material that he or she wishes.

Using Search Engines. Literally millions of pages of information can be found using the Internet. How can you sift through that much information? How can anyone find anything in such a cyber pile of material? Without a method or effective strategy to help your search, this could take the better part of your college career to complete.

Search engines provide that strategy. They may be used for on-campus collections found in the library, or they can be found on the Internet to assist in gathering pertinent information from the many databases on the World Wide Web. Search engines speed the search process by allowing you to instantaneously find material that is related to the area of your research.

The Internet offers a variety of search engines. You possibly have already used some of the following:

www.google.com

www.yahoo.com

www.altavista.com

www.dogpile.com

www.lycos.com

www.ask.com

Once you arrive at the home page of a search engine, it will be beneficial to look for a "Help" link that will explain how to navigate the site. Each search engine has its benefits and liabilities—and each will have its own quirks and operating features. For instance, Table 9.1 indicates where you will find the "Help" link on each of the sites.

Just like people, search engines have their unique appearances. Some open with a page full of columns, colors, and information. Others prefer a more minimalist approach, showing a few basic links on the home page. Which is best will depend on your personal preferences. Do you like a site that looks clean and neat but requires you to dig down a few "layers" by clicking through one, two, or three pages to get what you want? Or would you prefer a site that provides a lot of information with a variety of links right on the home page? Some sites you will find very easy to navigate; others will appear to be a maze of sensory overload.

Besides the look of the site, you will come to prefer a site based on the good fortune you experience each time you search for information.

Conducting Keyword Searches. Once you know what you are looking for, you may turn to your campus library or conduct an Internet search from your personal computer. One of two things usually happens: Either you find very few sources, or you quickly turn up hundreds—if not thousands. In the first instance you may be frustrated by the lack of pertinent material. The other scenario provides so much information that you become overwhelmed by the sheer volume.

Exploring the holdings of your campus library or the Internet can be maximized with a **keyword search,** using a word or phrase to help you find material on your topic. It can uncover books, periodicals, and nonprint materials.

For example, let's say you decide to type in the words *consequences of World War II* for a keyword search—and your search turns up *zero* possible sources. At this point you might try to narrow your search by typing in *Cold War.* This time your search of the campus library catalog[7] turns up sixty-nine "hits" that include information in all formats. This means that this particular library collection holds sixty-nine sources in either print or nonprint format. The point is that with a more refined search (more precise wording) the number of "hits" you get may increase.

Table 9.1
Locating help with a search engine

Search engine name	Information about the engine's "help" feature*
www.google.com	On the home page click "About Google." The next page will provide four links with information about different search features for this engine.
www.yahoo.com	Click "Help" on the home page. The next page provides a list of more specific links to help with searching this engine.
www.altavista.com	On the home page click "Help." On the next page click "Search." The next page will provide links on how to search as well as information about the features of this engine.
www.dogpile.com	On the home page click on "Tools and Tips." The next page will have a list of links to help you search effectively.
www.lycos.com	A "Help" link is located at the bottom of the home page.
www.ask.com	Click "About" on the home page. On the next page you will find information on how to conduct a search.

*All sites accessed on July 29, 2006.

There are a few simple strategies that will allow you to narrow or broaden your computer search strategies for source material. These will work on a campus library system or on the World Wide Web.

One such strategy is known as *Boolean logic,* by which you can either broaden or narrow your search using one of three words: *AND, OR,* or *NOT.*[8] (Some search engines or databases require that these connector words be typed in all uppercase letters.) Using the word *OR* will expand your search to turn up as many hits as possible. On the other hand, the connector words *NOT* and *AND* will limit the number of hits received on a topic; they are valuable to use if your initial keyword search turned up more sources than you wanted.

- *Example:* Going back to our example, typing the phrase *cold war AND united states* will reduce the sixty-nine sources to forty-five. Only those sources that contain all of the keywords will be listed. (*Note:* Capitalization is not required for such a search.)

- *Example:* Typing the phrase *cold war NOT soviet union* will help you locate source material that has the words "cold war" in the title but not "soviet union." This tool could help eliminate material you will not need for your paper. (*Note:* Some search systems may use the symbols "+" or "−" to do the same as *AND* or *NOT.*)

The use of quotation marks (" ") is another strategy that may help limit your search to just those words and just in that order. For instance if you conducted a keyword search using the words *consequences of world war II,* your "hit" list would include all source material that contains any of those words. But if you were to place quotation marks around the words ("*consequences of world war II*"), your search will uncover only sources with those words in that exact order.

© *Image Source Limited*

- *Example:* Typing the words *consequences of world war II* into one Internet search engine yielded more than fifteen *million* hits. Placing quotation marks around the words limited the results to less than fourteen *thousand.* Now, that is still a considerable number (and would need to be further limited), but it does graphically show the value of limiting a search with the use of quotation marks.

There is a downside, however, to any keyword search: If your keywords are not broad enough, you may miss a significant portion of information. To compensate, you may wish to look for additional subject headings. (These can be found in the library's online catalog.) For instance, other subject headings that may relate to the topic of the Cold War include *nuclear weapons, foreign relations–Soviet Union, world politics–1945 to 1989, Cuban Missile Crisis,* or *diplomatic history.* Be aware of your many options. Your reference librarian can help.

Keywords also can help you locate images and photos online with a click of your mouse. For instance, when you arrive on the Google home page,[9] click on the link "Images." Then type in the term or name you wish to search.

- *Example:* Go to the Google image search page and type in *"cold war"* (including the quotation marks). How many images are available?

- *A second example:* Type in a name—yours, a friend's, a family member's, or a celebrity's. What do you locate?

Step 3: Evaluating information

Once you locate information on the Internet, a natural tendency is to use it immediately. After all, wasn't that the purpose of the search in the first place? Yes it was—but another step remains: evaluating the information. How do you know if the information you found is credible? On the Internet, there is no guarantee of a "consistent and reliable" peer review process.[10]

When evaluating information, consider these four criteria:[11]

1. *Accuracy and authority:* Is the site precise and expert? What experience (credentials) does the author have? Is there a sponsoring site or organization?

2. *Objectivity:* Is the site evenhanded and impartial? Is the material factual, unbiased, and in-depth? Is the coverage balanced? Is the site one of advertisements, or is it scholarly?

3. *Currency:* Is the site up-to-date and current? Is there a copyright date? (This only indicates *ownership;* it does not indicate credibility or accuracy.) Are there references (bibliography and footnotes if appropriate)? Has the site been recently updated, or is the information old?

4. *Scope:* Is the range of coverage small, or vast? What is the "breadth and depth" of the site? That is, does it provide an in-depth review of the topic, or is it a superficial overview with broad general statements?

KEYWORDS AND SEARCH ENGINES

In Activity 9.2 you performed step 1 of information literacy, determining what information you need to find. This activity gives you practice in step 2, accessing that information.

1. Return to Activity 9.2. List five keywords that might help you find information about the topic of your assignment.

   _____

   _____

   _____

   _____

   _____

2. Choose two of the search engines mentioned in Table 9.1. Once you reach the home page for each, type in a keyword. Answer the questions below for each search engine used.

   a. Name of search engine: _____

   Once you typed in the search phrase, how many "hits" appeared? _____

   How easy or difficult was it to navigate this search engine? _____

   _____

   What kind of information did the initial "hits" page provide to you *and* how helpful would this information be in guiding your search? _____

   _____

   _____

   b. Name of search engine: _____

   Once you typed in the search phrase, how many "hits" appeared? _____

   How easy or difficult was it to navigate this search engine? _____

   _____

   What kind of information did the initial "hits" page provide to you *and* how helpful would this information be in guiding your search? _____

   _____

   _____

3. Finally, of the two search engines used, which one did you find to be the most beneficial? Why?

   _____

   _____

EVALUATING A WEBSITE: INTERNET CAREER SITE REPORT

The Internet provides a wealth of great information. But some sites are not very accurate or credible. This short activity will help you review the Internet with a critical eye, incorporating the four criteria of accuracy, objectivity, currency, and scope. Please find an Internet site that addresses a career area that interests you and then answer the following questions:

1. What is the common name of the site? (This is usually found on the home page of the site.)

   _____

2. What is the *exact* URL? This is the address (location) of the site. It will typically begin with *http://* or *http://www.* (*Note:* When entering the URL be sure to type it *exactly* as it appears. If only one character is incorrect, the site cannot be located.)

   _____

3. What is the career that the site addresses? List three things the site presents about this career.

   _____

   _____

   _____

4. *Accuracy and authority:*   Can you rely on the information you find on this site?

   a. Who is the author of the site?

      _____

   b. What evidence exists that the author is qualified to publish this material?

      _____

      _____

   c. What are the credentials of the author? Include any affiliations (e.g., university professor, government agency). If none are listed, state that.

      _____

      _____

   d. What is your opinion of the credentials of this author? Why do you, or don't you, trust this site?

      _____

      _____

      _____

5. *Currency:*   Is the site current? When was it last updated? _____

6. *Scope:*   Explore some of the hot links of this site. A *hot link* is a link that takes you immediately to another page (or another place on the same page) simply by clicking your mouse button. What types of links exist?

   _____

   _____

   _____

(*continued*)

EVALUATING A WEBSITE: INTERNET CAREER SITE REPORT (continued)

7. *Objectivity:*   Specifically discuss one of these links. Is the information biased or slanted in any way?

_____

_____

_____

_____

8. Would you recommend this site to other students with the same career interest? Why or why not?

_____

_____

9. Briefly summarize what you learned from this site. Are you still interested in this career? Why or why not?

_____

_____

_____

_____

10. What other questions do you still have about this career? Who could help you with these questions?

_____

_____

_____

Step 4: Using information

Information is power. As with any form of power, though, information must be used responsibly—and it must be conveyed in a clear and convincing manner. Whether you deliver a classroom presentation, write an analysis of a current event, or describe the features of a new video game, what and how you communicate the information will have an impact on how it is received.

Consider the history term paper described earlier in the chapter. Let's assume you completed that paper as an actual assignment. You put in a number of hours figuring out exactly what you were going to research; you found appropriate information either in the library, on the Internet, or both; and then you determined what information was suitable for your final product. At this point, keep one question in mind: Do you want to waste all of that hard and worthwhile work with a hastily crafted paper that looks like it had been thrown together in the wee hours of the morning?

The presentation—how you use your information—is critical. No matter how much you may know, if it is not clearly and thoroughly presented its impact will be minimal. Let's review some basic steps for organizing and presenting your hard work. (See chapter 7 for more detail.)

- Be sure to provide the final product in the form required by the assignment: length of the paper, cover page, illustrations, bibliography, and so forth.

- Outline the presentation before creating the final version. Plan carefully.

- Ask someone you respect to critically review your paper, evaluating the organization of the presentation as well as grammar and mechanics.

- Before you turn in your final product, be sure that what you have written reflects what was asked for by the instructor.

RESPONSIBILITIES OF THE INFORMATION AGE

Academic integrity

Although chapter 7 explained the importance of **academic integrity,** it is appropriate at this point to reflect on that issue once again.[12]

Violations of academic integrity are not new. Ever since there have been schools, there have been students looking for shortcuts to complete assignments or exams. Plagiarizing papers, cheating on exams, and copying homework were not created by today's students. If anything is "new" it is, perhaps, the technological methods that make plagiarizing easier. Whether it is copying material from a Web site and directly pasting it into a student paper (without proper citation), or buying a paper from any of the various "dot-com paper mills" on the Internet, cheating has moved to cyberspace.

And more colleges and universities are rising to the challenge. At the very least, violations of academic integrity typically result in a failure for the particular assignment. But the punishments can, and do, become more severe. Students can fail a course, be suspended for a term, or be expelled from school. Some schools have created a new grade that reflects failure due to violation of academic integrity.

E-mail responsibilities

E-mail has revolutionized communication. As long as there is an Internet connection, one person can instantaneously contact another on any continent of the globe. Information can be rapidly

YOUR SCHOOL'S ACADEMIC INTEGRITY POLICY

1. Locate and read your school's academic integrity policy. What are the possible punishments a student can receive for violating the academic integrity policy?

_____

_____

_____

_____

Table 9.2
Cyberspace do's and don'ts

Cyberspace don'ts	Cyberspace do's
Don't type in all capital letters (the equivalent of online SHOUTING!).	Do adhere to rules of grammar, punctuation, and capitalization in all e-mails. An e-mail represents you in cyberspace.
Don't send inflammatory notes.	Do be courteous.
Don't abuse distribution lists and don't send spam. You may think the latest joke or inspirational story is great, but the fifty people in your address book may not have the same taste. You could also be sending someone a computer virus.	Do respect the privacy of your e-mail recipients. If you use a distribution list, put the names in the "blind copy" (bcc) space when composing your e-mail. Everyone will receive the e-mail but no one's e-mail address will be displayed for others to see and use.
Don't give out private information in cyber chat rooms or on cyber bulletin boards. This includes address, phone, photos, and other identifying characteristics.	Do protect your own privacy. The Internet is a wonderful tool but it also attracts its share of predators. Be ever vigilant.
Don't compromise your dignity or integrity (part 1).	Do maintain the highest level of academic integrity.
Don't compromise your dignity or integrity (part 2).	Do choose an e-mail address or screen name that portrays a respectful self-image. What you think is a cute e-mail or screen name may be perceived in a negative way: "foxylady," "spoiledrotten," "studpuppy," and "Uwannabeme" may sound creative and adorable but they do not impart the image of a serious student—or potential employee.
Don't be sarcastic. Since the facial expressions behind the e-mail cannot be seen, your words must speak for themselves.	Do use clear language. Judiciously use emoticons* to indicate the emotion behind a statement if the wording is not clear. (Better still, if the wording is not clear, rewrite or eliminate the passage altogether.)

*An *emoticon* uses the computer keyboard characters to represent an emotion. For instance, a smiley face can be depicted as :>) by using the colon, caret, and close parenthesis keys.

accessed and just as quickly passed along to another location. E-mail communication is quick, paperless, and free.† It is also faceless and open to abuse. Therefore, remember to observe e-mail *netiquette* (the rules of behavior for using the Internet). Table 9.2 provides a brief list of e-mail do's and don'ts that the information literate person observes. (Also see chapter 10.)

†At the writing of this book, e-mails can still be sent without having to pay postage or some type of access fee (not counting the cost of an Internet Service Provider). There have been limited conversations about the possibility of charging for e-mails, mainly in conjunction with ideas on how to limit *spam* (unwanted e-mail solicitations and correspondence).

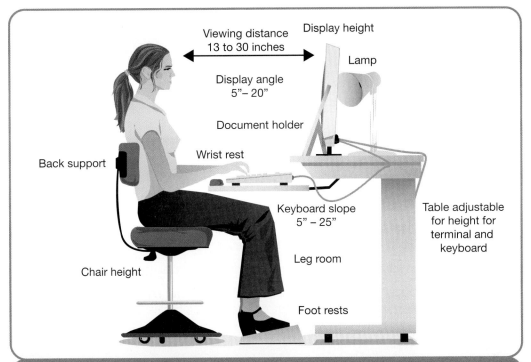

FIGURE 9.2 • Computer workstation suggested ergonomics.
Source: Library of Congress (Integrated Support Services, Workforce Ergonomics Program), "Ergonomics and VDT Use," *Computers in Libraries* 13 (May 1993). From a flyer prepared by the Library of Congress Collections Services VDT Ergonomics Committee, 1991–1992.

Avoiding repetitive strain injuries (RSI)

In addition to being responsible for the academic integrity of your work, take time to be responsible for the health and condition of your body. Although hours sitting at the computer workstation may not appear to be demanding, they can have a debilitating effect on your body.

Repetitive strain injuries (RSI)—also called *repetitive stress injuries*—commonly occur to people who spend long hours typing at a keyboard and staring into a computer monitor. As the name implies, the injury results from repetitive (continual) motions or actions. Typing at a keyboard for a prolonged period of time, for instance, has been cited as a cause for carpal tunnel syndrome (CTS). The repeated keystroke activity can lead to a swelling of the thumbs and wrists if care is not taken. Various sources provide a checklist of activities that can be followed to minimize the risk of RSI.[13] Perhaps your school has such information available. There may be ergonomic* workshops offered on your campus. Such instruction typically addresses proper positioning of your monitor, keyboard, and chair to reduce eyestrain and muscle fatigue (see Figure 9.2). Remember to take appropriate stretch breaks and eye breaks. Simply standing up and walking away from the computer screen for a couple of minutes can reduce fatigue.

---

*Dictionary.com defines *ergonomics* as "The applied science of equipment design, as for the workplace, intended to maximize productivity by reducing operator fatigue and discomfort." See http://dictionary.reference.com/search?q=ergonomics (accessed January 1, 2006).

SUMMARY

PUTTING YOUR CYBER KNOWLEDGE TO WORK FOR YOUR ACADEMIC, PERSONAL, AND CAREER CHOICES

Before you leave this chapter, keep the following points in mind:

- The information explosion has not only increased the availability of information, but it has also increased the types and locations of the information.

- Information literacy requires a person to know *what* information to look for, *how to find* that information, *how to judge* the information's credibility and quality once it has been found, and *how to effectively use* the information once it has been found and evaluated.

- Locate and use school resources that will sharpen your information literacy skills.

- Academic integrity demands a strict code of conduct (moral expectation) that governs the manner in which students and professors do research and behave in class.

- E-mails represent you in cyber space.

tuning your life-strings

the 4 Rs

self

change and personal growth

Your SELF:
Personal growth
and balance

The following activities will allow you to reflect on the three levels of student success as they apply to the major concepts introduced in this chapter. Each activity will give you an opportunity to reflect and apply the chapter concepts in a way that is meaningful to you during this transitional phase of your life.

The 4 Rs

Describe a personal example of how you used each of the 4 Rs to efficiently and effectively evaluate information.

1. *Reflection* (Example: Perhaps you recently studied a product you wanted to purchase.) _____

_____

_____

_____

_____

_____

2. *Respect* (Example: When completing a research project, which of your past skills did you use?) _____

_____

_____

_____

_____

_____

3. *Responsibility* (Example: Perhaps you sought assistance with using a database in the campus library.) _____

_____

_____

_____

_____

_____

4. *Renewal* (Example: After completing a research assignment you rewarded yourself.) _____

_____

_____

_____

_____

_____

The Change Cycle

Reflect on one of your information literacy challenges. What can you do (or have you done) to change this from a challenge to a strength?

1. What challenge have you identified? _____

_____

_____

_____

2. What led you to recognize that this challenge needed to be addressed? _____

_____

_____

_____

3. What was (or will be) your plan to make the change a reality? _____

_____

_____

_____

4. If you have put the plan into action (executed it), how are you progressing? If not, how will you begin to execute your plan? _____

_____

_____

_____

5. Once the change has become a reality, how do you plan to enjoy this achievement? _____

_____

_____

_____

Tuning Your Life-Strings

Before you move on to chapter 10, pause for a moment and reflect on the balance—or lack of balance—in your life at this point in the school term. Use this activity to apply newly acquired information from this chapter to gauge the level of strength in the various facets of your life. You may wish to refer to your responses in previous chapters.

Life-string	Questions to ask yourself	What possible activities could help you tune this string?	How can information literacy help you tune this string?
Social	• Do you participate in chat rooms? • Do you use e-mail to stay in touch with family and friends?		
Occupational	• What information have you been able to find on the Web that relates to your major and/or career interests?		
Spiritual	• Have you found any Internet sites that address your spiritual beliefs?		
Physical	• Do you take stretch and eye breaks frequently when engaged in seated work (whether computer-based or book-based)? • Is your computer workstation placed in an ergonomically correct position?		
Intellectual	• How does being information literate enhance your critical thinking skills?		
Emotional	• Is your computer a source of joy or a source of frustration?		

Rhythms of Reflection

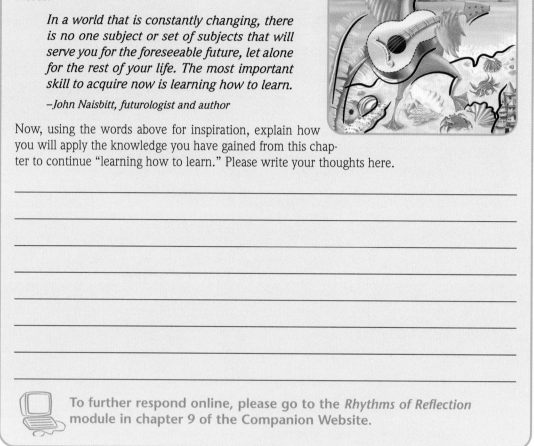

To complete this chapter, please reflect on the following words:

> *In a world that is constantly changing, there is no one subject or set of subjects that will serve you for the foreseeable future, let alone for the rest of your life. The most important skill to acquire now is learning how to learn.*
>
> *–John Naisbitt, futurologist and author*

Now, using the words above for inspiration, explain how you will apply the knowledge you have gained from this chapter to continue "learning how to learn." Please write your thoughts here.

_____

_____

_____

_____

_____

_____

_____

_____

To further respond online, please go to the *Rhythms of Reflection* module in chapter 9 of the Companion Website.

ENDNOTES

1. Peter Lyman and Hal R. Varian (senior researchers), "How Much Information? 2003," School of Information and Management, University of California at Berkeley, 2003, 1–12.

2. Association of College and Research Libraries (a division of the American Library Association), "Information Literacy Competency Standards for Higher Education," 2006, http://www.ala.org/ala/acrl/acrlstandards/informationliteracycompetency.htm#ildef (accessed November 30, 2005).

3. From Michael B. Eisenberg, Carrie A. Lowe, and Kathleen L. Spitzer, *Information Literacy: Essential Skills for the Information Age*, 2nd ed. (Westport, CT: Libraries Unlimited, 2004), 7–11.

4. "Internet," NetLingo the Internet Dictionary, http://www.netlingo.com/lookup.cfm?term=Internet (accessed December 14, 2005).

5. See Ann Marlow Riedling, *Learning to Learn: A Guide to Becoming Information Literate* (New York: Neal-Schuman, 2002), 72.

6. See "Global Availability of MSN Messenger and MSN Spaces Connects People Around the World," Microsoft PressPass, http://www.microsoft.com/presspass/press/2005/apr05/04-07GlobalMessengerSpacesPR.mspx (accessed December 14, 2005).

7. This example used the Florida Community College at Jacksonville library catalog (LINCC), http://www.fccj.org/library/ (accessed December 4, 2005).

8. Riedling, *Learning to Learn,* 28–32.

9. For an interesting article providing ten search tricks on Google, see Peter Grad, "Rev Up Your Engine," NorthJersey.com, December 3, 2005, http://www.northjersey.com/page.php?qstr=eXJpcnk3ZjczN2Y3dnFlZUVFeXk3MDcmZmdiZWw3Zjd2cWVlRUV5eTY4Mjg5NzEmeXJpcnk3ZjcxN2Y3dnFlZUVFeXk3 (accessed January 1, 2006).

10. Riedling, *Learning to Learn,* 61.

11. Riedling, *Learning to Learn,* 62. These are basic criteria that most information literacy resources list.

12. I would like to thank Amy Baldwin of Pulaski Technical College in North Little Rock, AR, for comments she made during her presentation, "Preventing Plagiarism, Advocating the Art of Scholarship, and Strengthening the Culture of Academic Integrity" (Pearson Prentice Hall Symposium on Student Success, Chicago, IL, November 4, 2005).

13. For one example of such a list, see Paul Marxhausen, "Computer Related Repetitive Strain Injury," 2005, University of Nebraska-Lincoln Electronics Shop RSI Web Page, http://eeshop.unl.edu/rsi.html (accessed January 1, 2006).

PART THREE WELLNESS

WHAT'S ON YOUR MIND?

Thoughts from Fellow Students

Thinking back on the first three months of our first year in college, we are amazed at what we accomplished. We had adjusted to a new campus, rigorous classes, professor expectations, and, for some of us, roommates. But with all that, we still had questions as we moved into the final month of the term. Maybe you, too, have questions similar to these:

- I have had to do a lot of group work in my classes and it has been very frustrating. Every group has had problems. What is it that I am supposed to get from these groups? (chapter 10)
- I must be a problem magnet. The whiners and complainers always seem to find me. Is there a polite way to avoid these people? (chapter 10)
- Between sitting and partying, my "freshman ten" may be closer to the "freshman fifteen or twenty"! I don't think I've ever been this heavy. What can I do to control my weight and feel healthy again? (chapter 11)
- I have received a lot of offers for credit cards. I've heard it is a good idea to build a credit history. Would it be a good idea to get a couple of these cards and start using them? If so, how can I keep track of my finances and avoid debt? (chapter 11)
- I'm not sure I'll make it to the end of this term. I'm exhausted. How can I push myself to survive the rest of the term? (chapter 11)

We all discovered our own answers to these questions, in our own way and on our own timetable. We are confident that you will, too. Continue to enjoy your campus life!

When you respect someone, you avoid violating that person. You treat the person with dignity. In fact, all positive, meaningful, and loving relationships are based on respect. Without respect, the relationship is one of manipulation and degradation. This applies to others as well as ourselves. When you encounter individuals and groups, you confront differences—gender, ethnic background, racial makeup, religious beliefs, academic abilities, political philosophies, and socioeconomic backgrounds, to name a few. The way in which you interact with others goes a long way in framing your reputation. Based on the way you treat others, people will see you on a continuum from *gracious, dignified, and accepting* to *boorish, dishonorable, and discriminatory.*

And if you do not treat *yourself* with respect, then you squander the most precious resource you have. Trite and cliché as it might sound, you are the only *you* that you will ever have. This part of the book will explore healthy relationships and how you take care of yourself.

- **Chapter 10: Building Nutritious Relationships.** You benefit by maximizing your contact with energizing people and minimizing time spent with energy thieves. Maximizing relationships does not equate to "using" people or "taking advantage" of their good graces. It refers to ways in which both you and the people you come in contact with can enjoy a fulfilling, healthy relationship. Whether the association is a short-term group project or significant intimate bond, respect for yourself and others will help to build meaningful relationships. Keep this question in mind as you read the chapter: *Do you know how to maximize your potential when working with people?*

- **Chapter 11: Personal Integrity.** Although every chapter contains great nuggets of information, this one will provide a bucketful of gold. Integrity, in its broadest sense, means conducting oneself in an honest, responsible, and respectful fashion. Do your actions show respect for yourself as well as for those around you? Four facets of integrity will be described: personal, health, financial, and academic. Keep this question in mind as you read the chapter: *How will you benefit from living a life of integrity, impeccability, and health?*

So far in this book, you have reflected on your reason for being in college. From there you demonstrated how to carry out the classroom responsibilities that come with being a successful college student. Now, let's take time and examine how you can treat others and yourself with the respect that is deserved.

10 Building Nutritious Relationships

Harmonious Connections

REFLECTIVE QUESTIONS

Keeping the following questions in mind will make this chapter more meaningful:

- How can you identify and surround yourself with "nutritious" and energizing people?

- What makes group work challenging?

- What are the benefits of active listening?

- What is the difference between assertive behavior and aggressive behavior?

- How can conflict be a positive force in your life?

KEY TERMS

active listening
assertiveness
collective monologue
conflict
elephant in the corner
energy vampires
hostile work environment
nutritious people
quid pro quo
sexual harassment
trust

GUEST SPEAKER

MEET **KAYE BRAGG**

Director of the Faculty Teaching
and Learning Center

California State University

Bakersfield, California

College is all about answering two questions: Who are you? and What do you want? Your college experience can transform your "dreams" into "goals." Your college experience gives you a wealth of opportunities to add to your knowledge base and expand your social network. Don't be afraid to try new and different activities because that will help you grow as a person. Enjoy the courses, the sports and cultural events, and lectures offered at your college.

My top three suggestions to get the most from college by developing relationships and making connections:

1. Find a faculty member who can become your mentor—someone who listens to your questions, gives honest advice, and encourages you. Your mentor will help you confront obstacles you encounter so you can succeed.

2. For each class, take time to get to know other students. They have the same problems, questions, and fears that you are experiencing. Working with other students builds a support group.

3. Take care of your physical, mental, and spiritual well-being. Learning to balance these three areas will build a strong professional self.

INTRODUCTION

You are the author of your own life. You make decisions that lead you in certain directions. Although it is true that many times you cannot control or stop change, it is just as true that you have a choice on how you address that change. The manner in which you handle situations gives clues to those around you as to the type of person you might be. Are you impulsive, thoughtful, cheerful, demeaning, or encouraging?

How you engage in an activity, with whom you associate, the manner in which you respond (or do not respond) to a question, and the types of written and oral expressions you use contribute to how you appear to others. Tom Peters, a motivational speaker and author, reminds us that "what you value is unmistakably reflected in precisely how you spend your time, the nature of each contribution [you make, and] who exactly you hang with."[1]

More than likely, when you were a young child you were told by parents, grandparents, uncles, or teachers to "play nice" with the other children. That simple piece of advice holds true as an adult—probably even more so. For that reason, this chapter will address the concepts of healthy interpersonal relationships, effective communication, and conflict management.

POINTS TO CONSIDER

- **What can you do to maximize relationships with other people?** Unless you plan on living the life of a hermit, dealing with people will be a reality for the rest of your life. You will have personal intimate relationships, you will have casual social relationships, and you will eventually become involved in important professional associations. Learning how to communicate a message of confidence and competence will have an impact on how people perceive you. Maximizing relationships does not equate to "using" people or "taking advantage" of their good graces. It refers to ways that you and the people you interact with can enjoy a rewarding experience. Whether the association is a short-term group project or one of enduring intimacy, respect for yourself and others will help you make meaningful connections.

- **How can you benefit from being in energizing relationships?** Think of the people you know. Some of them bring a smile to your face just at the thought of their name. You will gladly spend time with them. The mere thought of some other people, however, may bring you to a cold sweat. You are not sure what it is about these individuals, but every time you are near them you feel tired and lack energy. Perhaps the problem lies with them, or maybe it is due in part to the way in which you react and interact with these people. Why do some people fill our energy fuel tanks, while others seem to siphon our energy for their own uses? This chapter will help you learn to maximize your contact with energizing people and minimize time spent with energy thieves.

- **How can you recognize and manage conflict situations?** Conflict will always be present. It is part of the human drama—but it can be a positive force in your life. The key to dealing with conflict successfully is first to recognize when and why it is happening, and then to have a healthy plan for managing and resolving the conflict. This requires practice, patience, and persistence. This chapter will help you learn to confront and resolve the conflicts in your life.

INTERPERSONAL RELATIONSHIPS: HOW TO "PLAY NICE" WITH OTHER PEOPLE

Who are the "energy vampires" of your life?

Authors of personal success and growth books often write about "toxic" people. Very simply, these people "poison" our lives. This can happen on various levels. Perhaps it is a physically abusive relationship; maybe it is a psychologically demeaning relationship. In whatever manner they come to us, these toxic people seem to take the life right out of our bodies.

In her book *Positive Energy*, Judith Orloff writes of **energy vampires**[2]—people in our lives who are continually draining us of energy. They whine about their lives, berate us for our actions, and monopolize conversations. When they finish with us, *they* feel more energized; *we* feel exhausted, having had our energy zapped.

The metaphor of an "energy vampire"[3] is powerful. After hanging onto us, these people move on and leave us feeling tired and wasted. It could be a roommate, a classmate, an instructor, a friend, a coworker, or even a family member. The experience may be subtle—you are not really sure what happened, but you feel more tired than you did before a particular person talked with you. At other times, however, you can literally feel the energy draining from your body as the person moves closer to you and begins to speak.

Energy vampires do not typically engage in conversations, as that would indicate a two-way exchange. No, the energy vampire typically delivers a monologue about his or her maladies, opinions, or prejudices. The consequence of the encounter reveals itself once they walk away. You feel like you need a nap or even a cold shower to wash away the residual effects of the encounter. In short, these people spray toxins into your environment just as real as if you immersed yourself in a polluted river.

Two cautionary notes must be added to this description. First, as with many things in life, there are shades of gray; not every situation is black or white. Obviously, a friend who comes to you in distress about a traumatic event that just occurred is not the same as the person who *continually* drains energy from your relationship. Second, any encounter is a two-way street. If you continually find yourself in draining relationships, it would be wise to evaluate *your* actions. Do you do something that draws these types of people to you and encourages their behavior?

How to guard against energy leaks

After you identify the source of your energy leak, what can you do to plug the hole? Orloff provides a number of prescriptions—antidotes to the toxin—including redirecting the conversation, setting limits, or simply spending less time with the person. A few of her suggestions are summarized in Table 10.1.

IDENTIFYING THE ENERGY VAMPIRES OF YOUR LIFE

This activity is particularly personal. The intent is not to ridicule or denigrate another person. Rather, it will help you to identify those people in your life who are tiring *on a regular basis.* Only after that has been accomplished can you work to take ownership and remedy the situation.

Think of people in your life who drain your energy on a regular basis. How do you know these people drain your energy? Specifically, what do they do and what emotional or physical reactions do you experience after having encountered these people?

1. What do they do?

_____

_____

2. Emotional consequences for you:

_____

_____

3. Physical consequences for you:

_____

_____

Table 10.1
Patching energy leaks

The cause of the energy leak—what the person does to drain energy from you	How to plug the energy drain—what you can do to minimize or avoid a loss of energy
The person constantly whines and rehashes past events.	Attempt to redirect the conversation.
No solution is really sought—the problems seem to give a purpose to this person's life.	Ask the person to stop rehashing the same scenarios over and over.
Everything constitutes a major crisis.	Try to set limits on the conversation. Take a deep breath.
The person is angry and negative.	When you can, limit your time with this person.
The person blames others for his or her misfortunes.	When you can't walk away from the person, set boundaries of appropriate conversation.
The person dumps problems on you and wants you to "fix" them.	You are responsible for your life—the other person is responsible for his or her life.

Source: From Judith Orloff, *Positive Energy* (New York: Harmony Books, 2004), 288–320. Chapter 9, "The Ninth Prescription: Protect Yourself from Energy Vampires," provides a clear description of nine energy vampires and specific suggestions for countering each one.

Finding "nutritious people" for your life

One way to protect your energy and sanity is to associate with **nutritious people.**[4] These people help to neutralize the poison spewed by the energy vampires. A nutritious person has three main characteristics that stand out:

- When this person sees you, he is genuinely glad to see you. His face brightens with a smile.

- When you speak, this person *listens* to you. She asks questions about what you have said and about what matters to you. She exhibits a genuine interest in what you have to say.

- The nutritious person accepts you as you are. He does not try to make you into someone he would like you to be.

The more nutritious people we have in our lives, the better. It is almost as though we can feel our energy level rising just by seeing their faces.

Politeness: It *is* a virtue

Nutritious people dine on a menu of politeness. They demonstrate considerate behavior, engage in civil discourse, and generally have kind regard for the people they come in contact with. They are not saintly, but they understand how to make people around them feel at ease and appreciated. Even a "free-spirited" person does not have to be rude.

HOW CAN YOU PATCH YOUR ENERGY LEAKS?

Review your answers in Activity 10.1 and then answer the following questions:

1. In the past, when you have been confronted with one of these energy-depleting individuals, what have you done? That is, did you do nothing and just let the situation escalate? Did you argue—and still feel depleted? Did you walk away? Did you do something else?

_____

_____

_____

2. How effective, or ineffective, were your actions?

_____

_____

_____

3. What new strategies might you try the next time you are confronted by an energy vampire?

_____

_____

_____

Consider the following behaviors as minimally accepted standards that will nurture your casual, long-term, and (eventually) business relationships. More than likely you can think of a humorous story involving a breach of any (or all) of these very basic examples of social graces.

Phone Etiquette. Clearly identify yourself when making a phone call— especially if you are leaving a voice mail message. Don't count on your unique voice to be your identifying feature. As with any form of oral communication, speak clearly and to the point. For instance, if a professor retrieves a student voice mail, she needs to know, at the very least, the name, phone number, and message the student has left. It would be a pity to leave a fully detailed message but fail to properly identify yourself. That includes last names. Simply saying, "This is Thomas in your ten o'clock class" will not help much if three young men in that class have the name of Thomas. Speak slowly, clearly, and leave all the basic information pertinent to your message.

E-Mail Etiquette. This topic was addressed initially in chapter 9. Basic netiquette*— especially to professors and prospective employers—expects that e-mails will follow grammatical rules. That includes proper capitalization, punctuation, and sentence structure. E-mail allows virtually instantaneous communication. It does not provide license for sloppy writing. Remember, that when you speak and write you are giving a glimpse of yourself. One other point: Just because an e-mail can be sent in a nanosecond does not mean the receiving person is waiting by the computer to instantly respond to your needs. Be patient. A response might not be forthcoming for a day or two—or more. Just like you, the receiving person has his or her own life and priorities to address.

Group Etiquette. Once again, the simplest and most basic rule to follow is one taught in the earliest years of our lives: "Play nice!" Groups present some very real challenges, but rudeness

---

*As mentioned in chapter 9, *netiquette* refers to the rules of behavior when using the Internet.

ARE YOU AN ENERGY VAMPIRE?

Pause for a moment and reflect on how you interact with other people, then answer the questions below. Ask someone who really knows you well to share his or her perception of your interaction with others. Remember: If you ask someone for honest feedback, be prepared to accept what is said. Do not request information and then argue with the person because you disagree. Consider feedback a wonderful gift.

1. When talking with people, do you continually "replay" your same stories over and over?
   ☐ Yes   ☐ No

2. Do you hold a conversation with people, or do you engage in a self-centered monologue about your life?
   ☐ Yes   ☐ No

3. When someone speaks with you, do you avoid asking meaningful and substantive questions? Do you lack interest in the other person's "stories"?
   ☐ Yes   ☐ No

4. When describing events that have occurred, do you typically describe things as being devastating and particular only to you? That is, do you believe no one could ever experience the hardships that you do?
   ☐ Yes   ☐ No

5. Do you start most of your conversations with "You are never going to believe what happened to me!" (or something similar)?*
   ☐ Yes   ☐ No

6. When in a group, do you always have to be center stage?
   ☐ Yes   ☐ No

7. Do you find your conversation peppered with insults, anger, and attempts to make others look bad?
   ☐ Yes   ☐ No

8. Any *Yes* answers may indicate that you have a tendency to drain energy from others. Think of the mental list you made of people who drained your energy. Do you think *your* name would appear on anyone's list of energy vampires?
   ☐ Yes   ☐ No

9. Based on your answers, what do you plan to do to make sure you do not drain energy from those around you?

   _____

   _____

   _____

*Orloff labels these types of people "drama queens"(*Positive Energy*, 299). And of course you will also find "drama kings."

WHO ARE THE NUTRITIOUS PEOPLE IN YOUR LIFE?

Write the names of three people in your life who you consider to be nutritious. Below each name, write a specific explanation as to why you find this person nutritious.

1. Nutritious person #1: _____

    Why is this person nutritious? _____

    _____

    _____

2. Nutritious person #2: _____

    Why is this person nutritious? _____

    _____

    _____

3. Nutritious person #3: _____

    Why is this person nutritious? _____

    _____

    _____

4. Finally, are *you* a nutritious person? _____

    What do you do that is nutritious for other people?

    _____

    _____

need not be one of them. A golden rule of group interaction is to respect your group members as you would want to be respected yourself. (There will be more on this later in this chapter.)

Residential Hall Etiquette. If you are living in a dormitory setting, no one needs to tell you of the adjustments required. Sharing a room, bathroom, laundry facilities, and dining facilities may have come as quite a shock. This is your home away from home—and it is the home of the other students in the residence hall. Treat it with respect; be mindful that other people will be affected by your behaviors in these close quarters.

Cafeteria Etiquette. Although some students might equate the campus dining hall with a cattle call for poorly prepared food, basic levels of decency still exist. Thanking the cafeteria workers for their help, removing trash from the table, and generally being respectful of other people in the cafeteria costs nothing but enhances the overhaul dining experience for everyone.

Classroom Etiquette. Distractions top the list here. If you arrive late to a class, courtesy dictates that you enter the room quietly. That includes holding the door so it does not slam, finding a seat quickly, and quietly opening your class materials once seated. If you must leave before class finishes, do the above in reverse order: Quietly pack your books, quickly and without fanfare move to the door, and then quietly close the door when you leave. As for cell phones—unless you are a doctor on call at the emergency room or are waiting for a call from your pregnant wife who is about to go into labor—turn your phone off. And sitting at your desk and text messaging your buddy fails on a couple of counts. For one, it is rude to the instructor and those around you. And, secondly, while you are busily keying in a message on your handheld wireless communication device, you have missed important nuggets about the next exam or tonight's homework.

WORKING WITH PEOPLE

The challenges of group work

By the time you find your way to college, you have already been involved in group work on various levels. Whether working on a community project or a school assignment, group work is a common experience for all students. Some groups last for a very brief period of time. For instance, teachers commonly assign students to groups for in-class activities. These groups typically wrestle with a question or problem and then present an answer before the end of class. Other class groups may exist longer. Perhaps the class has been split into two groups that will debate the pros and cons of a current political issue. Each side is responsible for preparation and a presentation. Such an activity would no doubt involve research, planning sessions, and rehearsals.

Groups also help the participants develop communication, collaboration, and conflict resolution skills. They prepare members to handle situations in which a group member fails to live up to his or her part of the group assignment. Most everyone can share one tale of a "nightmare group" that presented one problem after another.

Understanding group dynamics

Whether you work with a group on a short-term classroom assignment or become the member of a sports team for a longer period of time, certain stages of development are present. Merely knowing about these stages will not eliminate all interpersonal problems, but familiarity can help you anticipate what is to come and, consequently, be better prepared for what lies ahead.

Groups present an opportunity for two, three, or more people to share talents and develop a better product than one person could produce. But human behavior can be unpredictable and create some challenges along the way.[5] A common model views group development as a predictable five-stage process:[6]

1. *Forming:* Group members introduce themselves to one another and learn about the task they are to address. Apprehension and anxiety may be present.

2. *Storming:* Conflict typically arises as the members try to find a leader, assign tasks, and agree on rules. Groups can end up splitting up at this early stage.

3. *Norming:* Members become more comfortable and tackle their tasks. Trust may start to develop.

4. *Performing:* This is the productive stage as members work on their assignments.

5. *Adjourning:* The group task is finished and the group ends.

While there is a certain *predictable unpredictability* about groups, the five stages are common to all groupings. Depending on the purpose of the group, the stages may take place over months or years. Or in the case of a short-term group, all five stages may be exhausted in less than an hour.

Forming your own group

At times you may be assigned to a group by the instructor; you have no choice in determining your group members. The instructor may group students randomly or according to some prearranged criterion such as grade distributions. On other occasions you will be able to form your own groups. For instance, a study group forms when a few classmates decide to study for a test together. In such a case there is a desired way to choose the members—and *then there is the college reality*.

In reality, study groups are made up of friends or, if not friends, acquaintances from the same class. The only criterion for group membership, usually, is that the students have the same test, essay, or project to prepare for. Perhaps a student who scores well on exams will be asked to join the group. The members look for friendly faces to provide comfort until the task is completed. Truth be told, this informal "method" of selecting group members can produce the needed results on short-term assignments. The suggestions that follow, however, may maximize the productivity of a study group—especially for a long-term group project. And if you are not part of a study group, you might find yourself a member of the homecoming committee, campus speakers' bureau, or the student government issues committee. Whatever the purpose of the group, when you have the option to choose your own members, consider the following points:[7]

- Size matters. Keep the group a small, workable number.

- One size does not fit all. The team members need to have complementary skills. If you have a four-member team, the ideal composition would be to have a creative person, a facts-based thinking person, an organizer who will be able to pull together all the ideas and research into a logical whole, and a "people" person who has a talent for helping people work together.

- Know why you exist. Early on, agree on a common purpose for the group.

- Disagree. A passionate exchange, in which all speakers and views are respected, can energize a group.

- Accountability is a must. Ensure that all team members have a task—and that they are held accountable to the group for completing the assigned task.

- Don't ignore the **elephant in the corner.** The "elephant" is a metaphor for a problem that is so big that it is impossible to miss. The "corner" indicates the problem is being pushed to the side because no one wants to speak about it. If a problem is big enough that every group member knows it exists, do not ignore it. Address and deal with it before it sabotages your group.

Trust: Building on a shared experience

All successful teams share at least one key component: **trust.** Meaningful and passionate discussion—as opposed to shouting at one another—will be fostered when the members recognize that their main concern is arriving at a reasonable answer and not having to worry if someone in the group will attempt to undermine them with personal attacks and hidden agendas. You can disagree and argue about the issue, but do not make a personal assault on another member.

But many times individuals are thrust together with little or no knowledge of one another. Or perhaps the pieces of information they *do* have do not give an accurate view of each person. How do you come to trust people you don't really know? The simple answer to this complex question is that you must build trust over time. It cannot be built by giving money to people; it cannot be built with glitzy technology; and it cannot be built with motivational pep talks. Trust will be earned when the group members share an experience over a period of time. The experience can be positive, like winning a volleyball championship for the college. Or the trust can come from a harrowing experience, such as surviving a prisoner of war camp with the assistance of a cellmate. The commonality in each of these situations it that the people involved came to rely on one another. They anticipated each other's needs; they supported one another over a long period of time.

ARE YOU REALLY LISTENING, OR JUST TALKING?

The "art" of communication

Effective communication is an art form. One person attempts to consciously construct and pass along thoughts and feelings about a particular subject to another person. This can occur on a one-to-one basis when a friend sends you an e-mail, engages in a face-to-face discussion, or gives you a heartfelt hug. It takes place on a larger scale, as well. *Mass communication* refers to the transmission of information to large numbers (thousands and millions) of people. Examples include the community newspaper, the nightly television news, radio talk shows, and the Internet. When done well, a connection develops between the sender and the receiver. One conveys a message while the other listens (or reads).

WHO DO YOU TRUST—AND WHY?

Take a moment and reflect on those people in your life whom you trust. Your initial thoughts might be of a family member, a church leader, a close friend, or a sports team-mate. For this activity, however, please picture someone you have met *since you have been on campus.* It could be a classmate, a professor, a counselor, a fraternity brother or sorority sister—or anyone else.

1. Write the name of this trusted individual.

    _____

2. Why do you trust this person?

    _____

    _____

    _____

3. Review your answer. Can you point to a common shared experience that led to the forma-tion of this trusted relationship? If so, briefly explain the experience.

    _____

    _____

    _____

Dialogues versus collective monologues

Also, it has been said that communication is a lost art. The thought here is that people have lost the ability to meaningfully exchange ideas with one another. Tune in to a television or radio talk show and chances are great that you will hear *talking*—but *not conversation.* One person talks, another interrupts. The first person interrupts the second person by raising his voice to be heard. Inevitably a shouting match results in a headache for the listener. Just because two people are in the same room and talking *at* one another does not mean that conversation is taking place.

A dialogue presupposes that two people have engaged in a conversation in which one person speaks and the other *listens.* The second person then *appropriately* responds to the first *with comments relevant to the conversation.* The conversation continues, back and forth, one person listening and the other person speaking.

Unfortunately, what passes for conversation most times is not. Think of a recent time when you either observed a group of people talking or you were involved in a conversation with a few friends. Was there true communication? While one person was talking, were the other people qui-etly listening? When the person talking finished her thoughts, did the others respond to those words or did they start talking about something else, not even recognizing the other person had just spoken? Did people continually interrupt one another to get their own opinions into the con-versation? If so, what you experienced was a **collective monologue.** Many people were talking but no one was listening. When one person speaks, without any expectation of an answer from someone else, she is presenting a monologue. Comedians do this. The air vibrates with words but little in the way of communication has taken place.

It is probably safe to say you have engaged in a collective monologue at one time or another. Most times it just passes as typical conversation. At other times it can be frustrating and border on disrespect. As with any action that is repeated often enough, it can become a habit—a bad habit. A person who continually engages in collective monologues will eventually be considered a bore, at the least, and very likely rude or an energy vampire. Although this may be irritating in a social setting, it can prove to be disastrous in a group or professional setting.

Active listening

An antidote to collective monologues is **active listening** (see chapter 8). This requires the listener to pay attention to what the speaker is saying. Active listening cannot be done halfheartedly. It is work. Listening to the actual words as well as verbal clues (tone of voice) and nonverbal clues (posture, for example) requires a degree of focus that you may not typically use in daily conversation. But it is worth it as active listening is one of the three characteristics of nutritious people.

As you read the following characteristics of an active listener, conduct a mental checklist of how you measure up:

© *Image Source Limited*

- *An active listener has to be quiet and focus on the speaker.* It becomes increasingly difficult to listen to another person if you are talking yourself. Quiet your mouth. An old saying reminds us that we have two ears and one mouth, so we should listen twice as much as we talk.

- *The active listener needs to quiet her mind.* If she attends to the chatter in her own mind, she will miss what the speaker is saying.

- *An active listener pays attention to what is said.* In a face-to-face conversation, the active listener maintains eye contact, does not interrupt, and tries to understand what the speaker wants to convey.

- *The active listener lets the speaker know that he is listening.* He nods his head, says "I see" or in some other way indicates that he hears what is being said. The key is to be sincere. Nodding and saying "I understand" while really thinking about what you will be doing tonight is not actively listening—it is preparation for a collective monologue.

- *Active listeners not only hear the words, but "listen" to the body language.* Are there clues in the body position that would help understand the message being delivered?

- *The active listener often asks questions about what the speaker has just said.* The questioning is not meant to be confrontational; rather it is an attempt to make sure the message has not been misunderstood. Such questions indicate interest in the other person's comments.

- *Finally, the active listener will attempt to repeat what she has just heard to make sure the message is understood.* In this way the speaker feels affirmed. The listener does not have to agree with the speaker; she only conveys that she has correctly understood what was said.

AGGRESSIVENESS, ASSERTIVENESS, AND PASSIVENESS

As you have read throughout this chapter, interpersonal relationships present a number of challenges. Not only does *what* you say impact your audience, but also *how* you say it (tone of voice) and how you look (body language) while saying it. Whether speaking to one person or a hundred, communication is the sum total of many interrelated parts.

One key to successful communication is to speak with an air of confidence. A self-assured person will capture attention better than someone stammering for the correct words. Self-confidence will lead to an assertive communication style. To say that one communicates with **assertiveness** means that the person can stand up for herself. The person can face demands and can also make requests in a nonaggressive manner.[8]

Aggressive behavior, on the other hand, represents a harsher attitude. It can border on hostility or a bully-like approach to other people. Bullies take advantage of *passive* individuals—people

ASSERTIVE, AGGRESSIVE, AND PASSIVE BEHAVIORS

Read the short scenario below and then write a description of how you think an assertive, an aggressive, and a passive person would respond.

Eileen has a major biology exam in two days. Although she has been working diligently in this class, it has been a real struggle to maintain a C average. Even though Eileen has only managed a C, her thorough notes are legendary in the class; the notes are organized and capture the main points of each lecture and lab. Earlier today, Brian, a biology classmate, said he would like to borrow Eileen's class notes for the night. He promised he would return them to her in the morning, which would still give her one night to study for the exam. Brian is a pitcher for the baseball team and has missed a few classes due to road trips with the team. Eileen really likes Brian and would like to help him, but she knows that she needs all the time she can to review those notes. What should Eileen do?

1. Describe what you think would be the *passive* response by Eileen.

_____

_____

_____

2. Describe what you think would be the *assertive* response by Eileen.

_____

_____

_____

3. Describe what you think would be the *aggressive* response by Eileen.

_____

_____

_____

4. In this situation, which response do you believe Eileen should use?

_____

_____

_____

5. Briefly explain how this represents the best response for the situation.

_____

_____

_____

who will submit to verbal and, in some cases, nonverbal attacks without resistance. A fine line can separate passive behavior from assertive behavior, or assertive behavior from aggressive behavior. Although every situation presents unique circumstances, generally speaking, assertive behavior is seen as the favored road to travel.

Bullies

Mention the word *bullies* and people tend to think of the elementary school playground. A larger boy seeks out and finds a smaller fellow whom he proceeds to verbally and/or physically abuse. It is an all too common phenomenon that has been around as long as moms and dads have sent their children off to school each morning.

But school-age children do not have a monopoly on bullying behavior. It exists in the workplace—and it exists on college campuses.[9]

Bullying is a power game, although to the victim it is never a game: A *game* indicates a chance to win. Bullies repeatedly seek to control other people by physical or verbal aggression. The main reason for a bully's assault is simply that he or she *can* do it. The victim is seen as easy pickings. Bullying can arise in any situation where one person holds power over another. People can be bullied in the workplace by a coworker or supervisor. A student can be bullied because of his or her sexual orientation. A boyfriend can bully his girlfriend; and a girlfriend can bully her boyfriend. Domestic violence is bullying taken to another, more extreme, level. Faculty can bully students, and students can try to bully faculty. No one is immune.

If you suspect a friend is being bullied—or if you are the victim of a bully—seek assistance as quickly as possible. Find someone you can trust and get help.

Sexual harassment

Sexual harassment is a form of bullying. The U.S. Equal Employment Opportunity Commission (EEOC) broadly defines **sexual harassment** as "a form of sex discrimination that violates Title VII of the Civil Rights Act of 1964."[10] According to the EEOC, sexual harassment can take on many forms, including the following:

- Victims and perpetrators can be either men or women.

- Sexual harassment can occur between same-sex individuals.

- The harasser does not have to be a supervisor. The harassment can come from the actions of a coworker.

- The harassment has to be unwelcome.

- The victim can be the person harassed, or anyone else affected by the offensive conduct.

    Sexual harassment can occur in one of two ways:[11]

- **Quid pro quo.** This Latin expression means "you give me something and I'll give you something in return." For instance, if a supervisor bases a performance evaluation on whether an employee submits to or rejects a sexual advance, **quid pro quo** harassment has occurred.

- **Hostile work environment.** This level of harassment can be created by coworkers as well as supervisors. Requests for sexual favors, telling inappropriate jokes, making offensive remarks, displaying sexually charged photos or cartoons, and cursing can create a hostile environment. A person can claim a **hostile work environment** has been created even if he or she is not the direct target of the harasser's actions.

If you have been victimized by a sexual harasser, take positive action immediately. More than likely the harasser will not decide to desist on his or her own, so let the harasser know that the comments or advances are unwelcome. The possibility also exists that the perpetrator does not realize that the actions are objectionable. Speak with a counselor, professor, classmate, or dean.

SEXUAL HARASSMENT, OR JUST GOOD-NATURED TEASING?

Reflect on and then react to each of the following situations.

Situation #1: On the way to class each day, a young woman first stops in the student center to buy a cup of coffee. The same group of young men is always standing by the doorway. When the young woman walks past them, there is always at least one comment. Either someone states he would love to take her on a date or there is a low whistle and comments about her clothing. She has ignored these men hoping they would tire of the comments if she did not respond. That tactic has not worked and the comments have continued.

1. Explain why this is or is not sexual harassment.

   _____

   _____

   _____

2. What should the young woman do in this case?

   _____

   _____

   _____

Situation #2: Another student in your First-Year Experience class makes you feel uncomfortable. The student has not said anything offensive—but when speaking, this person stands uncomfortably close to you. You have also noticed that when this student looks at you, the look turns to a lecherous stare. You have started coming to class a few minutes late just to avoid any pre-class confrontations with this student.

3. Explain why this is or is not sexual harassment.

   _____

   _____

   _____

4. What should you do in this case?

   _____

   _____

   _____

CONFLICT MANAGEMENT: MANAGING RISKS

Conflict describes a state of disharmony where one set of ideas or values contradicts another. It can range from the fairly minor—a roommate who rises for morning jogs and disturbs your sleep each morning—to the serious—two group members getting into a shouting and shoving match about the group's work. There will be times when you will have to confront conflicts of various degrees of severity.

Are you having a disagreement, or a conflict?

Conflict is not the same as a disagreement. For our purposes, an argument about which college football team should be the national champion does not constitute a conflict. It is a difference of opinion to be sure, but this disagreement does not pit one belief system against another.

Conflict, on the other hand, rears its head when two or more deeply held ideas, values, or perspectives are contradictory.[12] The conflict can be between two or more people—or it can be an internal conflict between your values and your own actions. Think back to the discussion of belief systems and values in chapter 2. Suppose a young man has been reared with a deeply held value that having sexual relations before marriage constitutes a violation of personal integrity. If he finds himself in a situation that now challenges his deeply held beliefs, he will experience a period of conflict as he tries to reconcile the contradictory signals.

Conflict is not always a bad thing

Earlier in this chapter you read about the dynamics of group formation. *Storming* is a real and necessary stage that groups and teams will encounter. Conflict about the exact purpose for the team, who has the best talents to be the leader, and what tasks should be assigned to whom can expose contradictory values and perspectives. One of the *dysfunctions* of teams[13] occurs when passionate debate does *not* take place. So, whereas an absence of conflict may seem to be heavenly, it is an unrealistic goal in most human relationships—and it may even be unhealthy. The required ingredient is a mechanism to discuss why the conflict exists and how it can be managed and resolved.

Any time two or more people come together for any length of time, the risk for conflict presents itself. You do not need to enter every relationship with the dread of impending conflict. But it may be healthy to understand that when it does occur, the conflict itself can produce a positive outcome for you and the other person or people involved.

Ways people deal with conflict

Just as with problem solving (see chapter 5), there are many ways to deal with conflict. If five people are involved in a conflict, there will be probably *at least* five different solutions presented. If ten people are present, there is a good chance you will find at least ten ideas. For this reason, any listing of strategies to manage conflict will be necessarily incomplete. As you read the following strategies[14] and examples, think about how you might handle each situation.

Ignore the Issue. Some people will do anything to avoid a confrontation. They believe that peace at all costs is better than arguments and loud voices. This could lead to a lose-lose situation in which the initial flame of conflict gets worse because it has not been addressed. Eventually the conflict consumes all parties in a blazing inferno of controversy. This can result in ill feelings and resentment.

Example: One member of your group always complains about the project at hand. He drags down your energy each time you are around him. Rather than saying anything to him, your group quietly goes about its work, many times taking on tasks that he was to do. You all hope this person will change his ways or leave the group, but nothing is said or done.

Lock Horns. In this scenario, everyone knows a problem exists but no one willingly changes position. In fact, as the conflict increases people may become more entrenched in their views.

Depending on the severity of the disagreement, this lose-lose situation can bring a relationship or team to a grinding halt.

Example: There are four members in your group. Each believes his or her direction for the group is the best. No one is willing to concede on anything. No work gets done—and the deadline for the group product gets closer.

Give In to the "Demands."
In the interest of peace, once again, one person decides to do whatever the other person wants. This win-lose situation may leave the underlying issue of the conflict unresolved.

Example: Your roommate likes to party late into the night. Unfortunately, her late hours have been interfering with your sleep patterns. Each day you awaken tired. When you talk to your roommate about this, she begins to whine about how you do not appreciate what she does around the apartment. Your early morning routines, she says, have bothered her. She threatens to move out and leave you to pay the entire monthly rent. You give in—and buy some earplugs.

Compromise.
You give a little, the other person gives a little, and the conflict is minimized if not totally resolved. This creates a modified win-win situation, as each person has not been able to achieve all that he or she had hoped for. But for the sake of harmony, a middle course has been agreed upon. Because all situations do not reach the synergy level (see next strategy), sometimes compromise represents a very positive resolution.

Example: Your late-night roommate has agreed to enter the apartment quietly and not turn the television on when he returns after midnight. You agree to be quieter when you arise early each morning for your 8:00 a.m. class.

Synergy.
When two or more people hit upon a solution that actually is better than any of the previous ideas, a synergistic solution has been reached. A win-win situation results. Although highly desirable, this outcome requires considerable effort to achieve.

Example: You and your late-night roommate have discovered that two of your good friends are having the same problem—one is an early riser and one is a night owl. The four of you decide to switch roommates. The two early risers will now live together and the two night owls will room together. All friendships have been maintained; all four are happier than they had been prior to the new arrangement; and you are now able to get a great night's sleep.

CAN YOU THINK OF ANY OTHER APPROACHES TO CONFLICT MANAGEMENT?

10.8 ACTIVITY

1. Once you have read the five ways people address conflict, as presented in this chapter, reflect for a moment and then add any alternative strategies you have used.

   _____

   _____

   _____

   _____

   _____

   _____

SUMMARY

ARE YOU INVOLVED IN NUTRITIOUS RELATIONSHIPS?

Before leaving this chapter, keep the following points in mind:

- Beware of people who constantly drain energy from you—the energy vampires.

- Seek out nutritious people who will help energize you.

- Effective communication is an art form that has no room for collective monologues.

- If you want to be considered a nutritious person, then pay attention to how you work with other people.

- Conflict can be positive when appropriately managed.

tuning your life-strings

the 4 Rs

self

change and personal growth

Your SELF:
Personal growth
and balance

The following activities will allow you to reflect on the three levels of student success as they apply to the major concepts introduced in this chapter. Each activity will give you an opportunity to reflect and apply the chapter concepts in a way that is meaningful to you during this transitional phase of your life.

The 4 Rs

Describe a personal example of how you used each of the 4 Rs in relating to other people.

1. *Reflection* (Example: Perhaps you considered a way to resolve a conflict.)

_____

_____

_____

_____

2. *Respect* (Example: When speaking with a friend, you made a strong effort to ask questions and show an interest in what she was saying.) _____

_____

_____

_____

_____

3. *Responsibility* (Example: Perhaps you took on a leadership role in a class group.) _____

_____

_____

_____

_____

4. *Renewal* (Example: After you successfully resolved a conflict, how did you feel?) _____

_____

_____

_____

_____

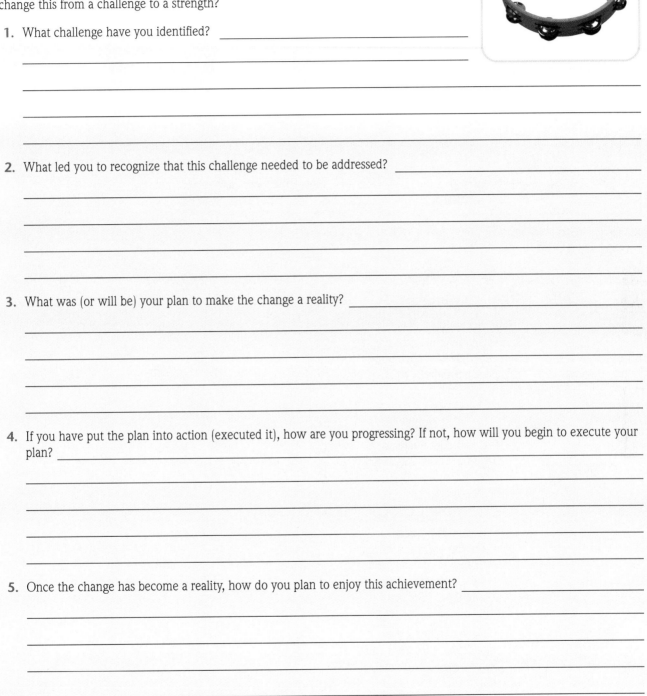

The Change Cycle

Reflect on one of your relationship challenges. What can you do (or have you done) to change this from a challenge to a strength?

1. What challenge have you identified? _____

_____

_____

_____

2. What led you to recognize that this challenge needed to be addressed? _____

_____

_____

_____

3. What was (or will be) your plan to make the change a reality? _____

_____

_____

_____

4. If you have put the plan into action (executed it), how are you progressing? If not, how will you begin to execute your plan? _____

_____

_____

_____

5. Once the change has become a reality, how do you plan to enjoy this achievement? _____

_____

_____

_____

Tuning Your Life-Strings

Before you move on to chapter 11, pause for a moment and reflect on the balance—or lack of balance—in your life at this point in the school term. Use this activity to apply newly acquired information from this chapter to gauge the level of strength in the various facets of your life. You may wish to refer to your responses in previous chapters.

Life-string	Questions to ask yourself	What possible activities could help you tune this string?	Who can help you tune this string?
Social	• How do you work in group situations? • How have you handled recent conflicts?		
Occupational	• When thinking about your possible career interests, how important will it be to have effective interpersonal skills in your area of interest?		
Spiritual	• Have you experienced inner conflict when addressing your spiritual needs?		
Physical	• Are you involved with any team sports activities? • Do you enjoy exercising with another person, or do you prefer to exercise in solitude?		
Intellectual	• Have you had any intellectual discussions that created conflict for you or other people? • Have you read any articles or books that address the issue of relationships or conflict management?		
Emotional	• What strategies have you used to effectively deal with stressful relationships?		

Rhythms of Reflection

To complete this chapter, please reflect on the following words:

> *Assumptions are the termites of relationships.*
>
> –Henry Winkler, actor

Now, using these words for inspiration, explain how you will apply the knowledge you have gained from this chapter about nutritious relationships. Please write your thoughts here.

_____

_____

_____

_____

_____

To further respond online, please go to the *Rhythms of Reflection* module in chapter 10 of the Companion Website.

ENDNOTES

1. Tom Peters, *Reinventing Work: The Brand You 50* (New York: Knopf, 2001), 2–3.
2. Judith Orloff, *Positive Energy* (New York: Harmony Books, 2004), 288–320.
3. The concept has also been referred to as "psychic parasitism." See Bruce Goldberg, "Energy Vampires," http://www.drbrucegoldberg.com/EnergyVampires.htm (accessed January 4, 2006).
4. For a clear review of this concept, see Richard Leider and David Shapiro, *Repacking Your Bags: Lighten Your Load for the Rest of Your Life* (San Francisco: Barrett-Koehler, 1995), chapter 7; and Richard Leider, *The Power of Purpose* (New York: MJF Books, 1997), 64.
5. Patrick Lencioni, *The Five Dysfunctions of a Team* (San Francisco: Jossey-Bass, 2002), vii.
6. Bruce W. Tuckman published "Developmental Sequence in Small Groups" in 1965. At that time he described the phases groups progress through from development to conclusion. His initial research included only the first four stages. In a later article, Tuckman and a colleague added and described the fifth stage. For more information, see Mark K. Smith "Bruce W. Tuckman—Forming, Storming, Norming, and Performing in Groups," *Infed: The Encyclopaedia of Informal Education*, 2005, http://www.infed.org/thinkers/ tuckman.htm (accessed December 26, 2005). Various other sites and books contain descriptions of this often-cited work. Also see "Five Stages of Group Development," George Mason University, Center for Service and Leadership, http://www.gmu.edu/student/csl/5stages.html, for a description of each stage (accessed December 26, 2005).
7. Numerous books address the power of teams. You may find the following helpful: Lencioni, *The Five Dysfunctions of a Team;* John R. Katzenbach and Douglas K. Smith, *The Wisdom of Teams: Creating the High-Performance Organization* (New York: HarperBusiness Essentials, 2003); and Jose Stevens, *The Power Path: The Shaman's Way to Success in Business and Life* (Novato, CA: New World Library, 2002). Also see Carol Carter, Joyce Bishop, and Sarah Lyman Kravits, *Keys to Success*, 5th ed. (Upper Saddle River, NJ: Prentice Hall, 2006), 273–274.
8. Hara Estroff Marano, "Assertive, Not Aggressive," *Psychology Today*, October 14, 2005, http://www.psychologytoday.com/rss/pto-20040206-000009.html (accessed December 29, 2005).

9. For one example, see Catherine Saillant, "A Bulwark Against Bullies," *LATimes.com*, December 5, 2005, http://www.bullybusters.org/press/latimes120505.html (accessed December 29, 2005).

10. "Sexual Harassment," U.S. Equal Employment Opportunity Commission, http://www.eeoc.gov/types/sexual_harassment.html (accessed December 30, 2005).

11. See "Definition," EEOC Notice No. N-915-050, March 19, 1990, http://www.eeoc.gov/policy/docs/currentissues.html (accessed December 30, 2005). For an example of one school's sexual harassment policy, see the University of Massachusetts at Lowell, http://www.uml.edu/equal/sexual_harassment.htm (accessed December 30, 2005).

12. Carter McNamara, "Basics of Conflict Management," 1999, http://www.managementhelp.org/intrpsnl/basics.htm (accessed December 30, 2005).

13. See Lencioni, *The Five Dysfunctions of a Team.*

14. See McNamara, "Basics of Conflict Management."

Personal Integrity
Hitting the Right Notes

REFLECTIVE QUESTIONS

Keeping the following questions in mind will make this chapter more meaningful:

- How do reflection, responsibility, respect, and renewal foster integrity?

- How do values, motivation, and integrity reinforce one another?

- In what ways does a life of integrity strengthen your six dimensions of well-being?

- What can student leaders do to lead with integrity?

- What is the connection between academic integrity, health integrity, and financial integrity?

KEY TERMS

academic integrity
aerobic exercise
binge drinking
credit
eating disorders
habit
integrity
obesity

GUEST SPEAKER

MEET **BILL MARTIN**

Executive Vice Chancellor

River Parishes Community College

Sorrento, Louisiana

The college experience enables a student to develop personal and professional qualities that will be valuable in the workplace and in life. Employers will expect graduates to be critical thinkers and effective communicators. However, they will also seek employees who have integrity. Integrity is not a single virtue but a collection of characteristics like honesty, fairness, and trustworthiness.

My top three suggestions for building integrity:

1. Honesty: Live up to the school's honor code. Employers who are looking for indicators of success in the workplace will examine college transcripts closely.

2. Fairness: Collaborative learning assignments, dormitory environments, and student organizations will provide opportunities to establish mutual agreements. Fairness will be found at the core of most successful mutual agreements, and it is a personal characteristic that will be invaluable in the workplace.

3. Trustworthiness: When accepting assignments, assume individual responsibility for completing tasks in a timely way and be prepared to receive suggestions for improvement. Being an accountable and dependable person will help to build trust among your peers.

INTRODUCTION

Eckhart Tolle begins his book *The Power of Now* with a tale describing the chance meeting of a beggar and a stranger. As the stranger passes by, the beggar, sitting on a box, holds out a hand and asks for some money. The stranger rebuffs the beggar saying, "I have nothing to give you." He then asks the beggar what is in the box on which he is sitting. The beggar says that he does not know, but he is sure there is nothing inside. After a little prodding, the beggar stands, opens the box, and finds the box filled with gold.

Tolle tells his readers: "I am that stranger who has nothing to give you and who is telling you to look inside . . . inside yourself."[1]

You have been asked to "look inside" throughout this book. The power of reflection represents a gift that each one of us can give to ourselves. Drawing on concepts from preceding chapters, you will have the opportunity to reflect once again upon those core values that make you the person you are—those values that drive you.

More specifically, this chapter will examine the concept of integrity and how it relates to your academic pursuits, your health, and your finances.

POINTS TO CONSIDER

- **What can you do to maintain a life of integrity?** Living a life of integrity is a full-time job. There are no shortcuts or cram courses on how to be a person of integrity. The main themes of this book—reflection, responsibility, respect, and renewal—foster integrity. *Reflection* allows you to think about what you have done and what you are about to do. *Responsibility* requires a person to fulfill obligations honestly. *Respect* indicates that you hold yourself and others in high esteem. (It is difficult to violate someone whom we hold in high esteem.) And *renewal* shows a respect for ourselves as we try to rejuvenate our mind, body, and spirit.

- **How can you identify situations that compromise your integrity?** When confronted with a difficult decision, ask yourself, "Can I do that?" If the answer is "No, I cannot do that because it violates my basic value structure," then you have found an issue that threatens your integrity. Listen to your intuition. When you feel, deep in the pit of your stomach, that pursuing a particular course of action would violate your principles, you have identified a situation that has the potential to compromise your integrity.

- **How can you benefit from living a life of integrity?** Chapter 10 introduced the concept of nutritious people. You will remember that these people share three characteristics: They are genuinely glad to see you; they sincerely listen to you; and they are not trying to make you into something they want you to be. You will find people with integrity to be candidates for the "nutritious person" label. Because of their honesty and responsibility, they earn the respect of others. Integrity cannot be faked. The person you are shows in what you do, how you talk, and with whom you associate. Ask yourself, "Would I rather associate with a person of integrity, or one who lacks integrity?"

WHAT IS INTEGRITY AND WHAT DOES IT HAVE TO DO WITH YOU?

Often, architecture will be described in terms of structural integrity. Such a description indicates to what extent the structure is *doing what it is supposed to do.* A bridge that has structural integrity does what it was built to do—provide for safe transportation from one point to

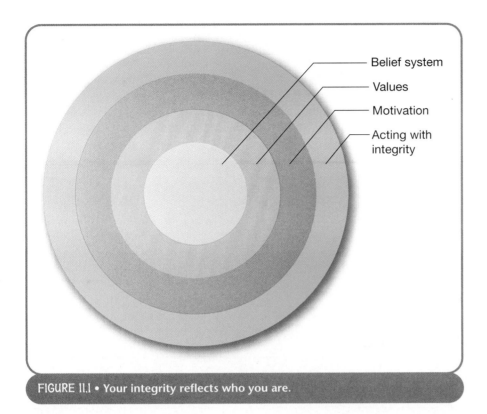

FIGURE 11.1 • Your integrity reflects who you are.

another. Likewise, a tall office building that safely houses its occupants has structural integrity.

A similar description applies to people. Chapter 2 described the connection between belief systems, values, and motivation. Our beliefs and values are at the center of our moral code (see Figure 11.1). They guide us—motivate us—to act with integrity, to do what is right and avoid what violates our code. We do what we are supposed to do.

Honesty, responsibility, and respect

Integrity, in its broadest sense, means conducting oneself in an honest, responsible, and respectful fashion. If you say you will do something, you do it. When something goes wrong, you admit your errors. Your actions show respect for yourself as well as for those around you. Integrity describes "what one has when one firmly adheres to and identifies with virtues for the right reasons and when no one is looking."[2]

In reality, a good argument can be made that only one type of integrity exists—personal integrity. Everything else (health, financial, and academic)* falls under that umbrella concept (see Figure 11.2). But because each category has particular issues that directly affect how and why we do what we do, they will be considered separately here.

Integrity of body, mind, and spirit

Chapter 1 posed the following question: How do you develop and practice a healthy lifestyle in your new school environment? You then examined a six-dimensional wellness model that represented broad aspects of your life.

---

*This division can be extended. For instance, "occupational integrity" can be added to address actions in the workplace.

ACTIVITY 11.1

For the purpose of this activity, consider the following situation: Your psychology class just completed a discussion on the topic of integrity. At the conclusion of class, you leave to go to an appointment. Three people remain in the classroom talking about the day's lesson and how they can apply the concept of integrity to the class. One is your best friend, one is your professor, and one is a classmate who only sees you twice a week in class. As you leave the room, you hear their discussion and a question comes to mind: "Do these people think I have integrity?"

1. What would your best friend say? _____

_____

2. Why would he or she say this? _____

_____

_____

3. What would your professor say? _____

_____

4. Why would he or she say this? _____

_____

_____

5. What would your classmate say? _____

_____

6. Why would he or she say this? _____

_____

_____

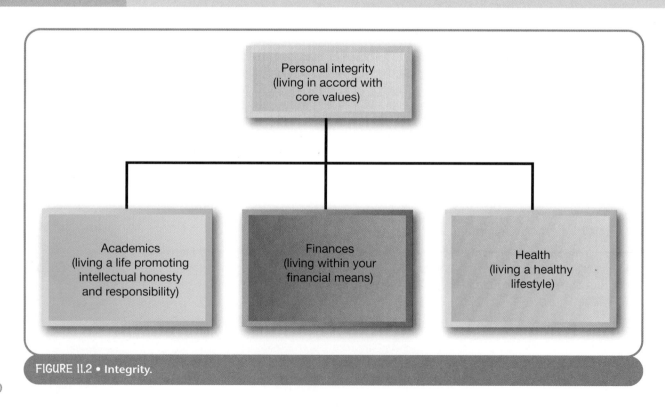

FIGURE 11.2 • Integrity.

The life-strings need to be strong in order to withstand the various stresses and pressures of life. In reality, when you develop and practice a healthy lifestyle, you act with integrity. Each of your six life-strings will become stronger when you act honestly, responsibly, and respectfully within each dimension. Table 11.1 charts this relationship.

Table 11.1 Connection between integrity and the dimensions of well-being	
Dimension of your well-being (Life-string)	Connection to your integrity
Social	You respectfully enter—and maintain—relationships. You speak with honesty when talking with or about other people. You do not put yourself or another person in foolish, risky situations.
Occupational	On the job (or in the classroom) you take care of your responsibilities in an honest fashion. You are honest with yourself about why you do what you do for work. You do not use other's resources (without their permission) for your own gain.
Spiritual	You respectfully attempt to understand differing spiritual beliefs. You seek to live your life according to a higher purpose.
Physical	You treat your body with respect. You follow a responsible diet and exercise regimen.
Intellectual	You do not engage in acts of academic dishonesty. You continuously feed your mind with responsible, thought-provoking material. You respectfully listen to and discuss differing points of view.
Emotional	You find healthy and responsible ways to handle stressful situations. You are respectful of your emotional needs as well as the needs of those around you. You understand how your emotional well-being has impact on other dimensions of your life.

ACADEMIC INTEGRITY

Chapter 7 examined academic integrity at length. Because this concept represents a critical component of education, it will be reviewed briefly once again. (You may find it helpful to review the appropriate pages and activities in chapter 7.)

In a straightforward definition, the Center for Academic Integrity (CAI) defines **academic integrity** as "a commitment, even in the face of adversity, to five fundamental values: honesty, trust, fairness, respect, and responsibility. From these values flow principles of behavior that enable academic communities to translate ideals to action."[3] The CAI published a pamphlet titled *The Fundamental Values of Academic Integrity,* which elaborates on this definition and can be summarized as follows:[4]

- *Honesty* is required in the classroom, the library, or on the playing field; is required of students and faculty; is a key component of "lifelong integrity."

- *Trust* is fostered by honest relationships; trust fosters collaboration and eliminates the fear of intellectual theft.

- *Fairness* requires that clear standards are present and equally enforced.

- *Respect* includes listening to other points of view, contributing to discussions, and properly citing sources of ideas and words.

- *Responsibility* demands honesty in one's actions and "discouraging and/or preventing dishonesty by others."

An educational community cannot long exist if these fundamental values are violated.

HEALTH INTEGRITY

Healthy living

Health is one of those topics where words do not necessarily match actions.* People *talk* about following a regular exercise program, or reducing their intake of junk food, or getting more sleep. But the challenge comes when the talk must be put into *regular action.* Quite a gap exists for most people.

How many times have you heard the following (or something close)?

- On your way to class one day, your friend complains about being out of shape and says he is determined to do something about it. As he is telling you this, he pushes the elevator button so he does not have to walk up a flight of stairs.

- Your roommate says she looks fat in last year's bathing suit. She vows to start watching her diet—*after* she finishes the bag of potato chips cradled in her arms.

- Sam has not been getting much sleep lately—and his performance on the baseball team has suffered. He planned on getting a good night's sleep tonight—but his friends just called and told him about a party. He went—and promised to start better habits *tomorrow.*

Living a healthy lifestyle requires the development of healthy habits. When you have a **habit,** it is something you cannot help but do. It has become second nature. If you have started every morning of the last five years drinking a can of caffeinated soda or a cup of coffee with your breakfast, it has become a habit. You feel as though you cannot function without that drink in your hands. The same goes for tobacco users. They wake up and reach for a smoke. Or perhaps each time you go to a movie, you just have to have a large tub of buttered popcorn. After all, what is a movie without popcorn and a soda!

---

*The information provided in this section of the chapter should not be considered medical advice or a substitute for the care of a health care provider. Always seek appropriate medical care, counseling, and treatment as needed.

"All right, I agree," you may say. "But what is the connection between health and integrity? I understand about personal integrity and academic integrity—but *health* integrity?"

The definition earlier in this chapter recognized that integrity requires honesty, responsibility, and respect. Can you think of three more important concepts when talking about the condition in which you maintain your body? If someone or something is treated honestly, responsibly, and respectfully, the integrity of that person or thing is enhanced. If you abuse your body, you are not treating it with integrity.

© BananaStock Ltd.

Diet

One of the key strategies to minimize weight gain—and probably the simplest to comprehend—is to balance your caloric intake with caloric expenditure. More intake than expenditure, on a regular basis, will eventually lead to fat. Likewise, if a person regularly does not consume enough calories to fuel activity, other problems, such as eating disorders, can develop.

But It Is So Hard to Eat Healthy Foods! Various factors make it difficult to avoid junk food. It is usually easy to find; the price can be very inexpensive; there is minimal work, if any, to prepare it; and it tastes so good!

OBESITY PREVENTION

Partner with a classmate and brainstorm what can be done about the problem of obesity in the United States. Is society to blame—or does the problem belong solely to the obese individual? Come up with at least five solutions and then identify which solution you believe to be the most practical solution.

1. _____

_____

2. _____

_____

3. _____

_____

4. _____

_____

5. _____

_____

ACTIVITY 11.2

THE CALORIE COUNTER

Budgets are useful tools to determine how we use a particular resource. A time management budget, for instance, will help you keep track of how your time is used (and possibly misused). A money budget allows you to see how much money is earned, spent, and saved. Once the facts of the budget are known, then it becomes easier to determine ways to improve the use of that particular resource.

For this activity, you will keep track of your "calorie budget" for seven days. You may wish to keep a small pad with you to record the information throughout the day and then transfer the information to this worksheet at the end of the day. For this to be meaningful, you must list *everything* you eat. Whether it is a full meal, a small bag of pretzels, a can of soda, or a piece of candy, write it down.

1. Using your information literacy skills, find a credible resource that will provide you with information about the *appropriate healthy caloric intake* for a person of your age, gender, and height.[11] You may see this referred to as the *required daily allowance* (RDA).

2. Write your healthy target calorie budget for a twenty-four-hour period here:

   _____

3. Find a site that provides information about the calories contained in various food items.[12]

Sometimes all of the advice about what to eat or not to eat can become quite confusing.* It does not need to be. Let's try to demystify the process of how to eat in a more healthy way:[5]

- Limit fat intake.
- Limit cholesterol intake.
- Eat whole grains.
- Avoid simple sugars and foods with lots of sugar. Sugar provides "empty" calories and may negatively impact your dental health and cause weight gain.[6]
- Eat vegetables.
- Limit your sodium intake.
- Limit alcohol intake.

Obesity. In recent years, **obesity** has become a national wellness issue. When one considers that *less than half* of the United States population is of a healthy weight,[7] it can be safely said that obesity has become an American health crisis. Since 1991, the incidence of American adults who are overweight or obese has significantly increased. In 1991, four states had obesity rates between 15 and 19 percent. (No state was above 19 percent.) In 2004, seven states had obesity rates of 15 to 19 percent; thirty-three had rates of 20 to 24 percent; and nine had rates greater than 25 percent (no data for one state).[8]

How can a wealthy nation like the United States end up with nearly 64 percent[9] of its adult population either overweight or obese? Some say it is precisely because of the lifestyle we lead.[10] Junk food is readily available (and widely marketed). Cars and elevators replace bicycles and walking. Video games and big-screen televisions substitute for participation in physical activity. And although genetics and medications may have an impact on weight gain, other controllable factors such as method of food preparation (frying), size of portions (all-you-can-eat), and lack of self-discipline can also contribute to obesity.

---

*These basic guidelines are offered here for informational purposes. A person should develop a diet that is geared to his or her needs and in conjunction with his or her own doctor's medical advice.

4. Enter your food choices in the chart below for one full week.

Food eaten	# of calories	Mon.	Tues.	Wed.	Thurs.	Fri.	Sat.	Sun.	Total
Totals for the day and the week									

5. What conclusions and insights did you gain from this activity?

_____

_____

_____

6. What steps do you need to take in order to achieve (or maintain) a healthy caloric intake?

_____

_____

_____

_____

Eating Disorders. On the other end of the spectrum from obesity are **eating disorders** that result in unhealthy—and even fatal—weight loss. Approximately 26 million Americans suffer from eating disorders.[13] The National Eating Disorders Association (NEDA) says, "Eating disorders are illnesses with a biological basis modified and influenced by emotional and cultural factors."[14] In other words, the causes of eating disorders go beyond mere individual willpower. While choice remains an important component in avoiding or curing a disorder, psychological and societal factors play a crucial role as well. Anorexia nervosa and bulimia nervosa are two disorders that are frequently discussed:

- **Anorexia nervosa.** People with this serious disorder are most often female, but males can suffer as well. They have an extreme aversion to weight gain—and perceive themselves as fat, overweight, or obese when, in reality, they are severely below normal weight. This serious disorder can be fatal.

- **Bulimia nervosa.** This potentially fatal disorder mixes frequent periods of binge eating with self-induced vomiting or the use of laxatives and fasting to purge the food from the body. Like the anorexic person, the bulimic person is fanatically concerned about body image.

For a more complete listing, visit the NEDA's Web site. If you or a friend suffer from an eating disorder, seek assistance immediately. A first stop might be a campus counselor or wellness center.

Tobacco

The dangers of tobacco have been chronicled in a variety of sources for decades. According to the American Lung Association, more than 430,000 Americans die each year due to "smoking-related diseases."[15] In addition to cost factors and health issues, it is becoming increasingly difficult for smokers to find public places where they can light up their cigarettes legally. Because secondhand smoke can also be harmful, more and more states have passed laws limiting where people can smoke. Some employers refuse to hire smokers—and even go so far as to fire workers—who smoke on *or* off the job.[16]

If you use tobacco products and have decided that the time has arrived to quit the habit, organizations and programs exist to help you. The federal government, for instance, has developed the Web site Smokefree.gov[17] to assist with tobacco cessation.

Once you have made the decision to quit, the acronym START[18] will remind you of the necessary preparation to actually quit:

S = *Set* a date to quit.

T = *Tell* a friend (someone who can be supportive).

A = *Anticipate* challenges and cravings.

R = *Remove* all tobacco-related items from your home, car, backpack, or any other place they might serve as a temptation.

T = *Talk* to your doctor for advice on quitting.

Quitting any habit can be difficult, but attempting to kick a nicotine habit has additional challenges. The critical period is the first three months. During that time old "triggers" will prove tempting[19] If you used to smoke a cigarette each morning with a cup of coffee, breakfast will be a trigger time. If you used to meet friends who smoked between classes, you may have to alter your routine. If you fail on your first attempt, don't beat yourself up. You will be that much stronger and well prepared for your next attempt. It *will* be difficult, but your will power and a strong support system can help you move to a tobacco-free lifestyle.

Alcohol—binge drinking

The National Institute on Alcohol Abuse and Alcoholism defines **binge drinking** as consuming four or five drinks in a row.[20] The number of binge drinkers has continued to increase on college campuses and the harmful effects of such behavior have not diminished. Binge drinkers, and those around them, suffer from physical and behavioral side effects. Besides the obvious symptoms of loss of consciousness, vomiting, and irregular breathing, secondary effects also have a negative impact.

It is not unusual for binge drinkers to use abusive language, engage in physical altercations, drive while intoxicated, and/or interfere with the study habits of nondrinkers. One study found that 26 percent of women experienced "an unwanted sexual advance"[21] because of binge drinking. Considering the impact that alcohol abuse also has upon class attendance, homework completion, and GPA, it is small wonder that "159,000 of today's first-year college students will drop out of school next year for alcohol- or other drug-related reasons."[22] Now, that is a *sobering* statistic.

If you or a friend has an alcohol problem, seek help immediately. Whether you talk with a counselor, residence hall assistant, clergyman, or family member, find someone who can direct you to the appropriate services.

Exercise

The American Heart Association reports that the leading cause of death in the United States is cardiovascular disease (CVD). Thirty-eight percent of all deaths have been attributed to CVD. And the leading cause of heart problems (as well as other health problems) is physical inactivity.[23]

Moderate cardiovascular activity of just thirty minutes per day can help reduce heart disease, lower cholesterol, control blood pressure, and relieve stress. Daily exercise will also enhance sound and restful sleep at night. There is no guarantee that physical activity will *prevent* health problems, but research indicates that even moderate levels of activity produce beneficial results.[24] As with any type of physical activity, of course, you should first seek medical advice to determine what is best for your age and personal health history.

As you develop your own personal physical program, consider a regimen that includes some activity from each of the following three categories:[25]

- **Aerobic exercise.** Typically **aerobic exercise** is defined as activity that increases your heart and breathing rates, as well as works your muscles. The American Diabetes Association suggests a total of thirty minutes per day for five days per week. Depending on your current level of physical conditioning, you may need to begin at five or ten minutes a day and then increase that as your body acclimates to this exertion. Swimming, kick boxing, biking, and jogging are examples of aerobic activity.

- **Strength or resistance training.** Whether it is Pilates, weight lifting, or yoga, when done appropriately a couple of times per week this form of activity helps to strengthen muscles and bones. If you have access to a gym, a staff member may be able to help orientate you to the equipment and provide some safety information about its use.

- **Flexibility training.** Injury can occur when muscles are not sufficiently warmed up and stretched. Flexibility training will not only reduce the possibility of injury, but it will also keep your muscles and joints flexible. Whether you engage in simple gentle stretching or take part in a more vigorous yoga practice, flexibility training limbers the muscles and quiets the mind.

A well-rounded and complete physical conditioning program will take time, but it will be time well invested to maintain the only body and mind you have. And remember, physical conditioning does not just occur in the gym or the athletic field. Incorporate it into your everyday life. When feasible, use the stairs instead of the elevator; park a little further from the door; walk or bicycle instead of driving; walk across campus between classes.

Managing the health risks of sexual activity

Years ago the term *VD* (venereal disease) was used to describe diseases passed on as a result of sexual activity. VD then became known as *STDs*—sexually transmitted diseases. Today, the commonly used label has become *STIs*—sexually transmitted infections. More than thirteen million men and women in the United States are infected with at least one of the more than twenty sexually transmitted infections. And nearly two-thirds of these infections occur in people *younger than twenty-five years of age.* Additionally, the incidence of STIs has been increasing due to personal choice and various societal factors including sexual activity at a younger age, the increasing divorce rate, and increasing incidence of multiple sex partners.[26]

At one time the main concern of unprotected sex was an unplanned pregnancy. Today, as the statistics just cited indicate, the stakes have increased. Perhaps you are sexually active now or are thinking of being sexually active. Maybe you are practicing the safe and sure method of "Just say

NO!"—but you have a friend who is active. Whatever situation you find yourself in, it will be wise to be aware of some of the many physical and emotional consequences of sexual activity in today's society. Table 11.2 lists some of the more prevalent sexual infections and diseases, along with a very brief description. Although abstinence is the surest way to prevent the spread or contraction of STIs, if you are sexually active seek competent medical advice to better protect you and your partner. If you, a family member, or a friend have contracted one of the diseases listed in the table—or any other STI—seek medical care as soon as possible. Your health care provider can also provide counseling concerning prevention of STIs.

Table 11.2
Sexually transmitted infections

Name of the infection or disease	Brief description
Chlamydia	Is one of the most common bacterial STIs in the United States. Can infect the reproductive organs and cause infertility in women *and* men. May lack any noticeable symptoms.
Genital herpes	Can infect the mouth as well as the genital areas. Symptoms are referred to as "outbreaks." Is not usually associated with serious health problems, although serious injury can occur to a baby born with herpes. Herpes sores can pass along the HIV virus.
Gonorrhea	Highest rates of infection are in women aged 15–19 and men 20–24. Women can develop pelvic inflammatory disease (PID); men can experience symptoms of pain and pus in the genital area. Infection with gonorrhea increases the chances of contracting HIV.
Human papillomavirus (HPV) and genital warts	HPV is estimated to be the most prevalent STI in the United States. Some types of HPV cause genital warts—raised bumps in the genital regions. Very contagious and spread by skin-to-skin contact. "Some types of HPV can cause cervical cancer . . . [but] most do not progress to cervical cancer." May cause problems during pregnancy.
HIV/AIDS	The human immunodeficiency virus (HIV) causes AIDS (acquired immunodeficiency syndrome). HIV compromises the body's ability to fight infection. AIDS is the last stage of HIV infection. HIV can be spread by sexual contact, sharing needles, and contact with blood. Early detection can help to "slow the decline of immune system function."

Table II.2 (continued)	
Name of the infection or disease	**Brief description**
Syphilis	Increases the likelihood of contracting or spreading HIV. The late stages of syphilis are potentially the most dangerous. Can cause miscarriages and birth deformities, as well as affect the brain.
Vaginitis due to vaginal infections	Three common forms: bacterial vaginosis, trichomoniasis, and vaginal yeast infection. "Scientific studies suggest that trichomoniasis is associated with at least a 3- to 5-fold increased risk of HIV transmission." May lead to low birth weight.

Sources: Adapted from "Sexually Transmitted Infections," December 29, 2005, National Institutes of Health, Division of Microbiology and Infectious Diseases, http://www.niaid.nih.gov/dmid/stds/#intro (accessed January 15, 2006). This site provides detailed information about symptoms, diagnosis, treatment and complications. Information about HIV/AIDS is adapted from "Introduction to Sexually Transmitted Diseases," 2006, myDNA.com, http://www.mydna.com/health/sexual/std/o/intro.html; and "Sexually Transmitted Diseases Treatment Guidelines 2002," Centers for Disease Control and Prevention, http://www.cdc.gov/std/treatment/1-2002TG.htm#HIVInfectionDetectionCounseling&Referral (both accessed January 15, 2006).

FINANCIAL INTEGRITY: MONEY MANAGEMENT

If not managed effectively, you can find yourself at the end of your money long before the end of your month arrives. Financial integrity requires that you honestly assess financial needs, responsibly adhere to a realistic budget, and respectfully take care of your financial obligations.

Credit: Buy now, pay later

Many students receive financial aid in the form of loans and/or scholarships. These loans are a double-edged sword: They provide the needed money to attend college, *but* they also represent debt that must be repaid upon graduation. In essence, with every college loan you acquire, you add to the post-college debt you will need to repay. The loans are an opportunity cost of attending college. Upon graduation, students will take their diplomas *and* their debt with them. In addition to the credit history that college years begin to establish, the ways in which you handle that debt after graduation (pay off timely versus default) reflects your integrity as a person. This will stay with you far beyond your graduation day.

For instance, soon after college graduation you may decide to finance a new automobile. The financial institution considering your loan application will rate you as a potential client on *character* (your

© Corbis

credit history), *capital* (your assets that can be used as collateral), and *capacity* (your ability to handle the added debt based on your current income, debt, and expenses). Character speaks to your integrity.

Of course, your student loans are only one part of the debt equation. If you don't yet have a credit card, be prepared for a deluge of card offers to flood your mailbox. Go to a campus sporting event and more than likely you will find representatives at a credit card table willing to give you a free T-shirt if you sign up for a credit card. When you buy clothes at the mall, you will be asked by cashiers if you would like to apply for a store credit card. "Sign up now and we'll automatically deduct 5 percent from your bill today!" may be a pitch you will hear. Yes, the big "C"—**credit**—is everywhere. It can be quite enticing and intoxicating.

Credit cards, when managed well by a self-disciplined individual, can be beneficial. Unfortunately, too often the cards are mismanaged. In a study by the Nellie Mae Education Foundation, 83 percent of all college students in the United States have at least one credit card. More than 20 percent of these cardholders maintain a credit card debt burden between $3,000 and $7,000[27]—and they do not have full-time paychecks with which to pay the debt. People who otherwise have sound common sense seem to lose their bearings once they receive one or more credit cards with their names imprinted on the front of each card.

It might be sobering—*before* you purchase an item on credit—to do a quick calculation of exactly how much the purchase will cost if payments are stretched over a period of time. At least one major credit card Web site provides a service to calculate your payments. Enter the purchase price, the interest rate charged by the card, and the minimum payment you want to make, and the total payment will be calculated.[28]

> *Example:* **You found a great deal on a new laptop. It has everything you want for just $800. You decide to buy it and pay $50 per month. If the credit card rate is 18 percent, how long will it take you to pay off this debt?**
>
> *Answer:* **It will take more than one-and-a-half years to pay off the computer. Interest charges will cost you about $120. (Keep in mind, there is a very good chance your computer will be outdated before you have paid it off.)**
>
> *Example:* **You got another great deal on a new credit card offered on campus. The interest rate is only 15.9 percent and you can make minimum monthly payments of just $25 per month. You receive the card just in time for Spring Break.[29] Some friends have found a great travel package that includes airfare, hotel, meals, and a concert ticket for only $1,500. It's your first year in college, and you have always heard how great these vacations are. You start packing your bags. How long will it take you to pay off this trip if you make the minimum payment of $25 per month?**
>
> *Answer:* **You will finally pay the trip off *ten years later* and it will have cost you, with finance charges, more than $3,000! Think about that. With a minimum payment, you will be paying for that first-year college vacation not only during your sophomore, junior, and senior years, but you will continue to pay for this trip for seven years *after* you have graduated. Now, that's one way to remember a trip well after you have returned!**

Protecting your credit history

Your credit history stays with you for life. Late payments or nonpayment of loans will have an adverse effect when you try to borrow money, finance an automobile, or mortgage a home. A poor credit history may even have a negative impact when you seek employment. The first way to protect your credit history is to avoid reckless spending habits. If you do incur a debt, paying your obligations in a timely manner will reflect well on your character in the future.

Three consumer reporting companies—Equifax, Experian, and TransUnion—have been mandated by the federal government to provide a free copy of your credit report, at your request, once every twelve months. Additional information may be found at the Federal Trade Commission's Web site *http://www.ftc.gov/bcp/conline/pubs/credit/freereports.htm*, or you may call 1-877-322-8228.

TIPS FOR AVOIDING CREDIT CARD DEBT

The reality is that most college students will plunge into the world of credit card debt. Credit cards can be beneficial *if* you know how to use them responsibly—and for some students that is a very big *if.* Suggestions to manage, if not totally avoid, credit card debt include the following:

1. Keep only one credit card with a small limit.

2. Use the card only for emergency purposes. A trip to the emergency room is an emergency; a late-night pizza party is not.

3. Depend on yourself to pay the balance—not your parents, uncle, or grandmother.

4. Know what you earn. If your job in the campus bookstore pays $7 per hour and you work 10 hours per week, you have $70 (minus taxes) coming at the end of the week. If you spend $200 on a weekend road trip, are you prepared to work for (at least) an entire month to pay for this excursion? One rule of thumb is to keep your monthly debt to 10 percent or less of your net (after taxes) monthly income. If your monthly net income from the bookstore amounts to $160, then your total loan and credit payments should be no more than $16 for the month.[30] That can be a sobering calculation.

5. Establish a budget and stick to it.

6. Use a debit card for purchases. A credit card extends *credit.* A debit card only works if cash is available in your account; no money, no purchase. One money management/debt counseling author proposes that people should have a "plasectomy." That is, cancel your credit cards and cut them up—never to be used again.*

7. Now, brainstorm other suggestions to manage or avoid credit card debt and write your ideas here.

_____

_____

_____

_____

_____

_____

_____

_____

_____

_____

_____

_____

_____

*Dave Ramsey writes and speaks about the dangers of credit cards. Take a look at his online store and you will notice that he only accepts debit cards. See "Dave's Store," http://www.daveramsey.com/shop/Debit_Card_Policy_W8.cfm.

BUDGET WORKSHEET

Before you spend your money, it would be wise to know how much you have to spend. A budget keeps tract of financial income and financial obligations. Sometimes people may have great intentions, but by the end of the week or the end of the month they just cannot figure out where their money has gone. Just like keeping track of time or caloric intake, a financial budget can help you "discover" where the money is going.

This activity includes two different tables. The first one asks for your monthly budget. The second will ask you to track your spending for one week.

Monthly Budget

Income items	$	Expenditure items	$
Primary employment		Tuition	
Other employment		Books	
Interest from bank accounts		Food	
Investments		Housing	
Spouse's income		Transportation: Bus fare	
Roommate's contributions		Transportation (car): Gas, insurance, repairs	
Parents' contributions		Clothes	
Loans		Phone	
Scholarships		Internet connection	
Other		Personal hygiene items	
Other		Haircuts	
Other		Medications	
Other		Recreation	
Other		Child care	
Other		Other	
Other		Other	
Other		Other	
Other		Other	
Other		Other	
Total income	**$**	**Total expenditures**	**$**

Total income: $ _____

Total expenditure: $ _____

Surplus or debt: $ _____

1. If you have a surplus at the end of the month, congratulations! How do you plan to wisely use or invest this money?

_____

_____

2. If you have a deficit (debt) at the end of the month, what responsible strategies can you use to erase the debt and regain financial integrity?

_____

_____

Weekly Accounting of Expenditures

As with most tasks of this nature, this is a time-consuming task—but one that can provide clarity as to how you are spending money, where you can eliminate spending, and how to increase your savings at the end of each week.

For each day, enter *everything* on which you spent money for that day. Whether it was gas for your car, lunch with a friend, a concert with a date, or just a bag of pretzels, enter the item and the amount you spent.

Mon.	Tues.	Wed.	Thurs.	Fri.	Sat.	Sun.
Total for the day: ___	**Total for the day:** ___	**Total for the day:** ___	**Total for the day:** ___	**Total for the day:** ___	**Total for the day:** ___	**Total for the day:** ___

3. How much did you spend for the entire week? _____

4. At the end of the week, reflect on your spending habits. What surprised you? Can you see any areas of waste?

_____

_____

_____

SUMMARY

LIVING A LIFE OF HONESTY, RESPONSIBILITY, AND RESPECT

Before leaving this chapter, keep the following points in mind:

- Integrity, in its broadest sense, means conducting oneself in an *honest, responsible, and respectful* fashion.

- Each of your life-strings will become stronger when you act honestly, responsibly, and respectfully within each dimension.

- An educational community cannot long exist if the fundamental values of academic integrity are violated.

- If you abuse your body, you are not treating it with integrity.

- Financial integrity requires that you honestly assess financial needs, responsibly adhere to a realistic budget, and respectfully take care of your financial obligations.

tuning your life-strings

the 4 Rs

self

change and personal growth

Your SELF:
Personal growth
and balance

The following activities will allow you to reflect on the three levels of student success as they apply to the major concepts introduced in this chapter. Each activity will give you an opportunity to reflect and apply the chapter concepts in a way that is meaningful to you during this transitional phase of your life. Use this opportunity to apply newly acquired information and also keep an ongoing journal of growth in the various facets of your life.

The 4 Rs

Describe a personal example of how you used each of the 4 Rs to enhance or maintain your level of integrity.

1. *Reflection* (Example: Did you recently have to consider an act that violated one of your core values?) _____

_____
_____
_____
_____
_____

2. *Respect* (Example: What have you recently done that reflected respect for one of the dimensions of your life?)

_____
_____
_____
_____
_____

3. *Responsibility* (Example: What have you done that involved taking responsibility for one of your actions?)

_____
_____
_____
_____
_____

4. *Renewal* (Example: How has living a life of integrity helped you to grow as a person?) _____

_____
_____
_____
_____
_____

The Change Cycle

Reflect on one of your challenges with integrity. What can you do (or have you done) to change this from a challenge to a strength?

1. What challenge have you identified? _____

_____

_____

_____

2. What led you to recognize that this challenge needed to be addressed? _____

_____

_____

_____

3. What was (or will be) your plan to make the change a reality? _____

_____

_____

_____

_____

4. If you have put the plan into action (executed it), how are you progressing? If not, how will you begin to execute your plan? _____

_____

_____

_____

_____

5. Once the change has become a reality, how do you plan to enjoy this achievement? _____

_____

_____

_____

_____

Tuning Your Life-Strings

Pause for a moment and reflect on the balance—or lack of balance—in your life at this point in the school term. Use this activity to apply newly acquired information from this chapter to gauge the level of strength in the various facets of your life. You may wish to refer to your responses in previous chapters.

Life-string	Questions to ask yourself	What possible activities could help you tune this string?	Who can help you tune this string?
Social	• Have you respectfully entered—and maintained—relationships? • Have you spoken with honesty when talking with or about other people?		
Occupational	• On the job (or in the classroom) have you taken care of your responsibilities in an honest fashion?		
Spiritual	• In what ways do your spiritual beliefs foster integrity?		
Physical	• Do you treat your body with respect? • Do you monitor your stamina and know when you are about to overextend yourself?		
Intellectual	• Do you continuously feed your mind with responsible thought-provoking material?		
Emotional	• Are you respectful of your own emotional needs as well as the needs of those around you?		

Rhythms of Reflection

To complete this chapter, please reflect on the following words:

> *"If the work we do lacks integrity for us, then we, the work, and the people we do it with will suffer."*
>
> –Parker Palmer, author of The Courage to Teach

Now, using these words for inspiration, explain how you will apply the information you have worked with in this chapter. Please write your thoughts here.

_____

_____

_____

_____

_____

To further respond online, please go to the *Rhythms of Reflection* module in chapter 11 of the Companion Website.

ENDNOTES

1. Eckhart Tolle, *The Power of Now* (Novato, CA: New World Library, 1999), 9.
2. Don Trent Jacobs and Jessica Jacobs-Spencer, *Teaching Virtues: Building Character Across the Curriculum* (Lanham, MD: Scarecrow Press, 2001), 39. Jacobs and Spencer maintain that the concept of *virtue* applies to those actions that make the world a better place.
3. "The Fundamental Values of Academic Integrity," October 1999, 4, Center for Academic Integrity, http://www.academicintegrity.org/pdf/FVProject.pdf (accessed January 8, 2006).
4. "The Fundamental Values of Academic Integrity," 5–10.
5. Perhaps your school has a campus newsletter that addresses wellness topics such as diet, exercise, and rest. This list is adapted from the "Foundations of Wellness: 14 Keys to a Healthy Diet," *Wellness Letter.com,* University of California at Berkeley, http://www.berkeleywellness.com/html/fw/fwNut01HealthyDiet.html (accessed January 12, 2006).
6. "Carbohydrates," January 6, 2006, Medline Plus Medical Dictionary, a service of the U.S. National Library of Medicine and the National Institutes of Health, http://www.nlm.nih.gov/medlineplus/ency/article/002469.htm (accessed January 19, 2006).
7. "Overweight and Obesity Statistics," August 18, 2005, Obesity Focused, http://www.obesityfocused.com/index.php (accessed January 13, 2006).
8. "U.S. Obesity Trends 1985 to 2004," November 8, 2005, Centers for Disease Control and Prevention, http://www.cdc.gov/nccdphp/dnpa/obesity/trend/maps/index.htm (accessed January 13, 2006).
9. "Overweight and Obesity Statistics," Obesity Focused.
10. Nance Hellmich, "USA Wallowing in Unhealthy Ways: Obesity Expert Points Finger at Fat-City Society," *USA Today*, August 22, 2002, http://www.usatoday.com/educate/college/firstyear/articles/20020823.htm (accessed January 13, 2006).
11. Pearson Education does not promote or endorse the use of the referenced sites. They are provided here for example purposes only; you are encouraged to find your own credible sources. For example, see FitDay.com, http://www.fitday.com/WebFit/Index.html; the Healthy Weight Forum, http://www.healthyweightforum.org/eng/calorie-counter/; or Nutrition.gov, a service of the National Agricultural Library, U.S. Department of Agriculture, http://www.nutrition.gov/.
12. Ibid.

13. "Statistics: Eating Disorders and Their Precursors," 2002, National Eating Disorders Association, http://nationaleatingdisorders.org/p.asp?WebPage_ID=286&Profile_ID=41138 (accessed January 13, 2006). For further information contact the National Eating Disorders Association's Information and Referral Helpline: 1-800-931-2237.

14. Introduction to "Eating Disorders Information Index," 2002, National Eating Disorders Association, http://nationaleatingdisorders.org/p.asp?WebPage_ID=294 (accessed January 13, 2006).

15. "Quit Smoking," 2005, American Lung Association, http://www.lungusa.org/site/pp.asp?c=dvLUK9O0E&b=33484 (accessed January 15, 2006).

16. "Severe Smoking Bans in Some Workplaces," December 9, 2005, CNN.com Transcripts, http://transcripts.cnn.com/TRANSCRIPTS/0512/09/lol.01.html (accessed January 19, 2006).

17. See Smokefree.gov at http://www.smokefree.gov/index.asp. The American Lung Association has a similar service, the Quit Smoking page on its site, at http://www.lungusa.org/site/pp.asp?c=dvLUK9O0E&b=33484.

18. Smokefree.gov.

19. Ibid.

20. "Binge Drinking in Adolescents and College Students," U.S. Department of Health and Human Services and SAMHSA's National Clearinghouse for Alcohol and Drug Information, http://www.health.org/govpubs/rpo995/#res2 (accessed May 16, 2006).

21. Ibid. Citing a study by Katherine Lyall, "Binge Drinking in College: A Definitive Study in Binge Drinking on American College Campuses: A New Look at an Old Problem," August 1995.

22. "School Daze?" Facts on Tap, Phoenix House, http://www.factsontap.org/factsontap/alcohol_and_student_life/school_daze.htm (accessed May 16, 2006).

23. "Fitness Resources: Frequently Asked Questions," 1999, American Heart Association, http://www.justmove.org/fitnessnews/faqs.html (accessed January 14, 2006).

24. Ibid.

25. Information of this sort can be found in a wide variety of sources. Your student center or campus fitness center may have suggested exercise programs. National health organizations like the American Diabetes Association provide fitness tips. See "Types of Exercise," American Diabetes Association, http://www.diabetes.org/weightloss-and-exercise/exercise/types-of-exercise.jsp.

26. "Introduction to Sexually Transmitted Diseases," 2006, myDNA.com, http://www.mydna.com/health/sexual/std/o/intro.html (accessed January 15, 2006). Also see "Sexually Transmitted Infections," 2006, Microbial Research Global Health, Division of Microbiology and Infectious Diseases, http://www.niaid.nih.gov/dmid/stds/#geninfo (accessed August 13, 2006).

27. Jamie Barrett, "Excessive Credit Card Use Causes Student Debt Woes," *Kansas State Collegian,* 2003, Young Money, http://www.youngmoney.com/credit_debt/get_out_of_debt/021007_03 (accessed January 14, 2006).

28. See "Credit 101: Calculate Your Payments," 2006, Visa U.S.A., http://www.usa.visa.com/personal/student/credit_101/calculate_your_payments.html?it=l2l/personal/student/credit_101/generate_good_credit%2Ehtml|Calculate%20Your%20Payments (accessed January 14, 2006).

29. This example is adapted from Barrett, "Excessive Credit Card Use Causes Student Debt Woes."

30. See "Budgeting: Plan Your Budget," 2006, Visa U.S.A., http://www.usa.visa.com/personal/student/budgeting/budgeting.html?it=cl/personal/student/budgeting/index%2Ehtml/img/text/lh_plan_your_budget%2Egif#anchor_7 (accessed January 14, 2006).

PART FOUR

APPLICATION AND LIFELONG LEARNING

WHAT'S ON YOUR MIND?

Thoughts from Fellow Students

If your first semester was anything like ours, you have made more decisions than you thought you would have to. Some, such as finding the best parking spot, were fairly insignificant. Others, like choosing a roommate, finding the best professors, juggling class responsibilities with family obligations, or adjusting your study habits, required more thoughtful reflection. The end of the semester always brought two feelings with it: *relief* that we completed the class assignments and *apprehension* that it all would start again in a few short weeks. Perhaps the following questions are running through your mind as you end this term:

- I've been told I need to declare a major *now*. I have no idea what I want to be, so how can I possibly pick a course of study? Where do I begin looking—who can help me? (chapter 12)
- What do I do if, after I declare a major, I decide I want to change that choice? Can I? If I'm not sure, I don't want to be stuck with the wrong decision! (chapter 12)
- I thought college was about exploration. Why would I want to lock myself into a major and career right now? (chapter 12)
- Ever since I was a kid, I knew exactly what I wanted to do. But how do I know if that is *really* what I want to do now? (chapter 12)
- This semester has really been great. I've met new friends and enjoyed the whole college experience. I don't want it to end. Will next term be as great—or will it become a boring routine? (chapter 13)
- My first-year experience instructor emphasizes the need to stay balanced in all aspects of my life. Isn't that a bit unrealistic? (chapter 13)

Our best advice is what we stated at the beginning of part 1: Take it one step at a time. Don't put yourself in a position where you need to make hasty decisions about important issues. Take a deep breath and enjoy the remaining days of this term.

You have just about made it. In a very short period of time this term will successfully conclude and a new one will soon begin. The ending of each term provides the opportunity to review successes and shortcomings. It is a time to celebrate victories and a time to reflect on choices made and consider goals for the coming term—and beyond.

This last section of *Rhythms of College Success* will gaze into the future. Your major course of study (and eventual career) will continue your journey of discovery, change, and mastery. With each step you make, you will be confronted with choices that will affect your life. Armed with critical thinking skills, you have the ability to make sound decisions that will have an impact on your eventual career choice.

- **Chapter 12: Exploration of Majors and Careers.** You may have entered college knowing exactly what you "want to be" when you graduate. Or you may have absolutely no idea and have declared your major to be "Undecided." Some students may even *change* their majors after a semester or two in school. This chapter will demystify the process of selecting a college major. You will learn not only what it means to major in a course of study but what it means to be an undeclared student. Whether or not you have chosen a major, this chapter's reflective activities will help you make (or reinforce) one of the most significant academic decisions you will make in college. It will be beneficial to keep this question in mind as you read the chapter: *How will you benefit from evaluating all of your options before carefully choosing a major?*

- **Chapter 13: The Choices You Make.** As you have read this book, you have moved along a journey of discovery, change, and mastery. This chapter will review the three levels of student success and how they have had an impact on the choices you made this term. No doubt you are a different person now—even if only a little—from the person you were four months ago. These changes reflect the choices you have made. Now, as you near the end of a successful term, it is time to also look to the future. What have you learned that will affect the choices you will make next term, next year, and the rest of your life? Choices change lives and with these choices you create the opportunity to master your life.

As you move into the last part of this book, consider this statement by *Harry Potter* author J. K. Rowling:

It is our choices . . . that show what we truly are, far more than our abilities.

Exploration of Majors and Careers

Making Music

REFLECTIVE QUESTIONS

Keeping the following questions in mind will make this chapter more meaningful:

- How does choosing a major course of study affect your life?
- How can you gather information about potential majors?
- What are you passionate about?
- What talents and skills do you have?
- What can you do if you are not satisfied with your major?

KEY TERMS

changing your major

declared

electives

general education
requirements (GER)

groupthink

major

portfolio

undeclared

GUEST SPEAKER

MEET **ROYCE B. DUNCAN**

Quality Control Partner

Rhodes, Young, Black, and Duncan, CPAs

Duluth, Georgia

One of the biggest decisions all students must face during their college years is the selection of a major field of study—a choice that will likely influence future career options. This important decision should be made only after significant deliberation and self-evaluation. Although there may not always be just one educational path to your career choice, you would be wise to ensure that a logical relationship exists between your major field of study and the educational requirements of your selected career choice.

My top three suggestions for effective career exploration:

1. Find a mentor. Establish a personal relationship with someone who can provide objective advice in the selection of a major, as well as provide meaningful career advice.

2. Utilize extracurricular activities. Frequently, outside college activities such as organizations and clubs will provide opportunities and experiences to help you determine if you have accurately gauged your interest and aptitude for a particular field of study.

3. Pursue internships and summer employment. Vocational exposure to the real-world work environment remains one of the most effective ways to determine if a career choice is a good match. Look for opportunities or contacts that can assist you in obtaining practical experience in your selected field of study.

INTRODUCTION

Some students enter college knowing exactly what they want to do after graduation. Arriving on campus with a clear career vision, these students know what courses they need to complete by graduation day. Focused and set on a particular outcome, they declare a major as soon as possible.

Other students have a vague idea of what they would like to study and what they would like to "become" upon graduation. They may not be as clearly focused as the first group of students just described, but they know their interests and what courses they want to explore during the first semester. They may declare their major before the first term of classes ends.

And then there are students who are just as committed to their college studies as their declared classmates, but they have yet to match their interests and abilities to a course of study or a long-term career commitment. Approximately 75 percent of first-year college students do not have a declared major by the time they reach college.[1] And one study found "that over 50 percent of students who choose a major will change their major at least once during college."[2] That's right—for every student you meet on campus who is pursuing a declared major, statistically there is another who has declared *and then changed* to a different major area of study.

POINTS TO CONSIDER

- **What are the guidelines and requirements for selecting a major course of study?** Choosing a college major is a three-level decision. There is the *what*—as in what will your major course of study be in college? There is a time component—*when* in your college career do you need to declare a major? And, finally, there is the process—*how* will you go about making this critically important decision? This chapter will explain the resources that will help you with the what, when, and how of choosing a major.

- **How does declaring a major benefit you?** Other than satisfying a college requirement to select a major, what does being a declared student mean? How does it affect your academic schedule of classes? This chapter will also examine the connection between your choice of major and a future career.

- **How will you know if you have chosen the correct road to travel?** College allows students to explore new ideas. This can lead to questions that challenge your fundamental system of beliefs (see chapter 1). So what happens if, after you declare a major, your explorations lead you down a new path, *away* from your major? Can you change direction? The short answer is yes. But school and in some cases state policies will determine whether such changes can be easily accomplished. Complicated or not, you need strategies that will help you make corrections on your way to graduation and the career world after that.

CHOOSING A MAJOR: WHAT DOES THIS MEAN FOR YOU?

College life presents one choice after another. So far this term you have had to make decisions concerning course selections, study methods, and personal relationships. Some choices may have been excruciatingly difficult, while others required little effort. One of the most important and perhaps most perplexing decisions for first-year students involves choosing a college major. The difficulty may be procedural, as you try to determine which bureaucratic hoops to jump through. Typical questions include: "Who can help me?" "Where do I get information?" "Are there forms to complete?" "Is there a deadline?"

A more common issue, however, is that many students simply do not know what they want to study in college. The college determines the *core requirements* that students must complete for a degree. Beyond that core, however, students may not know what to take—or even what their college or university has to offer. The vast listing of available courses can seem to be an overwhelming jumbled mess.

What is a major—and why should you care about it?

The word **major** in its most general sense refers to something that ranks high in importance or concern when compared to other things. A major event—like graduation from high school or a marriage proposal—represents a transitional moment in a person's life. What follows differs from what has just happened.

When students choose (or *declare*) a college major they commit to a particular course of academic preparation. Once the academic major has been **declared,** course work becomes more focused and more specialized. These courses will provide a depth of reading and discussion not found in the general education requirements of the college or university.

What should you do if you are still undeclared?

It can be easy to fall into the trap of thinking that if you are not absolutely sure what you want to be *for the rest of your life* then you must be deficient as a student. Nothing could be further from the truth.

Students who have not decided on a major fall into the category of "undecided," or **undeclared.** That is, they have not decided on a major; they have not declared their college course of study. *Undeclared* does not mean *uncommitted.* It means what it says—this student has yet to decide on a field of study. Nor does *undecided* mean *indecisive.* Undecided/undeclared students have not made a decision but that does *not* mean they are *incapable* of making a decision.

Reasons for not declaring a major abound.[3] Perhaps the undeclared student sees the college and university experience as a time for exploration, a time to investigate many areas of interest. Some students are, by nature, very deliberate in their thinking and decision making. They do not make snap judgments—especially about something that may eventually determine career direction. *Reflection* is a prized quality for these students. They want to gather as much information as possible; mull it over; and then make a decision. They are committed to making an *informed decision*—one they can live with. Like a singer searching for the right song to match her voice, these students want a major that will match their passions and desires.

© *EyeWire, Inc.*

Not all entering students require a prolonged period of thought and reflection. You will share classes with students who have had dreams of being a teacher, a doctor, an accountant, or a fashion designer since they were in elementary school. They see no need for further exploration. They *know* what they want to do with their lives.

But it is possible that some of these "I-already-know-what-I-want-to-be-after-graduation" students may have made either an uninformed or a premature decision.[4] Coming in with hard and fast ideas on careers *may* indicate narrow thinking or a decision heavily influenced by someone else.

For instance, the concept of **groupthink** refers to what happens when group thinking overshadows individual concerns. In order to get along with the others, the member agrees with what the group as a whole thinks; individual disagreement is stifled. A similar situation can occur if a family has decided what the best major will be for a son or daughter, leading the student to declare a major without a full exploration of alternatives.

Please do not misinterpret the foregoing paragraph. Simply because a student comes to college knowing what he or she wants—or has a family deeply involved in his or her education—does not spell disaster. Such confidence, coupled with a supportive family support circle, can be truly energizing and inspiring!

The point remains, though, that many first-year students may not be ready to make a quick decision concerning their major. They need to explore their desires and passions before making a meaningful commitment. These students—and you might be one of them—need time to grow into their major.

CHOOSING A MAJOR: MOVING FROM UNDECLARED TO DECLARED

Finding and then declaring a major does not have to be a mystical process. It can be straightforward and methodical. Your professors, counselors, family, and friends can provide critical input about what they see as your strengths, weaknesses, abilities, and possibilities. But the greatest resource lies within: What are *your* desires and passions?

Self-assessment: Finding your purpose

One career counselor describes *purpose* as "a source of energy and direction."[5] Any time you have wondered "What am I going to do with my life?" the question of purpose comes to the forefront. But this is "not a question that we can answer once and be done with it. We typically bring up the question of purpose about every ten years . . . [and] during major life transitions."[6]

College represents one of those "major life transitions" (see chapter 1)—and choosing a major is an integral part of that transition. Although your choice of major is *not* irreversible (as you will see later in this chapter), it *is* a critical decision that should not be taken lightly. The choice involves more than just picking a department and enrolling in courses. If done without thought and planning, it can be frustrating, time-consuming, and costly.

What are you passionate about?

Have you ever believed in something or someone with such fervor and intensity that you would gladly sacrifice for the benefit of that thing, issue, or person? Have you ever been in a class that was so exciting you literally lost track of time—the class ended, but you wanted it to continue? Do you have a class this term that is so energizing that you cannot wait to attend the next session? If the answer is yes for any of these, then it can be said you have a *passion* for that particular person, place, or thing.

Identifying your passions—what you love to do with your days—can help you understand why you get up in the morning. This is the purpose of your day. Sometimes, though, people pursue goals that do not connect to their passions, talents, and desires. In chapter 2 you identified goals you wanted to pursue. (One important goal is choosing your major, as illustrated in Figure 12.1.) Reaching a goal

WHY DO YOU WANT TO DO WHAT YOU WANT TO DO?

At this point of the semester, list three majors you would like to explore.

1. _____
2. _____
3. _____

Why do you want to do what you want to do? For each of the possible majors you listed above, reflect on why you want to pursue that major.

1. _____
   _____
2. _____
   _____
3. _____
   _____

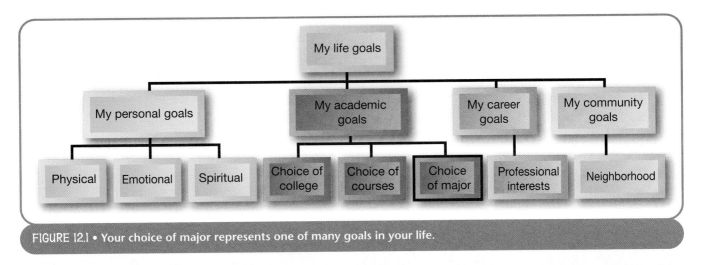

FIGURE 12.1 • **Your choice of major represents one of many goals in your life.**

will require resources and persistence. But have you ever wondered if a goal was *right* for you? Because you achieve a goal does not mean it furthers your life or otherwise has a positive impact on you. The same for your major. Once you have declared a major, how do you know it is the correct choice *for you?* Will it contribute to your overall balance and wellness?

The C.A.P. principle: Your advisor

A television commercial shows a man sitting at his dining room table. Before him appear a variety of knives. The front of his shirt is open, and he has the phone to his ear. On the other end of the phone, a doctor is giving the man instructions on how to perform surgery on himself. The man, with a worried look on his face, asks the doctor, "Shouldn't you be doing this?"

The "do-it-yourself" mentality does show fortitude and initiative but, at times, it can be foolish. That is especially true when it comes to the academic advising and counseling services your campus has to offer. Some students may view a visit to the counselor's or advisor's office much the same as going for an annual dental exam—necessary but dreadful. Other students do not even see it as necessary; they view course selection counseling as something they can do themselves. You might have heard a classmate say, "All I have to do is read the catalog, look at the current term's class offerings, and fill in the blanks. It is not exactly rocket science!"

This is an instance where perceptions do not necessarily reflect reality. Some colleges will put *blocks* on particular courses so that a student must see a counselor before registering for that class. Occasionally a professor's or dean's signature may be needed in order to get into a course. In these instances, students grudgingly make an appointment and see a counselor for the necessary paperwork. Like a visit to a doctor's office, these appointments never seem to be convenient and always take more time than the student is willing to give.

It might be helpful to view counseling and advising through a different set of eyeglasses. In fact, develop a goal (discussed in chapter 2) to *voluntarily* visit a counselor at least two times per term. A *mid-term* meeting gives you a head start on preparing for the next term registration process. You and the counselor can review the catalog requirements that direct your course of study. This allows you to make sure you are taking the correct courses. Maybe a course you need will be offered only once per year. Without the help of your counselor you might not know this— and you may end up waiting an additional year to take a required course. This mid-term visit would also be an appropriate time to discuss your grades, successes, and challenges.

An *end-of-the-term* meeting gives you an opportunity to review what has happened during the academic term. Did you make satisfactory progress? Have your goals changed concerning your major? Or maybe you have been "undeclared," and now you have decided to declare your major. This would be the time to discuss the requirements of the particular degree or certification program you would like to pursue. The academic counselor or advisor can answer your questions and direct you to appropriate sources in your career development center.

Other sources of information

Once you have thoroughly explored your interests and abilities, it is time to turn to other sources of information to assist with choosing your major.

PERSONAL ASSETS: A SELF-INVENTORY

How do you know whether your choice of a major—an academic goal—is right for you?[7]

Your Prospective Major

1. For the purpose of this activity, pick one of the three prospective majors you listed in Activity 12.1. Consider this an academic goal for which you will strive. Now complete the sentence below:

   By the time I graduate from college, I will have satisfactorily completed all the requirements for the major of _____

Your Personal Balance Sheet

2. In the four quadrants below, assess your own likes, dislikes, assets, and liabilities. Draw on your past work and school experiences.

Likes	Dislikes
What do you enjoy doing? _____ _____ _____	If you could list what you do *not* like to do, what would be high on your list? _____ _____ _____
What interests you? _____ _____ _____	What types of tasks bore you or "turn you off"? _____ _____ _____
What types of people do you like to associate with? _____ _____	What types of people do you find it difficult to be around? _____ _____
When working, what type of physical environment energizes you? _____ _____	Does routine bore you? _____
Do you like to work alone, or would you rather work with other people? _____	Does flexibility scare you? _____ Do you avoid speaking in front of people? _____
Do you like physical activity? _____	Do shortcomings in other people bother you? _____
Do you like spontaneity, or would you rather know what is going to happen in advance? _____	

What types of books, magazines or movies do you enjoy? _____ _____ _____ List other *likes* below: _____ _____ _____ _____	What types of books, magazines or movies do you avoid? _____ _____ List other *dislikes* below: _____ _____ _____ _____
Assets	**Liabilities**
What are your strengths? _____ _____ What can you do well? _____ _____ On which particular talent of yours have people complimented? _____ Is there a personality trait that has been of help to you? _____ What skills do you have? _____ _____ Are you able to focus clearly and persist until a goal is completed? _____ Are you optimistic? _____ Do you work well in groups? _____	What are your shortcomings? _____ _____ What do you have difficulty doing or completing? _____ _____ _____ Do you lack self-confidence? _____ Are you overly confident? _____ Do you procrastinate? _____ Is it difficult for you to be a creative thinker? _____ Are you pessimistic? _____ Do you have difficulty working with people who are different (race, ethnicity, social class, or gender) from you? _____

(continued)

PERSONAL ASSETS:
A SELF-INVENTORY (continued)

Are you a self-starter?	Are you self-absorbed?
List other *assets* below:	List other *liabilities* below:

Evaluate Your Choice of a College Major

3. Based on your responses, does your choice of a college major seem reasonable? For instance, if you listed your college major as *teacher education* but you identified working with children as a *dislike,* you may need to reevaluate your choice of majors. Write your reaction here:

_____

_____

_____

College Catalog. You can find a listing of the majors that your college or university has to offer by searching the school catalog (chapter 1). Four-year schools generally provide extensive information matching academic offerings to potential careers.

A two-year college's list of majors will not be as extensive, but you still have options from which to choose. Once again, differences exist from state to state and institution to institution, but the following academic options can be found at most two-year schools:

- *Associate of Arts (AA) degree.* Coursework focuses on a liberal arts* curriculum. Two-year schools may have an agreement with local or state colleges, allowing their AA graduates to transfer their course work to the four-year institution upon completion of the AA requirements. Generally, the two-year students would then complete the general education requirements of the college and any prerequisite (required) work for their major at the four-year level. See your advisor or counselor for more information.

- *Associate of Science (AS) degree.* Course work emphasizes the sciences. The catalog will provide information on what courses need to be completed successfully. As with the AA degree, course work can be transferred to a four-year institution. See your advisor or counselor for more information.

- *Associate of Applied Science (AAS) degree.* Course work prepares the student "for immediate employment and is identified with a specialty designation, such as computer technology or engineering technology."[8] An AAS is not a transfer degree to a four-year institution. Once again, see your advisor or counselor for more information.

---

*Liberal arts education refers to academic course offerings that provide students with a general knowledge in literature, history, sciences, and the arts. This base of knowledge can be an appropriate entry level for many occupations. This is different from many *certificate* programs, which provide vocational training for students in specific occupations.

- *Certificates.* These may be known as *professional certificates, technical certificates,* or some other descriptor. They are for students wishing to upgrade their employment skills. The college will spell out the specific course requirements needed to become certificated. Students who earn a certificate may find they have completed a portion of a degree—and may wish to complete that degree. Check with your counselor or advisor.

Campus Career Center. A visit to the campus career center can lead you to print resources, Internet sites, and contact with people in your areas of interest. Here you can find brochures, flyers, books, computer software, and specific Web sites designed to help you make an informed decision about your future course work. One such Web site, for instance, is FACTS.org (Florida Academic Counseling and Tracking for Students), hosted by the Florida Department of Education. From this site you can, among other options, receive help in choosing the right major.[9]

Career and Personality Inventories. The career center may also have specific computer programs that allow you to complete career, personality, and interest inventories. Personality assessments will *not* tell you what you *should be.* Rather, their purpose is to more scientifically help you understand yourself and how you relate to people and to specific tasks. Check with your advisor or counselor for more information.

Career Information. Choosing a major is not always synonymous with committing to a particular career. A major in history, for instance, does not mean you have to be an archivist in a museum; you could be a teacher, lawyer, or journalist. A sociology major does not have to prepare for a life of social work, but might explore criminal justice, law, or marriage and family counseling. Many majors will provide a broad course of study that can prepare you for many careers.

It is possible, however, to look at specific careers to help with your decision about a major. Think of this as working *backward.* Rather than choosing a major and then moving *forward* to the outcome, starting with the end in mind (the career) may help focus your choice of a major. For instance, you may be intrigued by the hospitality industry. Organizing conventions and major events appear to be exciting, challenging and creative. That may lead you to explore course work that would prepare you for such work.

The U.S. government annually publishes the *Occupational Outlook Handbook,*[10] which lists specific career areas. It can be found online (see Figure 12.2). Clicking on a career link will lead to

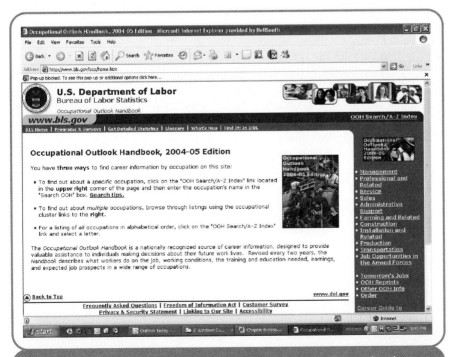

FIGURE 12.2 • Web site for the U.S. Department of Labor's *Occupational Outlook Handbook.*

information about the nature of the work, working conditions, employment statistics, qualifications needed, job outlook for the future, earnings potential, related occupations, and other sources of information about a given career area.

Specific Departments and Their Professors. As you seek help choosing your major, don't forget the *live* human beings. Take time to visit your professors (see chapter 7) and ask them about specific majors, including the preparation needed and the future career possibilities with such an academic background. Some college departments may have literature already printed and ready for distribution. A brochure with a title such as "What You Can Do with a Major in Science" will provide basic information. Ask the department secretary if a document exists for your area of interest.

Using Multiple Intelligences. The theory of multiple intelligences provides another piece of the puzzle as you seek help choosing your major. Occupations typically require the skills and talents of two or more intelligences. For instance, a teacher needs linguistic intelligence and interpersonal intelligence—and also logical-mathematical if she wishes to be a math teacher. Therefore that occupation could easily be listed in all three of those categories. Continue to develop all of your intelligences.[11]

Take a moment to review Activity 5.2 (chapter 5), where you reflected on the connection between multiple intelligences, majors, and careers. Based on new information you have learned since reading that chapter, do you need to add to the third column of the table in that activity?

NARROWING YOUR OPTIONS

Once you have gathered an abundance of information, it is time to begin narrowing the focus of your choices. Your goal will be to move closer to a declared major.

1. As a review, list the possible majors you have been seriously contemplating.

   _____

   _____

   _____

2. Of those you have listed, which ones can you *eliminate*? Perhaps you realized that a particular major no longer holds your interest; or perhaps one of your courses kindled such a strong interest that it has overshadowed all other choices. List the eliminated majors here, and next to each one briefly indicate why—at least at this time—you decided to eliminate it.

   _____

   _____

   _____

   _____

3. Now, at this point in time, which major has the most attraction for you?

   _____

4. Briefly explain the reasoning for your choice.

   _____

   _____

   _____

CAREER EXPLORATION

Using the information literacy strategies you learned in chapter 9, do an Internet search for Web sites related to the major or career area you are contemplating. Once you find an informative site, complete the following.

1. What is the Web site address?

   _____

2. What is the official name of the Web site?

   _____

3. What person or organization sponsors the Web site?

   _____

4. What is the career (or major) this site describes?

   _____

5. List three significant pieces of career information you learned from this site.

   _____

   _____

   _____

6. What questions do you still have about this career?

   _____

   _____

CHOOSING A MAJOR: WHAT DOES THIS MEAN FOR COURSE WORK?

Colleges and universities have a prescribed number of courses needed for a degree or certificate (see Figure 12.3). The exact number and nature of these courses may vary from institution to institution, but your course work will generally fall within three areas:

- General education requirements (called "core" at some colleges)
- Major requirements
- Electives

Following are brief descriptions of each of these three categories. Your college may have additional course work, as well as restrictions on types of elective courses allowed (if any). As usual, your school's catalog and academic advisors will be your best resources. Completing the requirements in a timely fashion moves you closer to the academic goal of graduation.

General education requirements (GER)

The **general education requirements (GER),** sometimes called *core* courses, consist of those courses your school believes to be important for *all* students, no matter what their major. Although these requirements will vary among schools, they generally consist of selected courses from a variety of disciplines. Students typically have to complete core courses in English (composition and/or

Degree earned

Major course work

Major core courses ——————— Major elective courses

General education
requirements
(GER)

GER core courses ——————— Elective courses

FIGURE 12.3 • Steps to a degree.

literature), history or political science (local, state, national, and/or world), math (basic computation), science (laboratory experience), and humanities (art or music appreciation). You may be required to complete work in a foreign language as well. For two-year college students, core requirements may account for as much as 50 percent of your course load. At the four-year level it will be less, due to the advanced course work in the major area of study required during the third and fourth years.

Major requirements

Whereas the GERs establish an educational base, the major requirements provide an in-depth study of your chosen academic area. At four-year institutions this course work takes place during the junior and senior years. At two-year schools, the major courses are often taken along with the GERs. Sometimes particular requirements must be completed before you can take certain courses in your major. Check with your counselor or advisor for a list of required major courses.

Electives

Depending on the program, you may have a handful of credit hours that you can take as **electives**—courses that you "elect" to take in addition to the GERs and those required for your major. For instance, students who must complete sixty credit hours for an Associate of Arts degree may be allowed to take twelve of those hours (three or four courses) in any field they choose. The same holds true for the four-year student, although the actual number of elective courses will vary. Some of these elective choices will be within the general education requirements, and others will support your major area of study. As always, a visit to your advisor is recommended.

© *EyeWire, Inc.*

MANAGING ACADEMIC RISK: ARE YOU TRAVELING THE CORRECT ROAD?

A certain amount of risk is involved with everything we do. Obviously the level of risk depends upon the activity; some risks can be deadly, others merely a momentary thrill. When we risk, we step outside our comfort zone; we take a chance.

Declaring a major has a certain amount of risk associated with it. Many students make this decision with far less than half of their college education completed. Then, after a semester or two of study, they may find that their chosen academic area is not what they had hoped. For whatever reason, the major does not fulfill or excite them.

The reality of change: What can you do if you are not satisfied with your major?

Perhaps you have heard the cliché that the only constant in life is *change*. No matter how much we might try to fight it, we *will* experience change time and again in our lives. The same thing may happen with your choice of majors. As you gain more information, your horizons widen, your belief system may be challenged, and your previous choices are reevaluated.

It happens to the best of students—and it can happen more than once. As stated at the beginning of this chapter, nearly 75 percent of college students will change their major *at least once* during their college career. Nearly 80 percent of freshmen have some career uncertainty.[12] As you have learned during this term, college students experience a number of life and academic transitions (see chapter 1). Exploring a major, declaring a major, and possibly **changing your major** are part of those changes and adjustments.

Consider the four-stage change cycle described in the Introduction to this book. Once you decide on a major you step into stage 2: *Plan* for the courses you will need to take (see Figure 12.4). When you enroll in these major courses, you are moving into stage 3: *Execute* the plan to

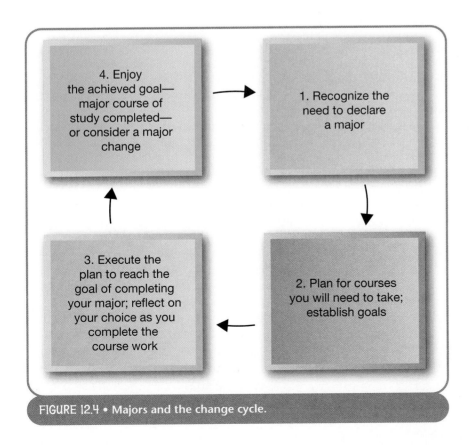

FIGURE 12.4 • Majors and the change cycle.

complete your major. In that stage obstacles present themselves; you have to confront the detours and then continue to move forward toward your ultimate goal (graduation).

And if you find that your declared major is less than satisfying, don't panic. If, as a result of new explorations and insights, you find yourself looking at an alternative course of study, welcome the new direction. You have not "failed" or "lost focus." Instead, you are about to embark on a new and exciting direction. You have not necessarily even made a mistake. Consider any detours as *learning opportunities!*

Major change: The positive side

If you get weak in the knees contemplating a major change, consider the following positive points:

- Some researchers have found that a student's graduation probability actually *increases* by 40 percent with a major change.[13]

- When you made your initial major decision, you may not have fully explored other areas of interest. You may have entered college with a childhood dream of pursing a certain career that you actually knew very little about—and then, upon deeper inspection, you discovered that the career does not inspire you after all. If you are "guilty" of anything, it would be premature articulation—you committed before you had all the facts.

- Changing your major may reflect not indecisiveness or immaturity, but "an underlying process of cognitive maturation."[14]

- Pursuing goals (see chapter 2) does not always move in a straight line. A change in direction may simply mean you have adjusted your goal to a more realistic outcome.

Changing a College Major

A Positive Story

In 1971, Steve graduated from high school, left home, and entered his first year of college. For as long as he could remember, Steve was going to "become a teacher." It was all he had ever wanted to be. When given the chance in high school, he taught parts of lessons for his teachers. He planned to get his degree and teaching credentials and then return to his hometown to teach.

During his first year in college, he worked toward completing his GERs. He looked forward to diving into teacher preparation. Steve had declared his major—history—and was dreaming of his own classroom. His goal was getting closer.

Steve found, however, that the best laid plans can change in a hurry and with no warning. During the summer between his freshman and sophomore years, he attended a picnic at his godfather's home. There he had an enlightening conversation with a man who had enjoyed a long and satisfying career in the federal criminal justice system. By the end of the day, Steve was thinking about a new direction for his education.

When he returned to campus in the fall, he changed his major from history to sociology and never looked back. He graduated as the valedictorian of his class and quickly landed a job in his adopted field of criminal justice. The major change proved to be a wise decision.

But the story does not end there. Six years after his college graduation, Steve once again found himself at a crossroads. Not satisfied with his career, he returned to school, earned his teaching credentials—and landed a job as a high school history teacher. Though the route had been circuitous, Steve found himself now enjoying the career he had initially pursued. It was a *ten-year* ride from college acceptance, to declaring a major, to changing a major, to beginning a career, and then to changing careers. His outcomes changed along the way, but his initial intent to help people discover their own talents and intentions was achieved.

A couple of graduate degrees later, Steve now teaches college students, facilitates workshops, and writes books—including this book you are now reading.

Major change: The downside

As with most decisions, of course, there can be negative repercussions as well, including these:

- Depending on when the decision is made, changing your major may lengthen your time in college—and thus the college education becomes more costly in terms of time and dollars.

- The longer the college education lasts, a potentially higher opportunity cost (see chapter 1) exists.

- In some state schools, changing your major can count against you, as there may be a restriction on the number of credit hours a student may attempt. Know your state policies.

- If you do not have a new major to embrace, you will fall back into the Undeclared category. This may mean more trips to the career center, taking more assessments, and conducting more research into a major—procedures that you have been through at least one time already. (This "downside" may turn into a "positive," however, as a second look may sharpen your academic focus.)

- You may feel pressure to quickly declare a new major—and once again make a less than informed decision.

Fix what? A final thought about changing majors

If you find yourself considering a major change, do not do it lightly. Think carefully about the situation. Is changing your major the *only* answer? Perhaps a discussion with a professor or advisor might clear up some concerns you have—concerns that may seem large and forbidding if you have not gathered correct information. Understand what you can "fix" with a major change—and what you cannot.

For instance, you *may* be able to "fix" the problem of content comprehension by moving from a math-oriented major to one that focuses on literature. But if you are experiencing difficulties with your major because you are homesick (see chapter 1), you can change your major monthly but the real problem—homesickness—will not have been addressed. *You have to know what to address* (see chapter 5).

Perhaps you have come to the conclusion that there are more students in your major area than there are potential jobs. For that reason you consider a change of major. Before adopting that "fix," though, you may wish to talk with the department chair, an academic advisor, or a career counselor. They might have job placement information that surprises you.

In their book *Selecting a College Major: Exploration and Decision Making,* Virginia N. Gordon and Susan J. Sears refer to a psychology major who lists a negative of her major as being too many students in psychology courses. The student can do nothing about that circumstance—she cannot "fix" *that* problem.[15] Just talking with a knowledgeable source can help put positive and negative issues into proper perspective.[16]

A LOOK TO THE FUTURE: BUILDING A PORTFOLIO

A *résumé* is a summary of your professional and work qualifications. It oftentimes accompanies an application for employment. It "sells" you to the prospective employer. Consider résumé writing a terminal or ending activity, one that generally has more urgency toward the end of your college career. For that reason, résumé writing will not be reviewed in this textbook. Of more importance at this level of your education is the collection of material to eventually include with your résumé. This collection of material about your background will be the beginning of a personal **portfolio.**

A portfolio checklist

When the time comes for résumé writing and job interview preparation you will already have a wealth of material to consult if you start working now on the items that follow. For our purposes here, let's keep it simple and look at some essentials you can begin to collect.

To begin, purchase five large (at least 13-by-10) manila envelopes. Label them as follows:

1. *Résumé material.* In this envelope place:

   - Copies of your college transcripts
   - A list of jobs you have had (including start date, end date, name of your supervisor, and your duties)
   - Copies of any certificates or awards you have received

2. *Letters of recommendation.* In this envelope place:

   - Any letter or commendation you have received from teachers or employers*
   - An ongoing list of people you will be able to use as references for prospective jobs (including their addresses and phone numbers, as applications may request this information)

3. *Products.* In this envelope place:

   - Information or samples of anything you have created that might favorably impress an employer (written work, software programs, artwork, and so forth)

4. *Skills.* In this envelope place:

   - An ongoing list (update it as you gain expertise) of your salable skills and talents

5. *Biography.* In this envelope place:

   - Personal information that one day might help on a job interview (Who significantly influenced your life or helped create an interest in a certain career? What types of books do you like to read? What are your career goals? Personal goals? How do you handle challenges?)

As you will discover with résumé writing, there are various formats for portfolios. Your school may offer a course on portfolio development.

SUMMARY

MATCHING PASSION TO YOUR CAREER— AN INCREMENTAL PROCESS

Choosing a major requires time and focus. This chapter introduced you to strategies, resources, and people you can use to help with the important process of selecting an academic course of study. Use your time in college to explore your passions, interests, and skills. Take each step mindfully and enjoy the journey!

Before leaving this chapter, keep the following points in mind:

- Choosing a major area of academic study requires time.

- A personal assessment of your likes, dislikes, abilities, liabilities, and passions can help you make a more informed decision about your academic major.

- Most students enter their first year of college without a clear direction of where their education can take them.

- Changing a major is a significant decision that should neither be taken lightly nor avoided.

- Start collecting material for your portfolio and résumé now.

---

*It is a good practice to ask for a letter of recommendation when you complete a *significant* activity such as an internship. If you serve on student government, ask your student activities director for such a letter upon the successful completion of your service.

tuning your life-strings

the 4 Rs

self

change and personal growth

The following activities will allow you to reflect on the three levels of student success as they apply to the major concepts introduced in this chapter. Each activity will give you an opportunity to reflect and apply the chapter concepts in a way that is meaningful to you during this transitional phase of your life. Use this opportunity to apply newly acquired information and also keep an ongoing journal of growth in the various facets of your life.

The 4 Rs

Describe a personal example as to how you used each of the 4 Rs as you considered your college major.

1. *Reflection* (Example: How have you learned more about majors this term?)

   _____

   _____

2. *Respect* (Example: What do your past experiences say about your passions?) _____

   _____

   _____

3. *Responsibility* (Example: Describe responsible steps you have taken to move toward "declaring" a major—or reinforcing your choice of a major.)

   _____

   _____

4. *Renewal* (Example: In what ways does thinking about your major energize you?) _____

   _____

   _____

The Change Cycle

Critical thinking skills (see chapter 5) play a vital role in the change cycle. Each of the four stages requires a critical evaluation of where you are and where you need to go. For this activity, reflect on a change that you are currently confronting concerning your major course of study.

1. What is the situation that requires change? _____

_____

_____

2. What led you to recognize this? _____

_____

_____

_____

_____

3. What is (or will be) your plan to address this situation? _____

_____

_____

_____

_____

4. If you have put the plan into action (executed it), how are you progressing? _____

_____

_____

_____

_____

5. Once the plan has become a reality, how do you plan to enjoy this achievement? How will you reward yourself?

_____

_____

_____

_____

Tuning Your Life-Strings

Pause for a moment and reflect on the balance—or lack of balance—in your life at this point in the school term. Use this activity to apply newly acquired information from this chapter to gauge the level of strength in the various facets of your life. You may wish to refer to your responses in previous chapters.

Life-string	Questions to ask yourself	What possible activities could help you tune this string?	Who can help you tune this string?
Social	• Is there a mentor in your college life who can provide information about a career area that interests you? • Are there any people in your social network who have helped (or can help) with your decision about an academic major?		
Occupational	• Have you made any decisions that will impact your major or your career interests?		
Spiritual	• What types of explorations have you been involved in that have helped you examine the deeper meanings of life—and your purpose in this life?		
Physical	• Have you taken a few moments for yourself to relax?		
Intellectual	• What did you do this week that provided you with more information about your major?		
Emotional	• What strategies have you used to effectively deal with your college stressors?		

Rhythms of Reflection

To complete this chapter, please reflect on the following words:

> *Life is not about finding yourself.*
>
> *Life is about creating yourself.*
>
> –*George Bernard Shaw,* playwright

Now, using the words above for inspiration, explain how you will apply the knowledge you have gained with this chapter so that you can go "about creating yourself." Please write your thoughts here.

_____

_____

_____

_____

_____

_____

_____

_____

 To further respond online, please go to the *Rhythms of Reflection* **module in chapter 12 of the Companion Website.**

ENDNOTES

1. Joe Cuseo, "Decided, Undecided, and in Transition: Implications for Academic Advisement, Career Counseling, and Student Retention," in *Improving the First Year of College: Research and Practice,* ed. R. S. Feldman, 27–50 (New York: Erlbaum, 2005).
2. Robert M. Orndorff and Edwin L. Herr, "A Comparative Study of Declared and Undeclared College Students on Career Uncertainty and Involvement in Career Development Activities," *Journal of Counseling and Development* 74 (July/August 1996): 634.
3. Cuseo, "Decided, Undecided, and in Transition," 27–28.
4. Ibid., 27–29.
5. Richard J. Leider, *The Power of Purpose: Creating Meaning in Your Life and Work* (New York: MJF Books, 1997), 1.
6. Ibid.
7. This activity draws from Ken Kragen, *Life Is a Contact Sport* (New York: Morrow, 1994), 41–45.
8. "Academic Credentials Offered at AACC," Anne Arundel Community College, http://www.aacc.edu/offer/academiccred.cfm (accessed November 19, 2005).
9. For more information visit the FACTS Web site, http://www.facts.org (accessed November 19, 2005).
10. The *Occupational Outlook Handbook* can be found online at the Web site of the U.S. Department of Labor, Bureau of Labor Statistics, http://www.bls.gov/oco/home.htm (accessed November 19, 2005).
11. For an in-depth review of MI and its practical applications, see Clifford Morris, "Linking Most General of Occupations to Multiple Intelligences," 2004, Thinking and Working Smarter Not Harder, http://www.igs.net/~cmorris/smo_comments.html (accessed November 19, 2005). This site provides an exhaustive list of occupation–MI connections.
12. From research by J. J. Kelly and E. R. White, and by L. Noel, both cited in Orndorff and Herr, "A Comparative Study of Declared and Undeclared College Students," 637.

13. Ted Micceri, "Will Changing Your Major Double Your Graduation Chances?" May 30, 2002, Policy Center on the First Year of College, First-Year Assessment Listserv, www.brevard.edu/fyc/listserv/remarks/micceri.htm (accessed August 1, 2005).

14. Cuseo, "Decided, Undecided, and in Transition," 3

15. Virginia N. Gordon and Susan J. Sears, *Selecting a College Major: Exploration and Decision Making,* 5th ed. (Upper Saddle River, NJ: Merrill/Prentice Hall, 2004), 78–79. This is an excellent workbook dedicated solely to the process of choosing a major. The extensive activities provide students with chances to reflect on strengths, abilities, and aspirations.

16. You may also wish to review the "plus-minus-interesting" (PMI) strategy introduced in chapter 5.

The Choices You Make

Looking Toward Your Next Engagement

REFLECTIVE QUESTIONS

Keeping the following questions in mind will make this chapter more meaningful:

- Are you satisfied with the choices you have made this term?

- What strategies have you used this term to maintain your physical and emotional well-being?

- What challenges do you anticipate to greet you in the future?

- What strategies do you have to help you address your anticipated challenges?

KEY TERMS

4 Rs
balance
change cycle
choices
self-aware
tuning your life-strings

GUEST SPEAKER

MEET STEVE PISCITELLI

Author of *Rhythms of College Success: A Journey of Discovery, Change, and Mastery* and *Study Skills: Do I Really Need This Stuff?* and Professor of History and Student Success

Florida Community College at Jacksonville

Jacksonville, Florida

You and I have covered a lot of ground in this book. In the first chapter I stated: "You already possess skills, knowledge, and strategies that will help you be successful in college." During this term you reflected on what you could do and took responsibility for what you needed to change. In short, you made choices that affected your life for this term—and for years to come. Respect where you have been; reflect on where you would like to go. And then continue to make responsible choices.

My top three suggestions about the choices you make:

1. You have the choice to change or not to change. When you choose to change, you take a risk—you show courage.

2. Living a life of wellness and balance is a lifestyle choice. Recognize that you have that choice—and make it.

3. You will be confronted with situations that are not of your choosing. Recognize that you *do* have the choice on how you handle and react to those situations.

Embrace your ability to choose and live each day honestly, responsibly, and respectfully.

INTRODUCTION

End-of-the-book chapters like this one run the risk of becoming cliché driven. Phrases like "preparing for the end," "a new beginning," "the next step," and "where do you go from here?" often appear as chapter titles. In reality, all reflect excellent sentiments and accurate thoughts. They let the student know that while the work is finishing for this term, more work and decisions are still to come.

This chapter will discuss those issues within the context of choices. In particular, you will be asked to do the following:

- Reflect on the choices you have made since the beginning of this school term.

- Consider the consequences your choices have had for yourself and others.

- Think about the choices that lie ahead of you.

POINTS TO CONSIDER

More specifically, you will be asked to consider your choices as they relate to the three levels of student success that have been the themes for this book. As a quick review, recall the three levels:

Level I: The 4 Rs

Level II: The Change Cycle

Level III: Tuning Your Life-Strings

Level I: The 4 Rs

As you studied the topics of each chapter, you were asked to:

- *Reflect* on the skills and challenges you brought to college.

- *Respect* the skills, knowledge, and strategies that you already had as a student.

- Assume the *responsibility* to make necessary changes to address your challenges.

- Develop and maintain *renewal* strategies that foster balance, wellness, and growth in your life.

How have you done in each of these areas?

Level II: The change cycle

No doubt you have made some changes in your life this term. Each change required you to recognize the need for change, plan for the change, execute the change, and then, hopefully, enjoy the results of that change (see Figure 13.1). This chapter will help you reflect on and evaluate those changes. You will also be asked to consider the changes that you may need to make in the near future—and what choices will help you through the change process. Your college life as a first-year student (or transfer student, or whatever classification you might have) is about to end. Recognition of this will lead you to more choices—and changes—for the next college term.

Level III: Tuning your life-strings

Renewal leads to personal growth—and this was continually stressed throughout each chapter. The Tuning Your Life-Strings activity at the end of each chapter graphically illustrated how continual personal renewal will strengthen the six dimensions of your life (see Figure 13.2).

Three levels of student success

Each of the three levels of student success has been intimately related to your growth as an individual (see Figure 13.3).

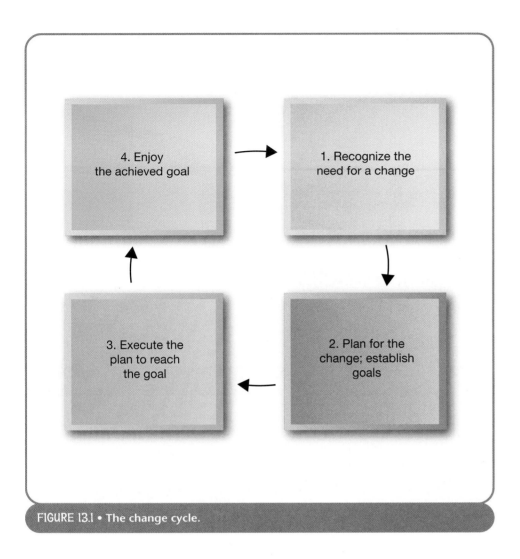

FIGURE 13.1 • The change cycle.

TUNING YOUR LIFE-STRINGS: WHERE HAVE YOU BEEN?

A number of months have passed since you arrived on campus. Along the way you have been able to celebrate successes and, in some cases, fret about challenges. No matter what the issue or circumstance, a part of your life—a part of YOU—had to confront the situation in one way or another. **Choices** had to be made—and were made—every day of the term. Even in those situations in which you chose to do nothing, you made a choice to do nothing.

Each choice involved the **4 Rs** of student success (reflection, respect, responsibility, and renewal). Each choice provided an opportunity to either stay with your current rhythms of life or make a change. In all instances, the choices have been yours to make. And each choice had an impact on one or more of the six dimensions of your life (social, occupational, spiritual, physical, intellectual, and emotional). You have been **tuning your life-strings.**

Social rhythms

Whether you tend to be introverted and stay to yourself, or are a gregarious individual who readily makes friends, the social dimension of your life has been touched this term in a number of ways. Consider the following:

- Some students moved away from home and took up residence in on-campus housing. Away from family and hometown friends, these students needed to establish a new social network.

- Commuter students had to learn to **balance** the college requirements with their family obligations. Family members continued to rely on them each day of the term.

FIGURE 13.2 • Tuning your life-strings.

FIGURE 13.3 • Three levels of student success.

- All students met new people in each of their classes. In-class groups were formed by the instructors and out-of-class study groups were formed by students. Class discussions required students to listen to views with which they might have disagreed. In some classes, students engaged in ideological debates.

- Campus activities brought people together. One week it might have been a concert, the next a sporting event, and the next a guest speaker. The student center, the cafeteria, the hallways, courtyard benches, and the parking lot all provided places for interaction.

- By the end of the semester, some students still never felt like they were part of the campus community. Alone and feeling alienated, they may be among students who now consider transferring or leaving college altogether.

- In some cases, relationships developed beyond the formal classroom associations. For some students, deep and lasting friendships have been developed and nurtured. For others, more intimate relationships were forged.

- Some students developed close ties with the community beyond the campus boundaries. Whether through campus clubs or service learning activities, these students have had a positive impact on the society around them.

Occupational rhythms

By this time in the term you may have decided on your major course of study, or you still may be undeclared. Even though your career might be a distant goal, the occupational dimension of your life has been affected over the past few months. Consider the following:

- During the term some students may have visited the campus career center to take interest or career assessment inventories.

- Whether because of a particular class, instructor, or community experience, students' knowledge and interests have expanded.

- Some students came to campus knowing exactly what they "wanted to be." However, after their experiences this term, they are no longer as sure about their career direction.

- For those students who have decided to major in a different area of study, they may have found out that this is not the college for them. They now consider transferring to another school.

YOUR SOCIAL RHYTHMS

As you reflect on this term, respond to the following questions.

1. What has been your biggest social adjustment?

   _____

   _____

2. In what ways have your choices in the social dimension of your life led to personal growth?

   _____

   _____

3. What questions do you still have about this dimension of your life?

   _____

   _____

YOUR OCCUPATIONAL RHYTHMS

As you reflect on this term, respond to the following questions.

1. What has been your biggest surprise concerning a major course of study?

   _____

   _____

2. In what ways have your choices in the occupational dimension of your life led to personal growth?

   _____

   _____

3. What questions do you still have about this dimension of your life?

   _____

   _____

Spiritual rhythms

You may have come to campus grounded, satisfied, and secure in your spiritual beliefs. After a term on campus your beliefs may have become stronger. Or perhaps your pre-college views have been shaken by material you have read, courses you have taken, or discussions you have had with other students. Consider the following:

- Some students had little or no exposure to different spiritual beliefs in their pre-college days. Once on campus, they read and heard about other practices and philosophies. For some students, this proved to be uncomfortable. For others, the new information opened their eyes to the diversity of the world around them.

- Some students may have attended a religious service or ceremony in the church or temple of another faith. As a result of the experience, they decided to learn more about that faith.

- Students at a religiously affiliated school may have found their faith to be strengthened.

- Maybe a student publication criticized a particular faith in a recent article—which in turn drew angry letters or protests.

- As a result of spiritual beliefs, some students may have become actively involved in community service work.

- Some students with deeply held religious beliefs may have been confronted for the first time in their lives with the views of agnostics and atheists.*

Physical rhythms

College life has put new strains on your physical condition. You could be a full-time student who lives on campus or a part-timer who takes one night class per week. Whatever the situation, healthy eating habits and regular exercise routines can quickly become a distant memory. Consider the following:

- For some students a college diet consists of doughnuts, fried foods, and pizza. They wash their food down with five or six sugar-filled and caffeine-laden sodas each day.

*An *agnostic* is skeptical about the existence of God. The *atheist* does not believe in the existence of God.

YOUR SPIRITUAL RHYTHMS

As you reflect on this term, respond to the following questions.

1. In what ways have your spiritual beliefs been challenged or reinforced?

   _____

   _____

2. In what ways have your choices in the spiritual dimension of your life led to personal growth?

   _____

   _____

3. What questions do you still have about this dimension of your life?

   _____

   _____

YOUR PHYSICAL RHYTHMS

As you reflect on this term, respond to the following questions.

1. In what ways have your diet, sleep patterns, and exercise been affected by college life?

   _____

   _____

2. In what ways have your choices in the physical dimension of your life led to personal growth?

   _____

   _____

3. What questions do you still have about this dimension of your life?

   _____

   _____

- Some students had sincere intentions to begin a regular exercise program once they got used to their class schedule and new environment. It is now three months later—and the running shoes are still in the closet.

- Many times commuter students rush from job to campus and then home to family. The healthy diet gets lost each night at the candy and soda vending machines.

- Some students want to get their degree requirements completed as soon as possible. As a result they decide to take a full load of classes—and still hold down a job or stay involved with a number of campus activities. The homework load keeps them up into the wee hours of the night. By the end of the term they are exhausted.

- Eating disorders plague students who seek to maintain an unhealthy weight.

- Some students have used poor discretion and abused alcohol and drugs. Others have engaged in sexually promiscuous activities.

Intellectual rhythms

While colleges and universities offer many diversions and attractions, their main reason for existence is to feed the intellect and challenge critical thinking skills. A rigorous course of study provides you with the necessary tools for the world after college. Consider the following:

- Since the beginning of the term, there have been numerous opportunities to increase your knowledge base and develop your skill base.

- College courses require critical thinking. No longer will rote memorization be sufficient to master course content or meet professor expectations.

- Some students recognize that their study skills lack the depth to meet the demands of college courses. They need to hone their current skills or develop new ones.

- In-class group work and out-of-class study groups expose students to new ways of thinking. Some left-brain thinkers are surprised by the creativity that a right-brain thinker can bring to the table. And the very creative thinkers need the help of the more linear thinkers when trying to put an idea into practice.

- Campus activities add to the students' knowledge and skill bases. Whether it is a class discussion, a professor sharing her latest research, or a guest speaker, the opportunities for growth surround the student body.

Emotional rhythms

Campus life provides the setting for a mixture of emotions from elation to despair. You are learning to recognize your stressors—and then to find healthy ways to eliminate or limit them. Consider the following:

- Some students have had to juggle work, family, and school obligations. At times the competing demands have been the source of stress.

- You may know students who have resorted to abusing alcohol or drugs in order to cope with the stressors of college life.

YOUR INTELLECTUAL RHYTHMS

As you reflect on this term, respond to the following questions.

1. In what ways have your knowledge and skill bases expanded while you have been in college?

   _____

   _____

2. In what ways have your choices in the intellectual dimension of your life led to personal growth?

   _____

   _____

3. What questions do you still have about this dimension of your life?

   _____

   _____

YOUR EMOTIONAL RHYTHMS

As you reflect on this term, respond to the following questions.

1. In what ways have you been able to effectively deal with your stressors?

   _____

   _____

2. In what ways have your choices in the emotional dimension of your life led to personal growth?

   _____

   _____

3. What questions do you still have about this dimension of your life?

   _____

   _____

- For some students, financial aid is the only way they can attend college. Trying to make ends meet is a constant struggle.

- Students who have been involved in intimate relations while attending college may have had to contend with the ups and downs of such relationships.

- Some students do not have emotional support from their families to attend college. In fact, some may face verbal or physical abuse for their decision to better their lives.

TUNING YOUR LIFE-STRINGS: WHERE ARE YOU HEADED?

As the preceding brief reflective activities indicate, you have made a number of choices this term. In addition to all of your academic successes, social networking, and career explorations, you have become a more **self-aware** person—even if just a little. Self-aware people take time to reflect on their actions, understand how those actions will affect themselves and others, and assume responsibility for the choices in their lives.

But self-aware people do not have all the answers. None of us do. In fact, you may have more questions now than when this term started. But self-aware people are, at least, more alert to circumstances around them—and how those circumstances may have an impact on themselves and their surroundings.

Have you ever shopped at a retail store and noticed a sign that announced, "Please pardon our dust—we are working hard to serve you better"? Renovations take time—and at times they create chaos. In some ways, this term may have been a time for your renovation and renewal—changes for the better. But you are a work in progress. Choices have been made—some good, some not as good. Each choice—and how you handle the results—gives you more awareness about yourself.

Even though you have become more attentive to what works for you and what does not work, you still may feel a bit confused about your direction. Let's take a look at some of the decisions you may have to make in the months to come. Once again, the discussion will be framed within the context of the six dimensions of your life.

© *BananaStock Ltd.*

Social rhythms: A look to the future

At one level or another during this term, you have been involved in group activities, talked with your professors, and met with advisors. Your social rhythms will continue to be challenged in a number of areas.

Team Skills and Collaboration. When you examined multiple intelligences (chapter 5), you found that some people have strong *interpersonal* skills. They can work effectively with other people. Perhaps this describes you—or maybe you would rather work individually.

A look to the future: One thing that you can count on in your college career will be the need to work with people. Whether or not you participate in a study group, you will be confronted with interpersonal relations on a variety of levels. For instance, there will be classroom discussions in which you will hear views that differ from yours. Your open-minded observations and reactions (chapter 3) will help you there. If you share a dorm room or an apartment with one or more people, your critical thinking and problem solving skills (chapter 5) will come in handy as you try to resolve differences of opinions and living styles.

Letters of Recommendation. Once you decide on a major course of study, apply for a job, or wish to become involved with campus activities, you will need to provide a list of references—people who can speak about your character.

A look to the future: The C.A.P. principle (chapter 6) recommended that you develop a working relationship with at least one classmate, one advisor, and one professor. Before the end of the term, ask at least one of your instructors if you could use him or her for a reference and future letter of recommendation.

Mentoring. Fortunate students have a mentor. It could be an instructor, an advisor, a classmate, or someone in the community. These people share their wisdom and add to your skill and knowledge bases.

A look to the future: Continue (or begin) to seek out people with experience who can help you with their wisdom. And when possible, consider being a mentor yourself—for a classmate or someone in the community who could benefit from your knowledge, skills, and wisdom.

Online Classes. Across the nation, colleges and universities have added online course offerings to their class schedules. These courses provide a level of flexibility that cannot be matched by traditional on-campus sections. This flexibility requires a level of self-discipline that exceeds what is normally required of a student. And there can be a sense of "I'm all alone in this," because you do not meet face-to-face with a group of students or an instructor.

A look to the future: Before you sign up for an online class, make sure you are capable of maintaining a disciplined study schedule—without the face-to-face urgings of a classroom instructor.

A look to the future: Some students believe—mistakenly—that online courses are an "easy way out." "After all," the reasoning goes, "since I don't have to go to class, I now have extra time to myself. Right?" Absolutely not. Online courses require more time. Remember that your online work requires a great amount of composition. What you may be able to share verbally in a classroom for a short period of time will require lengthy periods of time to type the same information. If you take an online course, manage your time appropriately (see chapter 4).

YOUR SOCIAL RHYTHMS AND FUTURE CHOICES

As you reflect on the term to come, respond to the following questions.

1. What do you consider to be the biggest challenge facing you in the social dimension of your life?

   _____

   _____

2. What choices can you make to help you address this challenge?

   _____

   _____

Occupational rhythms: A look to the future

While you may still be years away from pursuing your dream career, each semester brings you closer to the world of work. First you will be asked to declare a major (chapter 12). Or you might have decided to go in a totally new direction of study (see the profile "Changing a College Major: A Positive Story" in chapter 12). Your occupational rhythms will continue to be challenged in a number of areas.

Personal Satisfaction. More than likely your first term of classes included most, if not all, college-required courses. It is still quite possible that you learned about new topics, courses, and areas of study that held interest for you. You now may question what you want to study during your college years.

A look to the future: Refer to Activity 12.2, "Personal Assets: A Self-Inventory" (chapter 12). Have your passions changed? Have you gained some new assets this term? Have you identified some "new" liabilities?

Where Do You Belong? Colleges and universities use the term *student success* quite frequently. Many times it refers to a grade and whether or not a student successfully completes a course. Student success can also be achieved in a way that is not reflected on the grade transcript. For some, the first term or two in school raises a revealing question: "Is college the correct choice for me at this point in my life?"

A look to the future: Talk with your advisor; talk with an instructor; talk with a mentor. But talk with someone to help sort out your thoughts and doubts in a logical manner (chapter 5). Perhaps you are having doubts about your abilities—typical of many first-year students. Rather than run for the door, an objective observer may be able to point out the strengths you have that will help you succeed in college. Likewise, a reasoned discussion may lead you to consider another direction different from college.

A look to the future: Maybe you are considering transferring to another school. If you are, be sure to do *at least* two things:

1. Know why you think a transfer would be beneficial to you. Identify why you need to transfer. For instance, if you want to transfer because you have earned poor grades at your current school, what makes you think a new environment would be any better?

2. Thoroughly investigate any school you seriously consider to be a transfer candidate. Understand what course credits, if any, the new school will accept from your current school. Know what the school has to offer you in academics as well as social activities. Visit the campus. In other words, be an informed consumer.

YOUR OCCUPATIONAL RHYTHMS AND FUTURE CHOICES

As you reflect on the term to come, respond to the following questions.

1. What do you consider to be the biggest challenge facing you in the occupational dimension of your life?

   _____

   _____

2. What choices can you make to help you address this challenge?

   _____

   _____

YOUR SPIRITUAL RHYTHMS AND FUTURE CHOICES

As you reflect on the term to come, respond to the following questions.

1. What do you consider to be the biggest challenge facing you in the spiritual dimension of your life?

   _____

   _____

2. What choices can you make to help you address this challenge?

   _____

   _____

Spiritual rhythms: A look to the future

An 1850s letter from Chief Sealth (Seattle), to the president of the United States, states: "Man did not weave the web of life; he is merely a strand in it. Whatever he does to the web, he does to himself." His words indicate that we are connected to the universe around us. Your spiritual rhythms will continue to be challenged in a number of areas.

Life's Purpose. Perhaps your college experiences have brought you face-to-face with some deep personal questions concerning faith and your purpose on this earth. Or maybe your spiritual beliefs have been the rock on which you have been able to survive the trials and tribulations of the term.

A look to the future: In chapter 2 you examined your belief system and values. Respect the values that have brought you to this point in your life. Perhaps you have found scripture readings from your religious faith to be positive and reassuring—guideposts along your journey. Maybe, on the other hand, you are questioning your previous religious convictions. Find a trusted person with whom you can talk. It could very well be a roommate, a professor, a religious leader in the community, or a family member. Use your information literacy skills (chapter 9) in your search for answers. An effective college education does more than fill your mind with details and facts. It actually should open your mind to the world around you. How will you continue to revitalize your spiritual energy?

Physical rhythms: A look to the future

Now that you have completed (at least) one college term, you have a more accurate idea of the demands college life places on your physical well-being. Some students have superb self-discipline when it comes to exercise and rest. Others are not as mindful to what their body needs. Your physical rhythms will continue to be challenged in a number of areas.

End-of-the-Term Exhaustion. The end of finals week finds students celebrating in one way or another. With the term successfully behind them, they feel as though a huge weight has been lifted. At the same time, some students may feel that they could crawl into bed and sleep for the next week. Hectic schedules, poor diet, and nonexistent physical conditioning have created an exhausted and irritable person. And within a few weeks a new semester—and the same craziness—will begin again.

A look to the future: Examine what has worked and has not worked for you in the area of physical conditioning. The first place to look is your class schedule. Perhaps, driven by the desire to graduate as soon as possible, you registered for a larger course load than you could realistically handle. Carrying too many courses can be physically draining. And, in some cases, it deprives you of the full value of your college education. It is a bit like planting a seed and then getting on your hands and knees and urging the plant to hurry up and grow. Some things take time.

A look to the future: Before registering for classes, make sure you will have the time to devote to your studies. If you decide to sign up for five, six, or seven classes, that means five, six, or seven sets of exams, assignments, textbook readings, and class discussions or lectures. Do you have the time? In addition to the time spent in the classroom, plan for the hours needed outside of the classroom to complete required assignments. (Refer to chapter 4.)

A look to the future: Consider what you can do to keep your body in healthy shape. Maybe the student center, campus physical education department, or the local community center sponsors yoga classes, Pilates, weight training, or kickboxing. Or maybe you can set a goal to walk or jog on a regular basis. Your body can perform better if it is fueled and maintained in a healthy manner. Respect it and treat it with integrity (see chapter 11).

Intellectual rhythms: A look to the future

One of the true joys of higher education comes from the daily intellectual stimulation that surrounds you. The opportunities to expand your knowledge base and skill base are limitless. From the lecture hall to the laboratory to the student center, students share and learn. Your intellectual rhythms will continue to be challenged in a number of areas.

YOUR PHYSICAL RHYTHMS AND FUTURE CHOICES

As you reflect on the term to come, respond to the following questions.

1. What do you consider to be the biggest challenge facing you in the physical dimension of your life?

_____

_____

2. What choices can you make to help you address this challenge?

_____

_____

© Image 100 Ltd.

Lifelong Learning. The mind needs exercise just like the physical muscles of your body. Respect your mind just like you would your body. How will you make sure your mind dines on a healthy diet?

A look to the future: Your mind does not cease to need nourishment at the end of the term. Nor does a college degree mean the end of education. Your schooling may end, but your education will continue for the remainder of your life. Take advantage of all the opportunities to expand your experiences and add to your storehouse of knowledge. Attend as many events as you can, on campus *and* in the surrounding community. While fine-tuning this dimension of your life, you will be able to renew other dimensions. For instance, attending a yoga class can strengthen your body, relax your mind, and help you form bonds with other members of the class.

Mental Ruts. In his book *Making Choices That Change Lives,*[1] Hal Urban tells his readers to avoid mental ruts—tired ways of thinking that are never challenged or updated. A rut becomes the opposite of renewal. Rather than grow, a person in a mental rut stagnates.

A look to the future: What will you do to avoid mental ruts? Think of a young child, or even a puppy. Notice the joy and curiosity with which they experience the world around them. You won't find them in a rut. They see something different and they move toward it! You may want to review the strategies about open-minded observations (chapter 3) and creative thinking (chapter 5) once again. Look at old things in new ways; try new experiences; go to a type of movie you do not usually attend; walk a different route to class. In short, do what you can to keep the world around you fresh. Move toward new opportunities.

Emotional rhythms: A look to the future

Your emotional health will have an impact on the other dimensions of your life. Think about times you have suffered from distress. You might not have slept well, which had an impact on your physical health. Perhaps the way in which you handled the stress caused you to be short-tempered with those around you. Emotion, of course, can also be positive, as in feelings of joy. In such situations you feel so elated that people enjoy your company. Your ongoing task is to minimize stressful times and maximize the opportunities that bring satisfaction to your life. Your emotional rhythms will continue to be challenged in a number of areas.

Exhilarating or Debilitating? Each new college term will bring with it new demands. Once you move into your major area of concentration (junior and senior years, for instance) the

YOUR INTELLECTUAL RHYTHMS AND FUTURE CHOICES

As you reflect on the term to come, respond to the following questions.

1. What do you consider to be the biggest challenge facing you in the intellectual dimension of your life?

   _____

   _____

2. What choices can you make to help you address this challenge?

   _____

   _____

YOUR EMOTIONAL RHYTHMS AND FUTURE CHOICES

As you reflect on the term to come, respond to the following questions.

1. What do you consider to be the biggest challenge facing you in the emotional dimension of your life?

   _____

   _____

2. What choices can you make to help you address this challenge?

   _____

   _____

VALUES AND CHOICES[2]

Some of the first activities you did in this book (see chapters 1 and 2) involved examining your values. As you near the end of the book, let's return to your identified values.

1. Perhaps your values have changed during this term in college. Maybe the values you brought to college are stronger than they ever were. As with many things in life, you might find that you are somewhere in the middle—some have changed, others have not. List what you consider to be the five most important things to you right now.

   1. _____

   2. _____

   3. _____

   4. _____

   5. _____

2. In chapter 4 (Activity 4.1), you listed the activities that you spend time on each week. Review that activity and make any changes that are necessary. Once you have done that, list the five activities (other than sleep) that you spend most of your time on in a given week.

   1. _____

   2. _____

   3. _____

   4. _____

   5. _____

3. Compare the two lists. How do your weekly activities reflect what you say you value? Write your response here.

   _____

   _____

   _____

(continued)

VALUES AND CHOICES (continued)

13.13
ACTIVITY

4. What do the two lists say about the choices you have made during the past few months?

_____

_____

_____

5. Finally, what changes do you need to make as you look to the future?

_____

_____

_____

courses will become more challenging, the material more complex. While this can be an exhilarating time, it can be stress-producing as you try to master the material that will lead to your degree and possible career. How will you manage your emotional health?

A look to the future: As described in chapter 11, a habit is something that you cannot help but do. A person who has handled stressful situations with unhealthy strategies (alcohol, drugs, or temper tantrums, for instance) has developed habits—bad habits. With the help of a friend, family member, or mentor, identify some of the less effective strategies you have used in stressful situations. Use your problem solving strategies from chapter 5 and brainstorm ideas to replace the unhealthy emotional responses with healthy life-affirming strategies. Think about the strategies that have allowed you to remain emotionally calm, or at least allowed you to effectively manage stressful situations.

Patience Is a Virtue. Like learning to play a musical instrument, a college education takes time. Before you can play lead guitar for an internationally known band, you need to learn the basics of the instrument. One of those basics involves keeping the strings in tune. It takes patience to learn, but it is critical if the instrument is to be mastered.

A look to the future: Consider your emotional health as an important string to your overall personal well-being. Keep it tuned by learning to handle stress effectively. We live in a fast-paced, I-want-it-now society. Some colleges and universities cater to that mind-set by offering compressed courses in short terms so that students can get their degrees as quickly as possible. The good news: You get to finish these courses in half the time of the regular full-term offering. The bad news: You get to finish these courses in half the time of the regular full-term offering. Yes, the course is over quickly, but you will need to do double the amount of work since the class meets only half as often as the full-term offering. If you cannot handle that type of accelerated pace, do not place yourself in that position.

SUMMARY

MAKING CHOICES

Congratulations on having the perseverance to complete your studies this term. Whether you reached your goals in full or in part, you have moved closer to your destination. Even if that destination has changed, one thing is certain: You have become a different person from the one who came to campus a few months ago. You have grown in ways that you might not even recognize—but you have grown.

Before leaving this chapter, and this book, keep the following points in mind:

- No matter what situation you find yourself in, you bring past skills and knowledge to that situation.

- You may not be able to control every event that comes your way, but you can control the way you react to those situations.

- Self-aware people take time to reflect on their actions, understand how those actions will affect themselves and others, and assume responsibility for the choices in their lives.

- Each dimension of your life has an impact on the other dimensions. Carefully tune each of your life-strings so that your life-song is in harmony.

tuning your life-strings

the 4 Rs

self

change and personal growth

Your SELF:
Personal growth and balance

The following activities will allow you to reflect on the three levels of student success as they apply to the major concepts described in this book. Each activity will give you an opportunity to reflect and apply the book's concepts in a way that is meaningful to you during this transitional phase of your life. Use this opportunity to apply newly acquired information and also keep an ongoing journal of growth in the various facets of your life.

The 4 Rs

Describe a personal example of how you used each of the 4 Rs as you considered the choices before you.

1. *Reflection* (Example: How have you made informed choices this term?) _____

_____

_____

_____

_____

_____

2. *Respect* (Example: What do your past experiences say about your ability to make reasoned decisions?) _____

_____

_____

_____

_____

_____

3. *Responsibility* (Example: Describe responsible steps you have taken to tune your life-strings.) _____

_____

_____

_____

_____

_____

4. *Renewal* (Example: In what ways does thinking about your choices energize you?) _____

_____

_____

_____

_____

_____

The Change Cycle

For this activity, reflect on a change that you are currently confronting concerning one of the dimensions of your life.

1. What is the situation that requires change? _____

_____

_____

_____

_____

2. What led you to recognize this? _____

_____

_____

_____

_____

3. What is (or will be) your plan to address this situation? _____

_____

_____

_____

_____

4. If you have put the plan into action (executed it), how are you progressing? _____

_____

_____

_____

_____

5. Once the plan has become a reality, how do you plan to enjoy this achievement? How will you reward yourself?

_____

_____

_____

_____

Tuning Your Life-Strings

Pause for a moment and reflect on the balance—or lack of balance—in your life at this point in the school term. Use this activity to apply newly acquired information from this chapter to gauge the level of strength in the various facets of your life. You may wish to refer to your responses in previous chapters.

Life-string	Questions to ask yourself	What possible activities could help you tune this string?	Who can help you tune this string?
Social	• Is there a mentor in your college life who can help you find balance and wellness?		
Occupational	• Have you made any decisions that will impact your major or career interests?		
Spiritual	• What types of explorations have you been involved in that have helped you examine the deeper meanings of life—and your purpose in this life?		
Physical	• What kind of an exercise schedule do you maintain?		
Intellectual	• What did you do this week that provided you with more information about your major?		
Emotional	• What strategies have you used to effectively deal with your college stressors?		

Rhythms of Reflection

To complete this chapter, please reflect on the following quotation:

> *Live a balanced life—learn some and think some and draw and paint and sing and dance and play and work everyday some.*
>
> *–Robert Fulghum, author*

Now, using these words for inspiration, explain how you intend to live a balanced life. Please write your thoughts here.

_____

_____

_____

_____

 To further respond online, please go to the *Rhythms of Reflection* module in chapter 13 of the Companion Website.

ENDNOTES

1. Hal Urban, *Making Choices That Change Lives: 15 Ways to Find More Purpose, Meaning, and Joy* (New York: Simon & Schuster, 2006).
2. Urban, *Making Choices That Change Lives*, 155.

"Ability to Speak English: 2000." U.S. Census Bureau Quick Tables. *http://factfinder.census.gov/servlet/QTTable?_bm=y& geo_id=01000US&-qr_name=DEC_2000_SF3_U_QTP17&-ds_ name=DEC_2000_SF3_U&-redoLog=false* (accessed February 22, 2006).

"Academic Credentials Offered at AACC." Anne Arundel Community College. *http://www.aacc.edu/offer/academiccred.cfm* (accessed November 19, 2005).

Adler, Mortimer, and Charles Van Doren. *How to Read a Book.* New York: Simon & Schuster, 1972.

Armstrong, Thomas. *Multiple Intelligences in the Classroom.* Alexandria, VA: Association for Supervision and Curriculum Development, 1994.

Banks, James A. *Teaching Strategies for Ethnic Studies,* 6th ed. Needham Heights, MA: Allyn & Bacon, 1997.

Barrett, Jamie. "Excessive Credit Card Use Causes Student Debt Woes." *Kansas State Collegian,* 2003. *http://www.youngmoney .com/credit_debt/get_out_of_debt/021007_03* (accessed January 14, 2006).

"Binge Drinking in Adolescents and College Students." U.S. Department of Health and Human Services and SAMHSA's National Clearinghouse for Alcohol and Drug Information. *http://www.health.org/govpubs/rpo995/#res2* (accessed May 16, 2006).

"Budgeting: Plan Your Budget." 2006. Visa U.S.A. *http://www.usa .visa.com/personal/student/budgeting/budgeting.html?it=c\ /personal/student/budgeting/index%2Ehtml\/img/text/lh_ plan_your_budget%2Egif#anchor_7* (accessed January 14, 2006).

Caddell Crawford, Ann. "Customs and Rites." Chap. 6 in *Cultures and Customs of Vietnam.* 2000. *http://goasia.about.com/ gi/dynamic/offsite.htm?site=http://www.militaryliving.com/ vietnam2/index.html* (accessed February 15, 2006).

"Carbohydrates." Medicine Plus Medical Dictionary. January 6, 2006. *http://www.nlm.nih.gov/medlineplus/ency/article/ 002469.htm* (accessed January 19, 2006).

Carter, Carol, Joyce Bishop, and Sarah Lyman Kravits. *Keys to Success,* 5th ed. Upper Saddle River, NJ: Prentice Hall, 2006.

Checkley, Kathy. "The First Seven . . . and the Eighth: A Conversation with Howard Gardner." Association for Supervision and Curriculum and Development. *Educational Leadership 55,* September 1997.

"Clark State's Wellness Model." Clark State Community College. *www.clark.cc.oh.us/clinic_well.html* (accessed November 13, 2005).

"College Degree Nearly Doubles Annual Earnings, Census Bureau Reports," *U.S. Census Bureau News,* March 28, 2005. U.S. Department of Commerce. *http://www.census.gov/Press-Release/ www/releases/archives/education/004214.html* (accessed July 7, 2005).

Consumer Calcs. "What Is the Value of a College Education?" Financial Calculators Inc. *http://www.fincalc.com/* (accessed July 7, 2005).

"Countries of Birth of the Foreign-Born Population, 1850–2000," *Profile of the Foreign-Born Population in the United States: 2000.* U.S. Census Bureau, 2001. Pearson Education's Infoplease database. *http://www.infoplease.com/ipa/A0900547.html* (accessed February 8, 2006).

Covey, Stephen, A. Roger Merrill, and Rebecca R. Merrill. *First Things First.* New York: Simon & Schuster, 1994.

"Credit 101: Calculate Your Payments." 2000. Visa U.S.A. *http://www.usa.visa.com/personal/student/credit_101/calcul ate_your_payments.html?it=l2\/personal/student/credit_101/ generate_good_credit%2Ehtml\Calculate%20Your%20Payments(* accessed January 14, 2006).

Cummings, M. *The Value of an Education.* Monmouth Housing Alliance. *http://www.housingall.com/oldsite/STEPUP/ValofEdu.htm* (accessed October 23, 2006).

Cuseo, J. (2005). "Decided," "undecided," and "in transition": Implications for academic advisement, career counseling, and student retention. In R. S. Feldman (Ed.), *Improving the first year of college: Research and practice* (pp. 27–50). New York: Erlbaum.

de Bono, Edward. "Edward de Bono Biography." Edward de Bono's Web. *http://www.edwdebono.com/debono/biograph.htm* (accessed June 23, 2004).

———. *New Think: The Use of Lateral Thinking in the Generation of New Ideas.* New York: Basic Books, 1968.

Dinnerstein, Leonard, and David M. Reimers. *Ethnic Americans: A History of Immigration and Assimilation.* New York: Harper & Row, 1975.

Dunn, Rita, and Kenneth Dunn. *Teaching Students Through Their Individual Learning Styles: A Practical Approach.* Reston, VA: Reston, 1978.

"Eating Disorders Information Index." 2002. National Eating Disorders Association. *http://nationaleatingdisorders.org/ p.asp? WebPage_ID=294* (accessed January 13, 2006).

Eisenberg, Michael B., Carrie A. Lowe, and Kathleen L. Spitzer. *Information Literacy: Essential Skills for the Information Age,* 2nd ed. Westport, CT: Libraries Unlimited, 2004.

"Ergonomics and VDT Use." *Computers in Libraries* 13 (May 1993). Library of Congress (Integrated Support Services, Workforce Ergonomics Program).

Estroff Marano, Hara. "Assertive, Not Aggressive," *Psychology Today,* October 14, 2005. *http://www.psychologytoday .com/rss/ pto-20040206-000009.html* (accessed December 29, 2005).

Evans, Kelli. "The Rights of Gay and Lesbian Students." In *Making Schools Safe: Anti-Harassment Training Program,* by Jennifer Middleton and Joshua Freker. New York: American Civil Liberties Union, 2002. *http://www.aclu.org/ images/asset_upload_file681_24003.pdf* (accessed February 12, 2006).

Family Educational Rights and Privacy Act (FERPA). U.S. Department of Education. *http://www.ed.gov/policy/gen/guid/fpco/ferpa/ index.html* (accessed August 12, 2005).

Fields, Suzanne. "A Way out of the Balkans." *Washington Times,* June 13, 2004. *http://www.washingtontimes.com/op-ed/ 20040613-102532-4353r.htm* (accessed February 3, 2006).

"Fitness Resources: Frequently Asked Questions." 1999. American Heart Association. *http://www.justmove.org/fitnessnews/faqs .html* (accessed January 14, 2006).

"5 Stages of Group Development." George Mason University, Center for Service and Leadership. *http://www.gmu.edu/student/csl/5stages.html* (accessed December 26, 2005).

"Foundations of Wellness: 14 Keys to a Healthy Diet." University of California at Berkeley. *Wellness Letter.com. http://www.berkeleywellness.com/html/fw/fwNut01HealthyDiet.html* (accessed January 12, 2006).

"The Fundamental Values of Academic Integrity." October 1999. Center for Academic Integrity: Fundamental Values Project. *http:// www.academicintegrity.org/fundamental.asp* (accessed January 8, 2006).

Glater, Jonathan D. "To: Professor@University.edu Subject: Why It's All About Me." *New York Times,* February 21, 2006. *http:// www.nytimes.com/2006/02/21/education/21professors.html?ex=1298 178000&en=361f9efce267b517&ei=5090&partner=rssuserland&emc=rss* (accessed April 22, 2006).

"Global Availability of MSN Messenger and MSN Spaces Connects People Around the World." Microsoft Press Pass. *http://www.microsoft.com/presspass/press/2005/apr05/04-07Global MessengerSpacesPR.mspx* (accessed December 14, 2005).

Gordon, Virginia N., and Susan J. Sears. *Selecting a College Major: Exploration and Decision Making,* 5th ed. Upper Saddle River, NJ: Pearson/Prentice Hall, 2004.

Grad, Peter. "Rev Up Your Engine." *NorthJersey.com,* December 3, 2005. *http://www.northjersey.com/page.php?qstr= eXJpcnk3ZjczN2Y3dnFIZUVFeXk3MDcmZmdiZWw3Zjd2c WVlRUV5eTY4Mjg5NzEmeXJ pcnk3ZjcxN2Y3dnFIZUVFeXk3* (accessed January 1, 2006).

Gray, Elaine. *Conscious Choices: A Model for Self-Directed Learning.* Upper Saddle River, NJ: Pearson/Prentice Hall, 2004.

Hellmich, Nancy. "USA Wallowing in Unhealthy Ways: Obesity Expert Points Finger at Fat-City Society." *USA Today,* August 22, 2002. *http://www.usatoday.com/educate/college/firstyear/ articles20020823.htm* (accessed January 13, 2006).

Herrmann, Ned "Is It True That Creativity Resides in the Right Hemisphere of the Brain?" *Scientific American.com. www.sciam.com/print_version.cfm?articleID=00049843-7DBA-1C71-9EB 7809EC5* (accessed September 16, 2004; document no longer available on this site).

———. "The Four Quadrant Model of the Brain." *http://www.kheper.net/topics/intelligence/Herrmann.htm* (accessed September 17, 2005).

Hettler, Bill. "The Six Dimensional Wellness Model." National Wellness Institute. *http://www.nationalwellness.org/index.php?id= 391&id_tier=381* (accessed July 7, 2006).

"Information Literacy Competency Standards for Higher Education." Association of College and Research Libraries (a division of the American Library Association). *http://www.ala.org/ala/acrl/acrlstandards/informationliteracycompetency.htm#ildef* (accessed November 30, 2005).

"Internet." NetLingo the Internet Dictionary. *http://www.netlingo.com/lookup.cfm?term=Internet* (accessed December 14, 2005).

"Introduction to Sexually Transmitted Diseases." 2006. myDNA.com. *http://newsletter.mydna.com/health/sexual/std/o/intro.html* (accessed October 23, 2006).

Jacobs, Don Trent, and Jessica Jacobs-Spencer. *Teaching Virtues: Building Character Across the Curriculum.* Lanham, MD: Scarecrow Press, 2001.

Jones, Lafayette. "Marketing Realities for the 'Browning of America.'" *Black Collegian,* October 1998. *http://www.findarticles. com/p/ articles/mi_qa3628/is_199810/ai_n8823185#continue* (accessed February 12, 2006).

Katzenbach, John R., and Douglas K. Smith. *The Wisdom of Teams: Creating the High-Performance Organization.* New York: HarperBusiness Essentials, 2003.

Keefe, James. *Learning Style Handbook: II. Accommodating Perceptual, Study and Instructional Preferences.* Reston, VA: National Association of Secondary School Principals, n.d.

Kragen, Ken. *Life Is a Contact Sport.* New York: Morrow, 1994.

Lazear, David. *Seven Ways of Knowing: Teaching for Multiple Intelligences.* Palatine, IL: Skylight, 1991.

Leider, Richard. *The Power of Purpose: Creating Meaning in Your Life and Work.* New York: MJF Books, 1997.

Leider, Richard, and David Shapiro. *Repacking Your Bags: Lighten Your Load for the Rest of Your Life.* San Francisco: Barrett-Koehler, 1995.

Lencioni, Patrick. *The Five Dysfunctions of a Team.* San Francisco, CA: Jossey-Bass, 2002.

Lyall, Katherine. "Binge Drinking in College: A Definitive Study in Binge Drinking on American College Campuses: A New Look at an Old Problem." August 1995.

Lyman, Peter, and Hal R. Varian. "How Much Information? 2003." School of Information and Management, University of California at Berkeley, 2003.

Martin, Ann R. "College Student Devotion to Homework Debated." *Chicago Tribune,* January 4, 2004. *http://nsse.iub.edu/articles/ Chicago_Tribune_1_4_2004.htm* (accessed July 1, 2006).

Marxhausen, Paul. "Computer Related Repetitive Strain Injury." 2005. University of Nebraska–Lincoln Electronics Shop RSI Web Page. *http://eeshop.unl.edu/rsi.html* (accessed January 1, 2006).

Matte, Nancy Lightfoot, and Susan Hillary Henderson. *Success Your Style: Right- and Left-Brain Techniques for Learning.* Belmont, CA: Wadsworth, 1995.

McCrone, John. "Right Brain or Left Brain—Myth or Reality?" *New Scientist* 163 (July 3, 1999): 26ff.

McNamara, Carter. "Basics of Conflict Management." 1999. *http:// www.managementhelp.org/intrpsnl/basics.htm* (accessed December 30, 2005).

Mearns, Jack. "Social Learning Theory of Julian B. Rotter." Department of Psychology, California State University–Fullerton. *http://psych.fullerton.edu/jmearns/rotter.htm* (accessed March 7, 2004).

Meyer, Paul. "Creating S.M.A.R.T. Goals." Top Achievement. *http://www.topachievement.com/smart.html* (accessed on January 3, 2005).

Micceri, Ted. "Will Changing Your Major Double Your Graduation Chances?" May 30, 2002. Policy Center on the First Year of College, First-Year Assessment Listserv. *www.brevard .edu/fyc/ listserv/remarks/micceri.htm* (accessed August 1, 2005).

Middleton, Jennifer, and Joshua Freker. *Making Schools Safe: Anti-Harassment Training Program.* New York: American Civil Liberties Union, 2002. *http://www.aclu.org/images/asset_upload_ file681_24003.pdf* (accessed February 12, 2006).

Miller, William. "Resolutions That Work." *Spirituality and Health* (February 2005): 44–47.

Morris, Clifford. "Linking General Occupations to Multiple Intelligences." 2004. Thinking and Working Smarter Not Harder. *http://www.igs.net/~cmorris/smo_comments.html* (accessed November 19, 2005).

Motta, Janice. "Massachusetts Community Colleges Release Findings of Study on Economic Benefits of Community College Education on Graduates and the Commonwealth." April 6, 2004. Massachusetts Community Colleges. *http://www.masscc.org/pdfs/press_1759 econreportrelease2.pdf* (accessed October 1, 2005).

Occupational Outlook Handbook. U.S. Department of Labor, Bureau of Labor Statistics. *http://www.bls.gov/oco/home.htm* (accessed November 19, 2005).

Orloff, Judith. *Positive Energy.* New York: Harmony Books, 2004.

Orndorff, Robert M., and Edwin L. Herr. "A Comparative Study of Declared and Undeclared College Students on Career Uncertainty and Involvement in Career Development Activities." *Journal of Counseling and Development* 74 (July/August 1996).

"Overweight and Obesity Statistics." August 18, 2005. Obesity Focused. *http://www.obesityfocused.com/index.php* (accessed January 13, 2006).

Pauk, Walter. *How to Study in College,* 5th ed. Boston: Houghton Mifflin, 1993.

Peters, Tom. *Reinventing Work: The Brand You 50.* New York: Knopf, 2001.

Piscitelli, Steve. *Study Skills: Do I Really Need This Stuff?* Upper Saddle River, NJ: Prentice Hall, 2004.

"Policy Guidance on Current Issues of Sexual Harassment." March 19, 1990. Equal Employment Opportunity Commission. *http://www.eeoc.gov/policy/docs/currentissues.html* (accessed December 30, 2005).

Posen, David B. "Stress Management for Patient and Physician." *Canadian Journal of Continuing Medical Education,* April 1995. *http://www.mentalhealth.com/mag1/p51-str.html#Head_1* (accessed January 13, 2006).

Procter, Margaret. "How Not to Plagiarize." 2006. Writing at the University of Toronto. *http://www.utoronto.ca/writing/plagsep. html* (accessed January 15, 2006).

"Projections of the Resident Population by Race, Hispanic Origin, and Nativity: Middle Series, 2006 to 2010." Population Projections Program. Population Division, U.S. Census Bureau. *http://www. census.gov/population/projections/nation/summary/np-t5-c.txt* (accessed February 8, 2006).

Ramsey, Dave. "Debit Card Policy." Dave's Store. *http://www.dave-ramsey.com/shop/Debit_Card_Policy_W8.cfm* (accessed January 14, 2006).

Riedling, Ann Marlow. *Learning to Learn: A Guide to Becoming Information Literate.* New York: Neal-Schuman, 2002.

Saillant, Catherine. "A Bulwark Against Bullies," *LATimes.com,* December 5, 2005. *http://pqasb.pqarchiver.com/latimes/ access/936841751.html?dids=936841751:936841751&FMT= ABS&FMTS=ABS:FT&type=current&date=Dec+5%2C+2005& author=Catherine+Saillant&pub=Los+Angeles+Times&edition= &startpage=B.1&desc=A+Bulwark+Against+Bullies* (accessed October 23, 2006).

Sapadin, Linda, with Jack Maguire. *Beat Procrastination and Make the Grade: The Six Styles of Procrastination and How Students Can Overcome Them.* New York: Penguin Books, 1999.

"School Daze?" Phoenix House: Facts on Tap. *http://www. factson tap.org/factsontap/alcohol_and_student_life/school_daze.htm* (accessed May 16, 2006).

"Severe Smoking Bans in Some Workplaces." December 9, 2005. CNN.com Transcripts. *http://transcripts.cnn.com/TRANSCRI PTS/0512/09/lol.01.html* (accessed January 19, 2006).

"Sexually Transmitted Diseases Treatment Guidelines 2002." Centers For Disease Control. *http://www.cdc.gov/std/treatment/1-2002 TG.htm#HIVInfectionDetectionCounseling&Referral* (accessed January 15, 2006).

"Sexually Transmitted Infections." December 29, 2005. National Institutes of Health, Division of Microbiology and Infectious Diseases. *http://www.niaid.nih.gov/dmid/stds/#intro* (accessed January 15, 2006).

Sherfield, Robert M. *The Everything Self-Esteem Book.* Avon MA: Adams Media, 2004.

Smith, Frank. *To Think.* New York: Teachers College Press, 1990.

Smith, Mark K. "Bruce W. Tuckman—Forming, Storming, Norming, and Performing in Groups." 2005. In *Infed: The Encyclopaedia of Informal Education. http://www.infed.org/thinkers/ tuckman.htm* (accessed December 26, 2005).

Southern Poverty Law Center. "101 Tools for Tolerance: Simple Ideas for Promoting Equity and Diversity." 2005. Fight Hate and Promote Tolerance. *http://www.tolerance.org/101_tools/index.html* (accessed February 12, 2006).

Spring, Joel. *The Intersection of Cultures: Multicultural Education in the United States.* New York: McGraw-Hill, 1995.

"Statistics: Eating Disorders and Their Precursors." 2002. National Eating Disorders Association. *http://nationaleatingdisorders .org/p.asp?WebPage_ID=286&Profile_ID=41138* (accessed January 13, 2006).

Sternberg, Robert. *Successful Intelligence: How Practical and Creative Intelligence Determine Success in Life.* New York: Plume, 1997.

Stevens, Jose. *The Power Path: The Shaman's Way to Success in Business and Life.* Novato, CA: New World Library, 2002.

Straus, David. *How to Make Collaboration Work.* San Francisco, CA: Berrett-Koehler, 2002.

Swartz, Roger G. *Accelerated Learning: How You Learn Determines What You Learn.* Durant, OK: EMIS, 1991.

Taylor, Bill. "Integrity: Academic and Political. A Letter to My Students." n.d. *http://www.academicintegrity.org/pdf/Letter_To_ My_Students.pdf* (accessed December 17, 2005).

"Test and Performance Anxieties." Campus Blues, 2002–2004. *http://www.campusblues.com/test.asp* (accessed February 24, 2006).

Tinto, Vincent. "Taking Student Learning Seriously." Keynote address, Southwest Regional Learning Communities Conference, Tempe, AZ, February 28–March 1, 2002. *http://www.mcli.dist .maricopa.edu/events/lcc02/presents/tinto.html* (accessed March 29, 2004).

Toga, Arthur W., and Paul M. Thompson. "Mapping Brain Asymmetry." *Nature Reviews: Neuroscience* 4 (January 2003).

Tolle, Eckhart. *The Power of Now.* Novato, CA: New World Library, 1999.

"Types of Exercise." American Diabetes Association. *http://www.- diabetes.org/weightloss-and-exercise/exercise/types-of-exercise .jsp* (accessed January 14, 2006).

Urban, Hal. *Making Choices That Change Lives: 15 Ways to Find More Purpose, Meaning, and Joy.* New York: Simon & Schuster, 2006.

"U.S. Obesity Trends: 1985 to 2004." November 8, 2005. Centers for Disease Control and Prevention. *http://www.cdc.gov/nccd php/dnpa/obesity/trend/maps/index.htm* (accessed January 13, 2006).

VanderStoep, Scott W., and Paul R. Pintrich. *Learning to Learn: The Skill and Will of College Success.* Upper Saddle River, NJ: Prentice Hall, 2003.

Wilson, Susan B. *Goal Setting.* New York: American Management Association, 1994.

PROBLEM-SOLVING INDEX